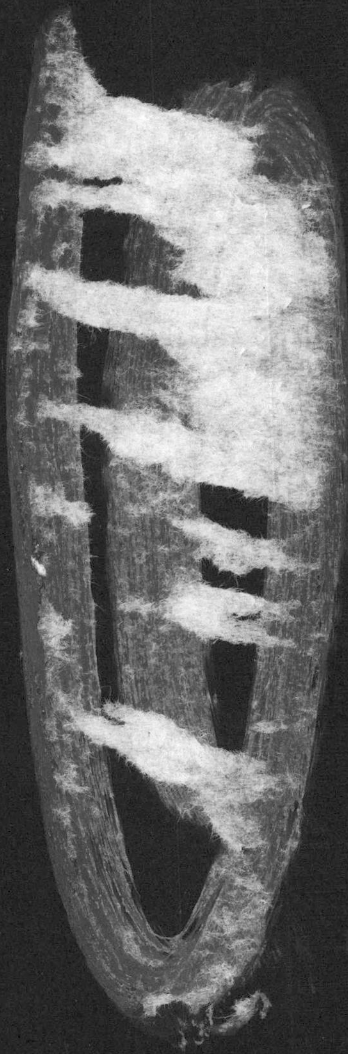

TO THE SUMMIT

TO THE SUMMIT

FIFTY MOUNTAINS THAT LURE, INSPIRE AND CHALLENGE

by Joseph Poindexter

BLACK DOG
& LEVENTHAL
PUBLISHERS
NEW YORK

Design by Dutton & Sherman Design

Photo Editor: Debbie Egan-Chin

Maps by David Allen & Catharine Wood
Technical Illustrations by
Nathan C. S. Frerichs

Published by
Black Dog & Leventhal Publishers
151 W 19th St.
New York, NY 10011

Printed in Hong Kong

Distributed by
Workman Publishing Company
708 Broadway
New York, NY 10003

ISBN: 1-57912-041-5

i h g f e d c b a

CONTENTS

ACKNOWLEDGMENTS

Many talents were marshaled in the creation of this book. It was originally brought to me by JP Leventhal and my editor, Jessica MacMurray; it was her energy, optimism and calm intelligence that kept the rest of us on this complex project from losing our way. JP backed the project from the start and kept it fresh with a constant flow of ideas and suggestions. The visual richness of this book is due in large measure to the boundless industriousness and tenacity of photo editor Debbie Egan-Chin. She in turn received invaluable assistance from Maria Spinella. Nathan Frerichs' drawings and maps by David Allen and Catharine Wood contribute information with a charm that words never could. Deborah Dutton & Joseph Sherman brought it all together with finesse and hard work during the design process.

Were it not for the timely intervention of long-time friend Bert Snyder, I would not have been invited to join this project. The encouragement and advice of Susan Bergholz, friend and writers' advocate nonpareil, helped me stay the course.

This book relies heavily on the route descriptions, observations and historical research of dozens of climber-writers. The works consulted in preparing the text are listed in a bibliography at the back of the book. Certain authors made a special impression on me with the richness of their insights or the depth of their research; these include Wilfrid Noyce and Ian McMorrin, Fred Beckey, Edwin Bernbaum, Steve Roper and Allen Steck, Andy Fanshawe and Stephen Venables, Helmut Dumler and Willi Burkhardt, Walt Unsworth, Nicholas O'Connell, David Roberts, Jon Krakauer, Al Alvarez and Tom Patey. Special thanks go to Greg Child for his thoughtful, brightly written and comprehensive reference work on climbing. Certain sections of the text gained depth and authority from the contributions of peerless free climber Todd Skinner.

My thanks to Janet Baldwin for the hospitality she extended us at the Explorers Club library, and to Gay Ellen Roesch, who gave us access to the American Alpine Club library even as its volumes were in transit to their new permanent home in Golden, Colorado. John Thackray, writer, climber and keeper of the AAC New York Chapter library, guided us to useful works in that collection and generously shared his extensive knowledge of mountaineering. Above all, I am indebted to Charley Mace, a world-class climber, who not only ferreted out most of the book's research but whose knowledge of mountains worldwide was like a firm rope on the many daunting pitches of this adventure.

I still think that nature

is a great teacher.

It's fair. There's gravity,

cold, avalanches, but

it's fair.

—Jim Whittaker

Mountains are not fair

or unfair. They are

dangerous.

—Reinhold Messner

For Holly

PREFACE

In July, 1976, I was standing on the summit of Pik Lenin. As it happens, I was there alone; my climbing partner, complaining of a severe headache, had returned to camp a few minutes after we had set out. Lenin requires no technical climbing—it's largely a matter of extracting oxygen from air that at 23,000 feet is excruciatingly thin. Getting down was a simple matter of following the footsteps I made on the ascent, except that as I was putting my camera back into my rucksack, it began to snow, and a cloud blanketed the summit. Suddenly, I was in a whiteout.

The shape of the broad west ridge, which descends to a shallow saddle and then climbs to the west summit, made route finding difficult. The air became nearly opaque as I hit the level section of the saddle, and, since I had neglected to take a compass, I was relying on a sort of inner gyroscope to keep me going in a straight line. After about an hour on the featureless ridge, the air lightened momentarily. A black outcrop emerged from the murk, and I recognized it: it was the rock rib that led to the summit. My descent had taken a long, 180 degree arc, and I was headed back up the mountain.

As I turned around, whiteout conditions closed in again and the rocks disappeared. Pushing forward, or whatever direction evolved from my efforts, seemed futile, so I stopped, dug a trench in the snow to conserve heat and lay down in it. I promised myself that I would not fall asleep—then promptly did just that. A brief dream—in which I saw a rescue party silhouetted on the western horizon—awakened me. Startled, I looked up and saw a disc, flat as a poker chip with the same texture as the surrounding whiteness but colored a dim pastel orange. It took me a moment to realize it was not the moon but the late afternoon sun hanging above the west summit. I blessed this disc, panicked when it faded from view, blessed it each time it reappeared—and followed it back to camp.

What it is that motivates people to exert themselves mightily to arrive at some of the least hospitable places on earth—and, having done that, seek harder ways to do it all over again—is a question that has been too much analyzed. Why not ask an amateur violist, say, why he spends an hour a day on finger exercises just to play a string quartet for which there are perhaps a dozen wonderful recordings? But at risk of adding to the verbal whiteout, here's my take on the mountain question: mountains are places that request—sometimes demand—that they be engaged on their own terms. Climbers succeed only when they yield control. Sometimes, of course, they fail even then, which is very much to the point. Mountains offer uncertain outcomes, novel experiences, surprise endings in a drama in which the climber gets to play a lead. For some people, that is an intoxicating enticement.

This book, then, is about theater: fifty places around the world, most of them cold, barren, starved of oxygen, subject to violent fits of weather—and beautiful—where human ambition collides with the glacial indifference of dangerous terrain. Stories abound in these places. When new stories are ready to be created, the mountains will not disappoint. They will be there.

Joseph Poindexter
Brooklyn, New York 1998

INTRODUCTION

I was seven years old when I had my first taste of climbing—an experience that would steer my life in unimagined directions. My family was at a picnic on a blazing hot August afternoon in 1965; I was a blonde tornado then, a freckle-faced tomboy with skinned knees and dirty elbows. After my parents spread our blanket on the grass, I ran off to look for some friends. A few hundred yards away, I noticed a group of boys swarming around a tall Douglas fir tree. I strolled up to see what was going on—they weren't only playing around the fir, but also inside, where lightning or blight had hollowed out the trunk. The cavern was large enough for five or six curious kids to squeeze into.

Squirming inside, I elbowed my way next to a small boy. "We're climbin' it," he explained. Indeed, one of the boys was doing just that. Hoisting himself to where the walls of the trunk curved inward, he spread his legs wide and braced himself, moving one Keds-shod foot then the other in jerky two-inch increments. He gained about a foot before his left Ked started to slip. "Gangway!" he called, and jumped down.

Two other boys met similar degrees of success; a third got a little higher, but none of them made it very far. As they grew bored and wandered away, I hoisted myself up and braced my feet against the walls of the tree trunk. "Aw, man," cried the boy who'd just collapsed onto the soft floor of the cavern. "A girl's gonna try it."

The remaining boys peered upward. Feeling their eyes on me, I pushed myself steadily up the walls, rocking my weight from one foot to the other. The trick, I learned, was to keep moving. Once you lost momentum, gravity would wrap its tentacles around your ankles. I rose higher. As the gap grew thinner, my legs were closer together, and it got easier. I was eight feet up, then ten, then twelve. At twelve feet the gap closed, but I found a large knothole and crawled out onto a branch. I stood there for a moment, leaning against the tree trunk. The boys gathered outside the tree, gazing up at me. "I made it!" I called down.

Little did I know the adventures that lay ahead.

It was my second summit attempt on Mount Everest in two years. The wind rushed past. I leaned on my ice axe. Steve Ruoss, Jim Frush, Pasang Gaylsen and I were climbing at 28,000 feet. We had one extra oxygen bottle and four people; budgeting at least three hours to cruise back down to camp, that made the entire trip approximately two hours beyond our oxygen supply. Maybe we could squeak by, maybe we could survive the trip without any oxygen—it had been done before.

I looked over at Jim, silently, and he shrugged.

"That's it, then." His voice was thin in his mask. "We go back down and try again tomorrow."

I looked up toward the summit, then back down the ridge, where we'd just struggled for the last two hours. There had to be a way. After all this time, all this effort, I wasn't going to turn around. The weather was perfect, and there was no guarantee that it could hold on for another twenty-four hours. After years of planning, hundreds of thousands of dollars, incredible commitment from people some of us had never even met…we had to get at least one person up there. No matter what anyone says, it comes down to one basic concept: an expedition either touches the summit or comes home ready to explain what went wrong. Steve, Jim, Pasang and I had reached the moment when that decision had to be made. I couldn't walk away: someone had to take the extra oxygen bottle and at least try. The question was, who would that person be?

All I could think to say was, "Let's draw straws."

My heart was racing. I felt as if I was floating out of my boots and up above the ridge, hovering over my climbing partners and the dilemma we faced. We were going to draw for it. Somehow, deep down inside, I knew beyond a shadow of a doubt that I was going to win—I was going to the summit.

"Pasang," Jim said, "choose a number between one and ten." Choose a number? What kind of a wacko Sahib game was this? But he did as he was asked. Pasang nodded to Jim, who turned to

Steve, waiting for his guess.

"Eight," Steve said.

They both turned to me.

"Four."

"I'll take six," Jim said. We all looked over at Pasang.

"Three," he said. "It's three."

The three of them looked at me. We'd already been standing for a few minutes. The cold was seeping through my boots, crawling up my toes and into my ankles. My fingers were numb. I could see the others shifting in their boots. We had to start moving.

Jim, Steve and Pasang could continue to the summit with me—they could risk running out of oxygen and continue their struggle to the top. Steve and Jim decided that for them, the summit of Mount Everest was not worth the risk; they turned back and began their descent. Pasang, however, was willing to join me in the final leg of our journey.

We made it—exhausted and cold but exhilarated. All of a sudden, everything that I had been working for had been accomplished: I stood at the top of the highest mountain in the world, smiling for the camera in my new role as the first American woman to summit Mount Everest. At that moment, I realized that in the end,

every summit boils down to what you're willing to risk to pursue your passion and make your dreams come true.

There is always risk. Even on seemingly easy terrain, when everything seems perfect, if the wind kicks up and the clouds descend the sense of danger is very real. But for most people who climb, the danger is not what draws them to the mountains; rather, it is the possibility of controlling risk. Climbers are drawn by the potential to test our skills, knowledge and judgment—the opportunity to push ourselves beyond our limits.

Climbing is about the unexpected. It doesn't matter how many times a mountain or rock face has been climbed, for each person it's a new experience: an experience in which the outcome is never guaranteed.

Climbing is about curiosity. What's over the next hill, around the next bend? Can it be done? Can I do it?

Climbing is about human relationships: developing bonds of trust and respect that demand honesty and strength—and inevitably tie you together with your partners through matters of life and in death.

For me, climbing is about expression. It's the key that unlocks my spirit, the clearest representation of who I am.

Before the British mountaineer George Leigh Mallory died on Everest in 1924, someone asked him a question: Why do you want to climb Mount Everest? He came up with an answer that was simple and almost Zen-like in its clarity: "Because it is there." It had the ring of manifest destiny, of a daring struggle and a hard-won victory. Although Mallory didn't intend for his words to become an epithet for conquest, they have come to characterize a man-against-mountain attitude that has, for many, characterized the perception of climbing.

But that's not why I climb.

I climb because I'm here.

I don't battle the mountains. I don't conquer anything, even when I do pull myself onto a summit. For me, the triumph comes in every step, in every breath and heartbeat along the way. It's the sheer pleasure of being on the planet, of seeing the mountains around me and, for a brief moment, being a part of them. I climb for a simple reason: because I'm alive.

This book takes us on a journey to fifty peaks around the world: from Mt. Hood, which is a mere forty-five minute drive from downtown Portland, Oregon to K2, the world's second highest peak, which lies at the end of a seven day trek from the nearest remote village.

You'll be awed by stories of courage, strength and wisdom as you read of climbers struggling through wind, snow, falling rock and avalanches to emerge triumphant on top—or sometimes lose their lives trying.

You'll catch glimpses of alpine glow casting its pink light on a snow covered peak, the swirling mist lifting to reveal the ethereal rock face, or the full moon as it gleams on ice and rock…leaving the climber and reader inspired at the magnificence and grace of our planet Earth.

I hope you'll also grow to understand and respect the sport of climbing itself. The dedication, hard work and skill that is involved. The sacrifices and joys, the losses and heartaches and the indomitable spirit that drives these climbers to ever greater heights.

Stacy Allison
Portland, Oregon 1998

WARNING

Alpine, ice and rock climbing are inherently dangerous activities, and carry with them the significant danger of personal injury or death. Do not attempt to embark upon any of the routes described in this book without extensive physical

training and formal instruction, a more thorough understanding of the terrain, knowledge of what is required of the human body in high-altitude environments, the understanding that your actions deeply affect your climbing partners, guides and any search and

rescue teams and the willingness to take responsibility for your actions and those of your party. This book is intended to inspire respect for the mountains and those who climb them responsibly; it is not intended as a guidebook or manual of any kind.

ASIA

The 1,500-mile arc of peaks reaching from the northern tip of Myanmar to Tajikistan and Kyrgyzstan contains the youngest mountains in the world. They seem still to be growing—at a rate of a foot or more every hundred years. They are already the world's largest mountains, by far. The Himalaya, reaching across Bhutan and Nepal, and the Karakoram, situated in northern India and Pakistan, together contain all of the world's 8,000-meter mountains. Add the Pamirs and the Tien Shan, hooking into Kyrgyzstan and western China, and the combined ranges have all the 7,000-meter peaks, too. Asia not only has the biggest mountains, it also has some of the most sacred: Fuji and Ararat, of course, but also Kailas in China and Machapuchare in Nepal—neither of which may be climbed. The sacred mountains of Asia are spell-binding, both for those who live in their shadows and for those who travel long distances to climb them. In the shadow of a great Himalayan peak, there are no non-believers.

K2

ELEVATION	LOCATION	FIRST ASCENT
28, 250 feet	*Karakoram, China/Pakistan*	*Achille Compagnoni, Lino Lacedelli, Italy, 1954*

Everest is higher—but K2 is harder. Both mountains present supreme challenges of endurance, but climbers on K2 encounter ice cliffs, seracs, rock bands and almost unrelenting steepness all the way to the summit, no matter which route they choose. To many, it is mountaineering's ultimate challenge.

K2 lies on the China-Pakistan border near the northwestern end of the 220-mile-long Karakoram Range. Unlike Everest, the world's second highest mountain does not have a monsoon season, so the preferred climbing months are July and August when the weather is most likely to be settled. The walk to K2 up the Baltoro Glacier from Aksole—arguably the most spectacular mountain trek on earth—is like visiting a great hall crammed with masterworks of art. To the east are the Trangos and the Gasherbrums, to the west is the Ogre and Broad Peak. Then, towering over a cirque at the head of the valley, looms K2, a stunning pyramid of granite, limestone and metamorphics. It was first sighted by westerners during the British survey of India by T.G. Montgomerie in 1856. Montgomerie provisionally assigned each peak surveyed the

ALSO KNOWN AS · Godwin Austen (1856 British Survey), Dapsang (Chinese)

> There's no nirvana on the summit....It's a goal, a goal met, but if you don't get down, it doesn't mean a thing.
>
> —*Scott Fischer*

letter K (for Karakoram) plus a number according to their location in the range. Eventually, Karakoram peaks were awarded the names given them by local peoples, but Balti villagers were unaware of K2, never having gotten close enough to it to have seen it. The English assigned the name Godwin Austen, but eventually it was dropped. The name K2 stuck.

The first attempt to climb the mountain was launched by Oscar Eckenstein, a British engineer and chemist who is credited with having invented the crampon. In 1902 he ascended to 20,000 feet on the northeast ridge, a knife-edged route so corniced it was not attempted again for seventy-four years. In 1909 the Duke of Abruzzi, the notable Italian adventurer who had already claimed first ascents on three continents, got no higher than 19,600 feet on K2 via the southeast, but it was his route, later called the Abruzzi Spur, that would finally lead to a first ascent.

Left: From a base camp on Broad Peak (the world's 12th highest mountain), the profile of K2 is caught in starlight. The normal route up the Abruzzi Spur follows the right hand skyline.

Bottom: The adventures on the way to Base Camp are often as unique as those found on the mountain—here climbers ride a cable across the Braldu River in Pakistan on the way to K2.

In the late 1930s two American assaults on K2 came close to reaching the summit. In 1938 a small close-knit group led by cardiologist Charles Houston climbed the Abruzzi Spur to almost 25,000 feet to the lower reaches of the Shoulder before diminishing supplies and threatening weather precipitated a retreat. The following year Fritz Wiessner, a U.S. immigrant from Austria and perhaps America's most ambitious climber at the time, got to within 750 vertical

feet of the summit with Sherpa Pasang Dawa Lama, but it was 6 PM and Pasang, fearful that spirits on the mountain would kill them if they were on the top of the mountain after dark, insisted on turning back. The poignancy of this near miss was overshadowed by the death of American climber Dudley Wolfe and three Sherpas who were sent to rescue him. Wiessner, a much stronger climber than the men he had assembled for the expedition, was blamed for the deaths because he had forged ahead of the rest of his team, thereby causing a crucial breakdown in communication.

In 1953 Charles Houston was headed back to K2 when word reached him that Everest had finally been summitted by the

British. An American success on K2 seemed all the more urgent. As in 1938, Houston selected a group of climbers as much for their compatibility as their talent and experience. By the beginning of August the eight-member American part had ascended to a high camp at 25,600 feet. In keeping with his democratic leadership style, Houston chose summit teams by secret ballot and then waited for the weather to clear.

Instead it worsened. After four days of violent storms, in which one of the tents was torn apart, the group began to discuss retreat. The decision was made for them the following day when team member Art Gilkey collapsed with bloodclots in his left leg. Houston knew immediately

Porters traverse the Godwin-Austen Glacier en route to base camp.

that Gilkey was doomed, but there was never any thought of abandoning him. He was cradled in tent and rope and lowered rope length by rope length down the slopes of the Shoulder by his seven exhausted teammates. But K2 wasn't finished with them. As the climbers approached a bivouac site, one of them lost his footing and, sliding out of control, pulled down four of the others. Only a superhuman belay by Seattle mountaineer Pete Schoening, who had buried the point of his ice axe behind a rock, saved them from plunging to their deaths. Then the moun-

tain delivered one more blow: Gilkey, left momentarily unattended as tents were erected, was swept off the mountain by an avalanche. His remains were not found for forty years. The American party returned home, dispirited and exhausted, having never reached their goal.

K2 was finally climbed in 1954 by a heavily equipped Italian expedition assisted by 500 Hunza porters. Achille Compagnoni and Lino Lacedelli reached the summit via the Abruzzi Spur near dusk on the last day of August and then survived a small avalanche as they descended in darkness back to their high camp.

No new route was opened on K2 until 1977 when Jim Wickwire, Lou Reichardt, Rick Ridgeway and John Roskelly

> SERAC: *An unstable tower of ice that forms in an ice fall. Also, ice pinnacles that result from the sculpting of sun and wind.*

Top: From Dasso, a roadhead village where porters are recruited, it is ten days walk to Concordia, a large campsite on the Baltoro Glacier from which K2, Broad Peak and the Gasherbrums can be reached.

climbed the northeast ridge first tried by Oscar Eckenstein to within 3,000 feet of the summit, then traversed to the Abruzzi Spur to finish the climb. It was the first U.S. ascent of K2; Ridgeway and Roskelly made it the first ascent by anyone without oxygen. In 1986 climbers Alan Rouse and Julie Tullis, a mountain cinematographer, made the first British ascents. But both died during the descent in what was at once a brilliant and devastating year on the mountain. Before the season ended, twenty-seven climbers had reached the summit–most via the Abruzzi Spur but also by difficult new routes on the South Face and the South–Southwest Ridge. Wanda Rutkiewicz of Poland and

Italian climbers wait out bad weather at the base of K2 during the first ascent expedition of 1954.

Lilliane Barrard of France were the first women to reach the top of K2, and Frenchman Benoît Chamoux, using camps and fixed lines that were already in place, went from advance base camp to summit in a single twenty-two-and-a-half-hour push. Yet with thirteen deaths in 1986, one climber died on the mountain for every two who summited.

Base camp for an ascent of K2 on the Abruzzi Spur is established on moraine below the South Face; advance base is two hours higher, where the top of an icefall meets the foot of the Spur. Camps 1 and 2 on a rock rib to the left of the Southeast Face take climbers to 22,000 feet, just above a short but vexing pitch solved in 1938 by William House and known thereafter as House's Chimney. Further up is a section of difficult rock called the Black Pyramid and above that lies a long and exposed slope

of snow and ice that leads to the base of the Shoulder. Camp 3 usually is placed here and Camp 4 on the Shoulder at an elevation of 26,000 feet.

Unfortunately, the most difficult climbing is still ahead. The Shoulder narrows to the Bottleneck, a steep couloir blocked at the top by huge seracs. These must be circumvented by an extremely exposed traverse above a 10,000-foot face. The route finally eases off, but the summit is still hours away in the painfully thin air of the earth's second highest and most merciless mountain.

Left: Its latitude— 35 degrees north—subjects K2 to harsher winters than the more southerly Himalaya. But, unlike those mountains, it does not have a summertime monsoon, so the normal climbing season is June to August.

Bottom: The forty-mile-long Baltoro Glacier, one of the world's longest, leads to base camps for K2, the Trango Towers and the Gasherbrum Peaks.

Brotherhood

FROM *K2: The Story of the Savage Mountain*
BY JIM CURRAN

All had gone well on this, the second American attempt to climb K2. But with the team poised to make a push to the summit, storms descended on the mountain. Then the Americans were hit by a greater calamity: One of the climbers, Art Gilkey, had developed blood clots in his left leg and soon was unable to move on his own. Suddenly the entire team, which refused to abandon one of their members, was in the gravest peril.

August 10 dawned cold, grim and windy. Conversations had to be yelled to be understood. Art had to descend, a clot was forming in his other leg and he couldn't survive much longer at that height.

Quickly the others packed up, taking the lightest of the tents, "in case of emergency," as Bob Bates wrote. (One has to wonder just what would constitute an emergency, if not their present predicament.) Then they set off. "Each of us realised that he was beginning the most dangerous day's work of his life."

The nightmare descent began. In freezing, numbing spindrift Gilkey was first pulled through deep snow then, when the angle increased, lowered. Every manoeuvre demanded the utmost concentration and the seven battered men began to realise the enormity of their task. Art Gilkey, strapped into a makeshift stretcher of a wrapped tent, a rucksack and a rope cradle, was uncomplaining but silent, his face a bluish grey. But whenever anyone asked how he was he would force a smile. "Just fine . . . just fine."

Painfully slowly they lost height. At one stage they set off a powder-snow avalanche which nearly swept Craig and Gilkey away, but the rope from above held. At last they got to a point on the rock rib where they could start to traverse across to the abandoned site of Camp VII. Pete Schoening was belaying Art Gilkey and Dee Molenaar. Above them were Houston and Bates and Bell and Streather. Craig had unroped from Gilkey and crossed to the shelf on which the camp had been placed.

Suddenly George Bell slipped on hard ice and fell out of control. Streather was pulled off and the two of them cannoned into Houston and Bates who were traversing below them. All four hurtled down the slope with nothing to stop them going all the way to the Godwin-Austen Glacier—nothing, that is, except the rope from Art Gilkey to Dee Molenaar, which somehow caught and snagged Tony Streather. Molenaar was plucked off and all five carried on falling until the strain came on to Art Gilkey and that in turn came on Pete Schoening belaying him above with an ice-axe jammed into snow behind a rock. Miraculously, Schoening held them all. Miraculously, no rope broke.

The whole jumble of tangled rope and bodies slid to a halt in total confusion. Far below George Bell minus rucksack, glasses and mittens staggered in confusion. Bob Bates and Dee Molenaar were tangled together and were almost cutting Tony Streather in half. And Charlie Houston lay crumpled and unconscious on a ledge poised over a huge drop. Bob Bates soloed down to him and Houston came round, concussed and confused. "Where are we?" he kept repeating. "What are we doing here?"

Bob Bates, knowing that if Charlie Houston couldn't help himself no one else could, looked his old friend in the eye. "Charlie, if you ever want to see Dorcas and Penny [his wife and daughter] again, climb up there right now!"

Mechanically Houston obeyed and climbed brilliantly. Bates followed slowly to reach Dee Molenaar, trying to answer Charlie's insistent question, "What are we doing here?"

Stunned, shocked, facing frostbite and, above all, exhausted, it was essential to get a tent up quickly. Gilkey, who had not fallen and was probably the warmest of them all, was anchored securely by two ice-axes in the gully he was being lowered into when the accident had occurred. The others moved across and tried to get Bell and Houston warmed up in the tent. Now Pete Schoening, the strongman of the party, seemed on the verge of collapse and was coughing uncontrollably. Art Gilkey had been shouting to them but in the wind they couldn't understand what he was saying. At last Bob Bates and Tony Streather returned to the gully to try and bring him down. Bob Bates wrote, "What we saw there I shall never forget. The whole slope was bare of life. Art Gilkey was gone."

Art Gilkey's death, however harrowing, undoubtedly saved them. Now they only had to fight for their own survival and it would take them the whole of the next day just to get down to Camp VI, which was still over 7000 metres. On the descent Tony Streather recovered a small bag, believing it belonged to Art Gilkey. But it didn't. It belonged to George Bell and miraculously contained a spare pair of unbroken glasses which cheered him up immensely. There was no sign of Gilkey except for some blood-streaked rocks, a tangle of ropes and an ice-axe shaft jammed in some rocks. No one mentioned this on the way down and it was not until the team was reunited that they all admitted they had seen those remnants.

CHARLES S. HOUSTON, M.D.

1913–

"On great mountains, all purpose is concentrated on the single job at hand, yet the summit is but a token of success, and the attempt is worthy in itself."

HOME BASE ▪ *Burlington, Vermont*

CLIMBING FEATS ▪ *first ascent, Mount Foraker, co-leader of first ascent expedition on Nanda Devi, foremost authority on altitude sickness*

In 1934 Charlie Houston was at base camp on Mount Foraker, having completed the first ascent of what was then the highest unclimbed peak in North America. Celebrating his triumph and his twenty-first birthday, Houston helped drain a bottle of Scotch and then retired to his sleeping bag. In the middle of the night he was brought rudely back to his senses as an earthquake destroyed the camp, causing him instantly to swear off alcohol. In a life devoted equally to medicine and mountains, this would become one of the few promises Houston would fail to keep.

The son of an international lawyer and climbing enthusiast, Houston grew up in New York City but by age twelve was spending summers on the spires of Chamonix. At Harvard he joined a remarkable group of climbers—Bob Bates, Brad Washburn, H. Adams Carter among them—who together moved to the forefront of American mountaineering in the years before and after World War II. Houston, the most ambitious of them, helped organize four Himalayan expeditions between 1936 and 1953, including the first ascent of Nanda Devi and two valiant attempts on K2. In 1950 he was among the first to reconnoiter the Western Cwm, South Col route on Everest.

Meanwhile, Houston found time to become a doctor, attending Columbia medical school after graduating from Harvard with the Class of 1935. During the war as a Navy medic, he conducted his first research into the effects of altitude on human physiology. Four volunteers were placed in a hyperbaric chamber and over a period of thirty-four days "climbed" to higher and higher eleva-

Dr. Houston and his wife, Dorcas, returning from a 1953 K2 expedition.

tions as the atmospheric pressure in the chamber was lowered. At the equivalent of 26,900 feet two of the volunteers requested oxygen. "But the other pair continued on, reaching 8,848 meters [29,028 feet]," Houston wrote in a research report on the study. "There is nothing critical, physiologically speaking," he concluded, "about the summit of Everest."

But there is much the human body needs to contend with at altitude, and Houston spent many years documenting what goes wrong and what to do about it. From 1967 to 1979 he directed research of human physiology at a lab at 17,500 feet on a flank of Mount Logan in the Yukon and is generally credited with having done more to unravel the mysteries of high altitude oxygen deprivation than any other man.

For those who have climbed with him, Houston represents another quality: a passionate commitment to amateurism and to mountaineering as a "fellowship dedicated to skill, enjoyment and trust," as he wrote recently. "When the goal is not the search for beauty, peace, serenity, but material things or national pride, is not the quest compromised?"

NANGA PARBAT

ELEVATION	LOCATION	FIRST ASCENT
26,658 feet	*Punjab Himalaya, Pakistan*	*Hermann Buhl, Austria, 1953*

TAJIKISTAN

CHINA

AFGHANISTAN

Karakoram Range

Pangi Range

K2

Nanga Parbat

Indus River

Trango
Towers

Islamabad

Srinagar

Ladakh Range

Rawalpindi

Zaskar Mts

PAKISTAN

INDIA

One of the most astonishing feats of survival in the annals of mountaineering took place high on the flanks of Nanga Parbat, the world's ninth highest mountain. On June 31, 1953, the leaders of a German-Austrian expedition to Nanga Parbat ("Naked Mountain" in Sanskrit) ordered climbers still on the mountain's northern Rakhiot Face to come down. They had gotten no higher than 20,000 feet, and the expedition was being abandoned. The mountain that had repulsed every attempt to climb it for 58 years had seemingly thwarted yet another one. But the climbers refused to come down. Instead, two of them, Hermann Buhl and Otto Kempter, moved up to a high camp below the Silver Saddle at 24,500 feet. Then on July 3, Buhl and Kempter set out for the summit. Kempter soon turned around, but Buhl kept going, and

at 7 PM he crawled, literally, onto Nanga Parbat's peak.

The ascent, however, was only a prelude to Buhl's real adventure. He had begun the descent with renewed energy and was circumventing a cliff of rock by way of an icy slope when his left crampon came off. Inexplicably,

Right: On July 23, 1953, twenty days after he stood alone on the summit of Nanga Parbat, Hermann Buhl (followed by expedition leader Karl Herrligkoffer) arrives in Rome en route to Munich and a celebration of his triumphant first ascent. A special boot protects his frostbitten right foot.

Bottom: Hunza porters carry across the Rakhiot Glacier to an advance camp on the 1934 German expedition. A storm smashed into the mountain, trapping sixteen climbers and porters at 24,500 feet. Only half survived the descent.

The Diamir Flank of Nanga Parbat separates the sunlit Diamir Face from the vast Rupal face to the south.

he had left his ice ax with a Pakistani banner tied to it on the summit, so now he had to scratch steps in the ice with the ski poles he still had with him. At 9 PM, with an abruptness that was frightening, darkness closed around him. Buhl could go no further until the light of a new day, but on the 60 degree slope, still at 26,000 feet, there was no place to recline or even to sit. He inched downward until he reached a narrow ledge with just enough space for his feet. It was here that he would have to wait out the darkness. Because he had cached his rucksack on the ascent to save energy, he had nothing with which to secure himself to his perch, and his greatest fear was that he would fall asleep and topple into the abyss below him. Cold, thirst and hunger stretched minutes into hours. He began to

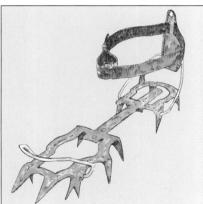

CRAMPON: *a boot-sole shaped framework of spikes that attaches to the bottom of the boot to provide purchase in steeply sloping snow and ice*

believe that the night would not end. "Then," Buhl wrote in his account of the climb, "behind a toothy mountain range in the far distance, a streak of light broadened and rose gradually higher. For me its light was the light of salvation." The hellish nightmare of darkness had finally ended. Forty-one hours after he had set out for the summit, Buhl stumbled back to his high camp

A base camp in the Karakoram, which contains four of the fourteen 8,000-meter mountains and some of the world's longest glaciers.

and the joyful embrace of his teammates.

Buhl had escaped. But Nanga Parbat, the most westerly of the 8,000-meter (26,240 feet) peaks, infamous for its storms and avalanches, had already claimed

The most westerly of the 8,000-meter peaks, Nanga Parbat is battered by storms from the Indus River basin, which feed the avalanches for which the mountain is notorious.

thirty-one lives. The death toll began in 1895 when famed mountaineer Alfred Mummery, who had reached to nearly 23,000 feet on the mountain, disappeared with two Gurkhas while crossing a spur to assess the viability of a different route. In 1934 a German expedition led by Willy Merkl pushed a route up the Rakhiot Face above the Silver Saddle to 25,250 feet, but six climbers and eleven porters were pinned down on the saddle by a vicious storm. Unable to hold out, all seventeen men ventured out into the blizzard; nine, including Merkl, died. In 1937 another German expedition suffered an even more appalling loss when seven climbers

and nine porters all perished in an avalanche that swept through their camp high on the Rakhiot Face. In 1938 German climbers, during another unsuccessful bid for the summit, came upon Merkl's body. In a pocket was a letter, written possibly in anticipation of being found unconscious, in which the doomed man begged for help.

The leader of the 1953 expedition, Merkl's stepbrother Karl Maria Herrligkoffer, returned to the mountain in 1962 to head a second ascent, this time on the western Diamir Face. He was back again in 1970 to tackle the awesome Rupal Face, which ranks with Denali's Wickersham Wall and the West Face of Dhaulagiri as the largest on earth. During this expedition another epic drama was written on Nanga Parbat's perilous slopes. The first to reach the summit via the Rupal Face were famed Austrian climber Reinhold Messner and his brother

Günther. Once there, however, Reinhold decided that a descent of the face would be too dangerous for his brother, who had taken ill on the ascent, and elected to go down an uncharted route on the other side of the mountain. After two harrowing days and nights, the pair had finally gained the easier lower slopes on the Diamir Face when Günther, lagging behind Reinhold, was swept off the mountain by an avalanche.

For a while, Reinhold Messner was so traumatized by the accident that he gave up climbing. But Nanga Parbat became an obsession. He returned the following year to search for Günther's body. In 1973 and 1977 he tried to climb the mountain solo—something that had never been done on an 8,000-meter peak. In 1978, as if to exorcise a demon, he was back again. This time he succeeded—alone, without oxygen, and with nothing more than ice axe and crampons.

There is no standard route on Nanga Parbat. The most frequently used is a route established in 1962 by Austrian Toni Kinshofer on the Diamir Face. Base Camp at 14,000 feet on the Diamir Glacier is best reached on a four-day walk from the roadhead at Bunar to the north. The route ascends a steep couloir, climbs a difficult 200-foot band of vertical rock, slants up toward the mountain's lower north summit and then breaks through a band of rock and seracs to a col between the summits called the Bazhin Hollow. At this point Kinshofer joined the Buhl route on the north ridge to the summit, but a variation which continues southward below the ridge to a snow slope on the west has proven to be easier.

From the summit mountains as far off as the Pamirs in Tajikistan are visible to the north; to the northeast is the stunning pyramid of K2. And to Nanga Parbat's west: the weather systems that have turned this mountain into a deathtrap for so many climbers.

This state of merging into infinity is a sensation I have frequently experienced on big mountains.... Up there, I didn't question what I was doing, why I was there. The climbing, the concentration, the struggle to push myself forward, those were the answers. I was my own answer, the question was canceled out.

—Reinhold Messner on Nanga Parbat

Creativity and Suffering

FROM *All 14 Eight-Thousanders*
BY REINHOLD MESSNER, TRANSLATED FROM GERMAN BY AUDREY SALKELD.

In 1986 Austrian Reinhold Messner, the most influential Himalayan climber ever, became the first person to summit on the 14 mountains in the world that exceed 8,000 meters (26,240 feet). He describes here the essential ingredients of that achievement.

To climb eight-thousanders is less a matter of skill and know-how, which is what rock climbing demands; far more, it requires an optimum combination of endurance, will-power, and instinct, and an ability to tolerate suffering. The right thing to do at any given moment is only learnt over decades. You can compare an expedition like this with a kind of Tour de France or Giro d'Italia. These long competitions last for weeks and exact the utmost from professional cyclists every day of that time.

On eight-thousanders it is not important whether you are a professional in the commercial sense of the word, as I am, or an amateur. It is like art. A pro has no more time to train than an amateur, than someone who works in any other field of life. Whether you climb in your free time and are able to go on expeditions in your annual holidays, or whether you divide your time between mountain activities, lecture halls and management is unimportant. The only thing that matters is how seriously you take what you do, and how creative you can be at it.

I finance not only my expeditions but also my life indirectly from climbing and directly from marketing the 'waste products' of climbing. But I have to spend the greater part of the time that I am in Europe at the writing desk, or standing on a platform, or consulting with business partners, or designing improved items of equipment. It requires considerable professionalism to manage such a job success fully; and professionalism takes application, skill and time, which is then lost to training.

Only if a climber keeps forcing himself to train, if he lets himself be driven by his own fanaticism to the outposts of his potential, can these limits be moved—his personal limits, that is, as well as the limits of Alpinism. To be fully stretched means being in perpetual momentum, being dragged along. Only thus is the climber capable of dismantling the inner barriers when he finds himself, after months of work and preparation, at the foot of a big wall. Only thus can he cope with the isolation, the apprehension and the spells of faintness that are much harder to overcome than all the rocks in the world. Good fortune and benign providence are presents from the gods, as the Tibetans say; they are an extra. But the prerequisites for success the climber has to acquire for himself—they are never given freely, anywhere.

TRANGO TOWER

ELEVATION

20,469 feet

LOCATION

Karakoram, Pakistan

FIRST ASCENT

Mo Anthoine, Martin Boysen, Joe Brown, Malcolm Howells, England, 1976

The Trango Towers rise out of the Baltoro Glacier region like ruined spires of a long-abandoned medieval city—at once inspiring and terrifying. Three of them ascend to more than 20,000 feet and contain more glacier-polished granite than in all of Yosemite National Park. At their center stands Trango itself, an awesome column of immaculate rock and arguably the most exquisite big wall on earth. Trango is so steep and lacking in

weakness that even to dream of climbing it might have, at one point, been deemed a rash and irresponsible act. But in 1956 British hardman Joe Brown sighted the obelisk during an expedition to the central Karakoram and began to dream.

It was nineteen years before Brown's vision was put to the test. In 1975, biology teacher Martin Boysen, perhaps the most

ALSO KNOWN AS • Nameless Tower

John Roskelly jumars up fixed rope to regain the height of the previous day's climb in a U.S. team first ascent of Great Trango in 1977.

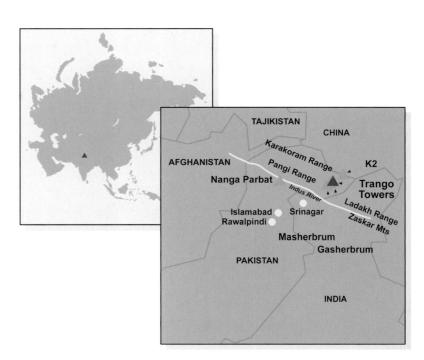

Well, I don't think getting to the top is all that important. You can always have another go. The things you remember after a trip are not standing on the summit but what went on while you were on the route. The nicest feeling is to know that you are relying on someone else and he is relying on you.

—*Mo Anthoine*

Mike Lilygren is bathed in morning sunlight at 18,500 feet on Trango Tower during the first free climb of the East Face.

precocious climber of his generation, legendary wildman Mo Anthoine, climber Malcolm Howells and Brown made an attempt on the Southwest Face of Trango. It nearly ended in tragedy. More than halfway up Boysen was leading a nasty pitch when he encountered an off-width crack, not wide enough for his body but too wide to grip a fist or a boot. So he wedged his knee into it. But as he tried to raise himself onto the next stance, the crack maintained a viselike grip on his knee. He pulled, twisted and cursed, but the knee wouldn't budge. After three desperate hours Boysen had one last idea. Using a piton for a knife, he cut away the pantleg around the knee and was finally able to extricate it. But all in all, the climbing had gone too slowly, and the team, running low on supplies, had to beat a retreat.

The following year the same foursome returned. Boysen took on his nemesis once again. This time he solved the off-width crack, and the team succeeded in a climb that was universally recognized as a tour de force.

Moonlight illuminates the Trangos from a base camp at 16,500 feet.

A psychological barrier had been breached and soon routes were being established on other of the Trangos. Two on Great Trango, Grande Voyage and Norwegian Pillar, are ranked among the hardest rock climbs in the world (Hans Christian Doseth and Finr. Daelhi fell to their deaths after having made the first ascent of the Norwegian Pillar). But the splendidly symmetrical Trango Tower remains the most popular spire in the area. One of its routes is so exacting that by the late 1990s it had never been repeated. It was created in 1989 by Germans Kurt Albert and Wolfgang Güllich, two supremely gifted technical climbers who were determined to apply the principles of rock climbing to what to then was considered a mountaineering challenge. They called their chosen route, an arête separating the Southeast and Southwest faces of the tower, "Eternal Flame", after an album by the Bangles, with each of its twenty-two pitches named for a song in

Steve Bechtel crosses the Braldu River on the way in to Base Camp in 1995.

the album. A pendulum move was called "Close Your Eyes"; a desperately hard finger crack, the crux of the route, "Say My Name"; and an even thinner crack at the top of the climb

HANGING BIVOUAC TENT: *a tent shelter designed to maintain its shape when suspended from a vertical wall*

PENDULUM: *An aid technique in which the climber traverses a blank section of rock by swinging from the rope after having clipped into a fixed point and then descended far enough to provide a radius of rope on which to swing.*

If we need rope ladders
to ascend a peak,
then we've climbed
our ladders, not the
mountain itself.

—*Todd Skinner*

from which Albert took several leader falls, "Ease the Pain." In fact, Albert, who had sprained an ankle on a lower pitch, was taking fistfuls of aspirin to complete the climb.

Since then, there have been other notable climbs on Trango. In 1995, history was made once again on the magnificent Trango Tower. Todd Skinner, a highly accomplished sport climber, led what he called "a team of cowboys from Wyoming" on the first free ascent of the daunting East Face. The team included the last-minute addition of Jeff Bechtel, a hunting guide with little climbing experience who was filling in for his brother Steve, who had fallen ill at base camp. They worked out the lower 1,000 feet from a camp on the shoulder at 18,500 feet, and the upper 1,000 feet from Hanging Camp: two tents that were clipped onto the face itself.

> **FREE CLIMBING:** *Rock climbing in which the ascent is made by way of the rock alone. Equipment is used only for protection.*

Climber's hands often take a serious beating on big wall climbs—to make matters worse, high altitude slows the healing process. Here, one of the members of the 1995 East Face ascent adjust a gri-gri, which is used as a brake on rappel. At right, Trango's East Face route.

Sticking it out through an epic storm, low supplies and the physiological challenges that come with spending sixty nights (they had only planned to be on the Tower for three weeks) above 18,500 feet, the team accomplished their goal: they had completed all thirty-four pitches and summited Trango Tower without a single piece of aid. When they reached the top, Bechtel took off his hat and dedicated their climb to the great state of Wyoming.

No matter what route or technique you use, Trango consistently offers no less than a supreme test of technique, stamina and courage.

20,469 feet

hanging camp

shoulder camp
18,500

NANDA DEVI

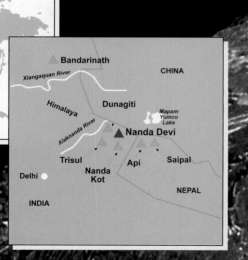

ELEVATION

25,645 feet

LOCATION

Garhwal Himalaya, India

FIRST ASCENT

Noel Odell, William Tilman, England, 1936

Willi Unsoeld and his daughter Nanda Devi Unsoeld climbed Washington's Mount Eldorado in 1972, four years before their fateful visit to the mountain for which Devi was named.

Ringed by peaks that rise to 20,000 feet and more, India's highest mountain ouside of Sikkim fills its visitors with awe. To many who have climbed in Asia, Nanda Devi is the most majestic Himalayan of all. Certainly it possesses one of the most poignant moments in mountaineering history. In 1976 a team of American and Indian mountaineers went to Nanda Devi to attempt the unclimbed North Ridge. Among the team members were Everester Willi Unsoeld, who considered the mountain the most beautiful he had ever seen, and the daughter he had named for it, Nanda Devi Unsoeld. The

ridge turned out to be harder than the climbers had anticipated, but in late August Americans Lou Reichardt, John Roskelly and Jim States finally pushed a route to the summit.

And now it was the turn of the second threesome, Andrew Harvard, Peter Lev and Devi Unsoeld. During the ascent to the high camp, Devi began for the first time to show the effects of diarrhea and an abdominal hernia that had developed early in the expedition. Her pace was slow and she didn't arrive until midnight. Fatigue and bad weather pinned them down for three days, and by then, Willi Unsoeld had joined the group in hopes of making the

summit bid with them. On the fifth day their camp was hit hard by a blizzard, and they decided to retreat. But as they were packing up, Devi, who had been up all night with intestinal distress, weakened and fell unconscious. Then with appalling swiftness she died. The three stricken men laid her to rest high on the North Ridge. Speechless and numb, they returned to base camp and informed the rest of the party of the tragedy. To some of the porters the death was full of portent. Devi, they said, had been the true "Bliss-Giving Goddess," her name in Sanskrit, and she had now returned to her mountain.

Nanda Devi has been an object of fascination for more than 100 years, but simply reaching the base of the mountain appeared to be an insurmountable challenge. In 1934 English climbers Eric Shipton and William Tilman finally discovered a weakness in the mountain's outer defenses, the Rishi Ganga Gorge that cuts through the western wall of the Nanda Devi Sanctuary. The two planned to return the following year but were deflected by an invitation to join a small Everest expedition. When Shipton returned to Everest in 1936, Tilman and three of his countrymen joined the first American team to venture to the Himalaya. Their objective: a first ascent of Nanda Devi.

The eight climbers encountered their first hurdle before they even reached the Sanctuary, when their porters refused to cross the swollen Rishi Ganga River. Tilman, cleverly he thought, forded the river himself, taking with him all the expedition's local currency and then telling the porters they would be paid on the other side. They would have none of it; they promptly turned around and went home. So the climbers themselves had to ferry supplies to their base camp at 17,000 feet under the South Ridge—a long haul for Sahibs unaccustomed to carrying at elevation—but the work put them in supremely good condition for the climb. By late August they had established four camps on the South Ridge, and then realizing they needed an expedition leader to choose a summit team, elected Tilman— unanimously—by secret ballot. Tilman, in turn, chose Noel Odell, who was on Everest in 1924 and was the last man to see Mallory and Irvine alive, and Dr. Charles S. Houston of the U.S., who had been one of the prime instigators of the expedition.

The two were poised for a push to the summit when Houston was stricken with food poisoning from a tainted can of corned beef hash. Tilman took his place, and he and Odell went to the top the following day. It was to date the highest peak ever climbed—and would remain so

Right: Tents on the Longstaff Col at 19,000 feet wear a thin dusting of predawn snow.

Bottom: Indian porters monitor the proceedings as loads are weighed for the carry to base camp.

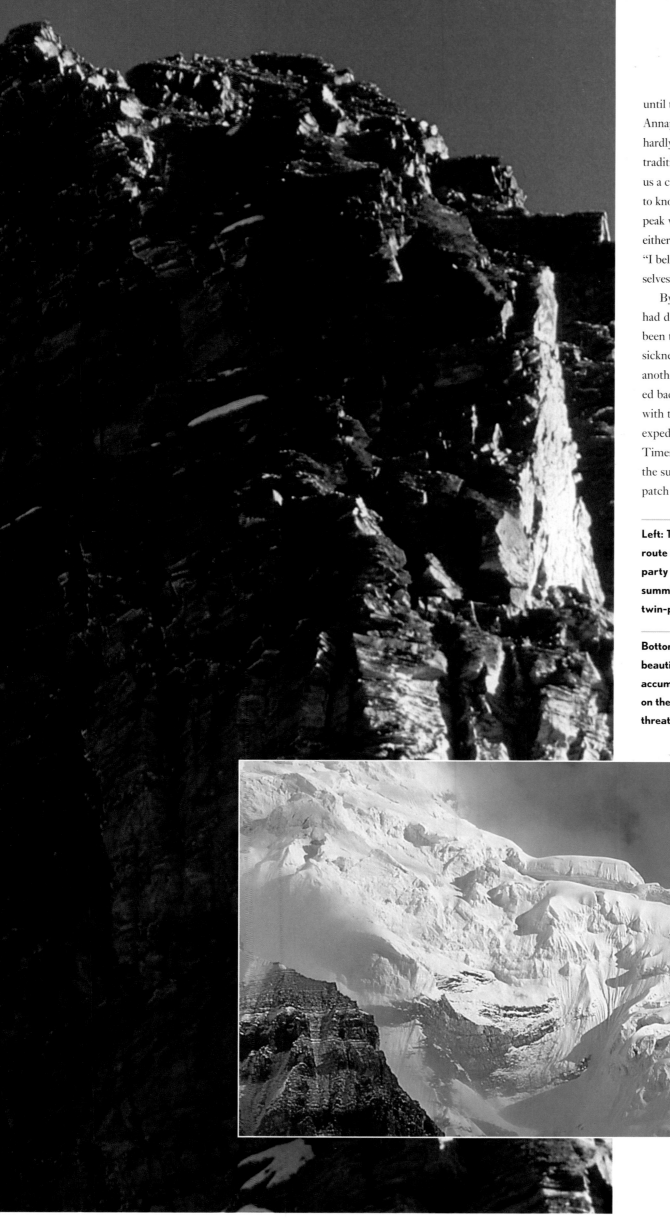

until the French ascent of Annapurna in 1950—but it was hardly an occasion to break with traditional British reserve. "It gave us a curious feeling of exaltation to know that we were above every peak within hundreds of miles on either hand," Tilman later wrote. "I believe we so far forgot ourselves as to shake hands on it."

By the time Tilman and Odell had descended, the team had been too weakened by altitude sickness and frostbite to send another pair up, so they all headed back to base camp. In keeping with the egalitarian spirit of the expedition, the team wired the Times of London: "Two reached the summit August 29." The dispatch gave no names.

Left: The elegant South Ridge, the route taken by the first ascent party in 1936, leads to the east summit, the highest point on the twin-peaked mountain.

Bottom: Cornices—although quite beautiful—indicate heavy snow accumulation; this corniced ridge on the east side of Nanda Devi threatens major avalanche activity.

Since then, most ascents of Nanda Devi have followed the 1936 South Ridge route. The walk-in from Lata up the Dhauli Ganga Valley takes about seven days. From base camp on the Dakshini Nanda Devi Glacier, the route circles eastward around the base of the heavily pinnacled Coxcomb Ridge and then ascends westerly onto the South Ridge. It follows the ridge to a saddle at 21,300 feet and up striated rock to a top camp at 24,000 feet. From here, the ridge narrows to a knife edge with huge drops to either side, as it rises stepwise to an upper snow slope. The final obstacle is a rock cliff just under the summit ridge.

The small, alpine-style approach of the first-ascent party was decades ahead of its time, as expeditions of the 1950s and 1960s tried to overwhelm big mountains with manpower and equipment instead of speed and agility. Shipton, who regretted having gone to Everest instead of Nanda Devi, called the Anglo-American effort, "the finest mountaineering achievement ever performed in the Himalaya."

Left: Jeff Petty clips into a fixed line at 20,000 feet to protect his descent of a steep section of the South Ridge.

Bottom: Petty demonstrates technique at advance base camp, while his teammates sort out fuel bottles and ice climbing gear.

Father and Daughter

FROM "NANDA DEVI FROM THE NORTH"
BY WILLI UNSOELD

After three Americans had summited Nanda Devi during the 1976 expedition celebrating the 40th anniversary of the first ascent, Peter Lev, Andrew Harvard and Nanda Devi Unsoeld moved up to Camp IV to make the second assault on the summit. On September 6, after the third summit team had disintegrated because of fatigue and illness, Devi's father Willi Unsoeld set out on his own to join the second team.

The familiar ground flowed smoothly past under my Jumars [ascenders] until I reached the snowfield. I was elated to see that to the mid-point it had taken only two-and-three-quarters hours actual Jumar time. There I added more food and a tent from the cache and put on my crampons for the traverse into the gully (called "Spindrift Alley" by the first party). My pack was very heavy now, but I found the beauty and boldness of the route totally exhilarating. The 400 feet of the gully were a ghastly slog with no certain footing in the depth of sugar snow which had accumulated. The final pitch to the lip at Camp IV was 200 feet of vertical going with occasional small traverse to attempt to keep the rope away from the nastier rock teeth which pro-truded from the wall. It was a definite relief to heave myself over the snow lip at the top.

September 7 was a pure blizzard at Camp IV and none of us moved from the tent. It was a day full of liquids and the easy talk which fills rest days at high altitudes. Devi was feeling better, but was still quite weak when measured against the energy output required for the summit try. It was decided that she should wait at Camp IV while the rest of us made our try and then descend with us the same day to Camp III.

However, that night was a bad one for Devi. Her stomach generated gas in such quantities that she simply could not sleep and spent most of the night sitting up to belch it forth. By morning she was extremely tired. Because of the high winds and continuing snow, we decided to head down at noon and wait for better weather in the relative comfort of Camp III. Pete, Andy and Devi had now been at 24,000 feet for nearly five days. We were packed for departure when at 11:45 Devi was suddenly stricken. She had time only to say with great calm, "I am going to die," when she lapsed into unconsciousness. We tried mouth-to-mouth resuscitation and CPR, but with no sign of success. Within fifteen min-utes I felt her lips growing cold against mine and I know that we had lost her. We continued our efforts to revive her for another half hour without result. As the enormity of our loss slowly sank in, the three of us could only cling to one another for comfort while tears coursed down our beards.

As our faculties gradually returned to us, we discussed what was to be done. We agreed that it would be most fitting for Devi's body to be committed to the snows of the mountain for which she had come to feel such a deep attachment. Andy, Peter and I knelt in a circle in the snow and grasped hands while each chanted a broken farewell to the comrade who had so recently filled such a vivid place in our lives. My final prayer was one of thanksgiving for a world filled with the sublimity of the high places, for the sheer beauty of the mountains and for the surpassing miracle that we should be so formed as to respond with ecstasy to such beauty, and for the constant element of danger without which the mountain experience would not exercise such a grip on our sensibilities. We then laid the body to rest in its icy tomb, at rest on the breast of the Bliss-Giving Goddess Nanda.

CHINA
(TIBET)

Makalu   Kanchenjunga

Everest   Pauhunri

NEPAL
         Gangtok   BHUTAN
Sapt Kosi

Darjeeling   SIKKIM   INDIA

         BANGLADESH

INDIA

                  BURMA

Bay of Bengal

KANGCHENJUNGA

ELEVATION

28,208 feet

LOCATION

*Kangchenjunga
Himal, Sikkim,
India*

FIRST ASCENT

*George Band,
Joe Brown,
Norman Hardie,
Tony Streather,
England, 1955*

George Band and Joe Brown had been on the flanks of Kangchenjunga for weeks, and now they were finally approaching the summit to claim a first ascent of the world's third highest mountain. But a few feet short of the summit pinnacle, they stopped and proceeded no higher. The very top of Kangchenjunga would remain untouched.

One of the world's most sacred mountains, Kangchenjunga—roughly translated, the name means "Five Treasuries of the Great

PRUSIK: *A knot adapted to mountaineering from violin string repair by Dr. Karl Prusik of Austria, that can be moved upward on a rope to which it is attached but holds when weighted downward. In emergency situations, it performs like the mechanical ascenders that have superseded it*

Snows"—can be climbed only on condition that no one trod upon the summit itself. As far as is known, none of the two dozen or so summit parties on Kangchenjunga's main peak has violated this agreement. Each of its five peaks is believed to be the repository of riches: gold, silver, gems, grain and holy books. The god of the mountain, depicted as a red deity, armor-clad and riding a white lion, is thought to be wrathful, capable of destroying crops, even entire villages with storms and floods. Even Western climbers, normally of a highly pragmatic nature, have come under Kangchenjunga's spell. English mountaineer Frank Smythe, with a 1930 expedition in which an avalanche killed a Sherpa and nearly wiped out the entire team, felt he was in the presence of a malevolent spirit. "Kanchenjunga is something more than unfriendly," he wrote, "it is imbued with a blind unreasoning hatred towards the mountaineer."

In 1977 Sikkim lamas were certain that the god had been angered. A large Indian military expedition was on the mountain when a huge boom was heard in the surrounding valleys. The avalanches and landslides that followed persuaded the lamas that the deity had been disturbed, a belief that was strengthened shortly thereafter by the death of a Sherpa in a fall.

Once an independent Buddhist Kingdom, Sikkim is now a tiny state of India; it measures only 2800 square miles. Although it is small, it offers extraordinary variety and beauty to trekkers—from its stunning monasteries to its more than 600 varieties of orchids, Sikkim is a jewel nestled between Bhutan and Nepal. Besides the Nepalese, who make up the majority of the population; there are two other distinct groups: the Lepsha and the Bhutia, both of which settled in this area over 400 years ago. The friendliness and welcoming

A basket of supplies, carried by a Sherpani porter, are on their way to Kangchenjunga base camp at 18,000 feet.

nature of the Sikkimese people is legendary; when Englishman Douglas Freshfield made a circuit of the mountain in 1899, villagers willingly accepted his foreign currency. The positive aspects to Sikkim are numerous and varied, but for the mountaineer, the focus is singular: Kangchenjunga.

Kangchenjunga's massive stature cannot fail to impress. Its ridges, radiating in all four directions, contain four peaks that exceed 8,000 meters in height. The main summit dominates the view from the hill station of Darjeeling, more than sixty miles to the south. Darjeeling and the Sikkimese capitol of Gangtok are the nearest towns, although many of the villages seen by early Western visitors to the region are no longer there. Sir Joseph Hooker, who visited eastern

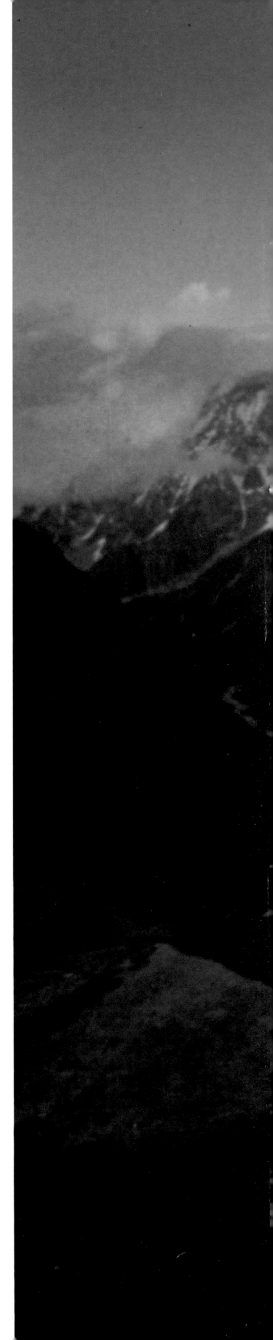

the Bay of Bengal—was to leave fixed rope on a few of the steepest pitches of the climb in case they were forced to make a rapid retreat. Their route, varied in some years to avoid rockfall from hanging glaciers, has been used by most of the subsequent parties on the mountain.

The walk-in from Taplejung, Nepal, which has an airstrip, to the wildflower-strewn Pangpema meadows takes about 10 days. Here at an elevation of 16,860 feet under the North Ridge is where the Anglo-French team set up base camp. Above them the ascent was defended by three cliffs set back from each other in a giant steps, seemingly designed, wrote Boardman, to

> **FIXED LINE:** *Rope that is left in place on steep snow slopes or rock faces to facilitate subsequent ascent and descent in an expedition-style climb.*

repel mountaineers. The British party circumvented the first step by climbing a steep slope to a col between Kangchenjunga and the double-headed Twin Peaks to the north. From there the team headed up the North Ridge and gained the Great Terrace via a difficult outcrop called the Castle. But their hard-won ascent to 26,000 feet was met by Kangchenjunga's vicious wind, which destroyed one of their tents at 26,000 feet and drove them back to Pangpema. After a few days of recuperation, the English climbers (Bettembourg stayed behind) re-ascended the North Ridge, cut westward above the Castle to gain the West Ridge and then to the summit through the red pinnacles.

The threesome took care, as

Climbers traversing a snow field on Pangpema keep the vast South Face of the third highest mountain at their backs.

had the successful teams before then, to avoid setting foot on the summit itself. "I had always thought that a mountain was magnificently indifferent," Boardman wrote in an account of the ascent. "But this year I began to discover how much your physical experience of a mountain depends on your mental attitude. At times Kangchenjunga seemed to have a mind. If you did not match up, you were quickly rejected. But if you approached with a mixture of confidence, respect and caution," he continued, "it was usually just possible to come through the worst, and discover a special reward."

Bottom: A typically colorful base camp under the north face of the mountain.

Each of its five peaks is believed to be the repository of riches: gold, silver, gems, grain and holy books. The god of the mountain, depicted as a red deity, armor-clad and riding a white lion, is thought to be wrathful, capable of destroying crops, even entire villages with storms and floods.

Nepal in 1850, reported that the village of Ghunsa just west of Kangchenjunga was a thriving trading community. Thirty years later three successive German expeditions found the communities in decline, but the fiercely difficult mountain itself continued to lure Westerners. It resisted every attempt until a British expedition of 1955. In late May a group under the leadership of Charles Evans climbed snowfields and icefalls on the Nepal side of the mountain, joining the red-pinnacled West Ridge near

Noted Italian photographer Vittorio Sella used thirty by forty centimeter glass-plate negatives to capture images like the one of this porter from Sikkim, taken during a circuit around the base of Kangchenjunga in the autumn of 1899.

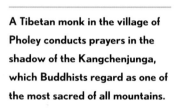

A Tibetan monk in the village of Pholey conducts prayers in the shadow of the Kangchenjunga, which Buddhists regard as one of the most sacred of all mountains.

the summit. Joe Brown, a supremely gifted rock climber, then surmounted a fearsome crack, the climb's final problem. The next day Norman Hardie and Tony Streather followed their route to the top, but circumvented Brown's crack by what Streather joked was "an easy walk round the back."

The ascent of Kangchenjunga's main summit was not repeated for twenty-two years. Then, the Indian team put one of its members and a Sherpa on top—again stopping just short of the summit. Two years later a new standard for Himalayan climbing was set when Englishmen Chris Bonington, Peter Boardman and Joe Tasker, joined by Frenchman Georges Bettembourg were the first to attempt on an 8,000-meter peak in alpine style: no stocked camps, no porters or Sherpas above Camp 1, no bottled oxygen. Their one concession to Kangchenjunga's notoriously bad weather—as the most easterly of the 8,000-meter peaks, it is nearest to the moisture-laden air coming off

Spectacular cascades, like this fall on the north side of Kangchenjunga, abound in the Himalaya.

Tattered prayer flags adorn the Himalaya. Sherpas and climbers alike string the colorful flags as an offering; as the words that are printed on them fade in the sun, snow and wind, the prayers are delivered to the mountains.

ANNAPURNA

ELEVATION	LOCATION	FIRST ASCENT
26,545 feet	*Annapurna Himal, Nepal*	*Maurice Herzog, Louis Lachenal, France, 1950*

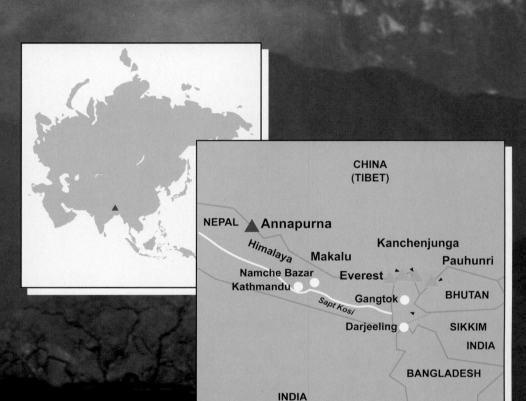

> As the dew is dried up in
> the morning sun, So too are
> the sins of humankind by
> the sight of the Himalaya
> —*From an ancient*
> *Indian legend*

The history of Himalayan climbing is written on the ridges and faces of Annapurna. It was the first of the world's fourteen 8,000-meter peaks to be climbed; its 10,000-foot South Face saw the first of the Himalayan face climbs; and it was the first Himalayan peak to be climbed by an all-female team. Yet when Maurice Herzog started it all by embarking on one of the greatest

A lookout tower used by Park Rangers in the Annapurna Sanctuary.

mountaineering adventures of all time, he didn't exactly know where he was going. It was early spring 1950 and the French Mountaineering Federation had set its sights on an 8,000-meter summit in the central Himalaya, but the exact destination—Annapurna or neighboring Dhaulagiri—still had not been determined. With their success on Annapurna the Herzog team achieved a remarkable mountaineering trifecta: exploration, reconnaissance and ascent of the world's tenth highest mountain in a single season.

Annapurna (which is Sanskrit for "filled with sustenance," or more idiomatically, the "Harvest Goddess") lies on the western end of a central Himalaya range known as the Annapurna Himal, a snow- and ice-capped wall of mostly 7,000-meter peaks that include,

from west to east, Annapurna III, Annapurna IV and Annapurna II. Annapurna South is a prominent peak on a spur running south of the main ridge. And to confuse matters further, Annapurna itself has three summits, East, Central (the high point) and Main.

After extensive exploration of approaches to Dhaulagiri, nineteen miles west of

In 1993 Frenchman Benoit Chamoux summited Annapurna in his quest to climb all fourteen 8,000-meter peaks.

Annapurna, proved disappointing, the French expedition turned to Annapurna and placed a base camp at the edge of the North Annapurna Glacier. Over the following weeks the team, which included such French

Top: Sherpa guides are a vital part of climbing in this region.

stars as Lionel Terray, Louis Lachenal and Gaston Rébuffat, forged a route up the vast, sickle-shaped glacier, placing a high camp at 24,500 feet. On the morning of June 3 Herzog and Lachenal made their push, with-out benefit of supplementary oxygen, for the summit. At 2 PM they stood, exhausted and suffer-ing the onset of frostbite but triumphant, the first men to reach the summit of one of the world's fourteen highest moun-tains.

As the two men began their descent, Herzog stopped to take something from his rucksack— he never recalled what—and then watched horrified as the gloves he had removed began to tumble down the face of Annapurna. Without gloves Herzog would soon lose the use of his hands. Nevertheless, he and Lachenal straggled into their high camp and were met by Terray and Rébuffat, who had come up in support. The next morning the four men set out for Camp 4 but were caught in a whiteout. Confused about the direction of the tents, they were still wandering the glacier as darkness fell. As Herzog worried about surviving a night of expo-sure to the storm, Lachenal sud-denly was swallowed up by a crevasse—just deep enough to accommodate the four of them until daybreak.

That morning, delirious and near death, the four were rescued by another member of the French team, Marcel Schatz, who had heard their shouts. They had spent the night only 200 yards from Camp 4.

On the team's descent to Camp 2, Annapurna delivered one more assault: an avalanche. Herzog, roped to the two Sherpas, was knocked from his feet and nearly strangled by the rope, which had somehow gotten wrapped around his neck. When he came to a stop 500 feet below, he was swinging head down on the slope of a steep couloir.

Bottom: An approach camp looks onto the massive South Face of Annapurna. The sacred mountain of Machapuchare, right of center, has never been summited, and the Nepalese government has placed the mountain off-limits to climbers.

Extricated with the help of the Sherpas, Herzog finally reached the safety of Camp 2. Though his ordeal continued as the expedition doctor performed amputations of frozen toes and fingers en route to a hospital in India, Herzog survived to write *Annapurna*, still regarded by

Nepalese women serve alongside the men as high altitude porters.

many as the classic of the mountaineering literature.

By 1964 the last of the "eight-thousanders,"—the fourteen mountains, all of them in either the Himalaya or the Karakoram, that reach above 8.000 meters (26,240 feet)—had been summited, so Himalayan climbers raised the ante. They began attacking these mountains with smaller parties and less equipment, notably without the use of the supplemental oxygen once thought to be indispensable above 8,000 meters. And they started to seek out more difficult routes. In 1970 a British team headed by veteran expedition leader and writer Chris Bonington ventured into the Annapurna Sanctuary, an otherworldly cirque ringed by Hiunchuli, Annapurna South and the spectacularly fishtailed Machapuchare. The mammoth South Face at the head of the

cirque—only Nanga Parbat's Rupal Face and Denali's Wickersham Wall compare to it in size—was Bonington's objective. After a siege of several weeks, two of Britain's best, Don Whillans and Dougal Haston, made it to the top. The face climb, following the westernmost spur on the wall, was not repeated for eleven years.

In the 1980s the alpine style of ascent, lightly equipped small teams moving swiftly without fixed lines and multiple camps on the route, came into vogue on Annapurna. Such an approach could often take advantage of brief spells of settled weather, but it introduced an element of hazard. Because the spurs on Annapurna's South Face were too barricaded to permit unsecured ascents, alpine stylists were forced onto the slopes between them, which were easier but more exposed to sometimes

British hardman Don Whillans summited Annapurna with Scotsman Dougal Haston (who took this snapshot) in their 1975 epic climb of the South Face—the first major face climb in the Himalaya.

fatal avalanche and rockfall. In 1982 Englishman Alex McIntyre, descending after a failed alpine-style attempt on the South Face, was struck by a rock and killed. Ten years later Christophe Lafaile of France, left high on the face with only thirty-three feet of rope when his partner Pierre Béghin fell to his death on rappel,

ALPINE STYLE: *An approach to multi-day climbs in which a team or an individual progresses toward the summit in one continuous push, using neither stocked camps or fixed ropes in the ascent.*

Storm clouds fill the Annapurna Sanctuary, a spectacular cirque surrounded by 20,000-foot peaks that has become a favorite of trekkers in Nepal.

barely escaped repeated cascades of stones during a desperate descent. In 1984 Catalonians Nil Bohigas and Enric Lucas succeeded in a brilliant six-day assault by climbing the most dangerous lower segment of their route at night when the snow was most likely to be consolidated.

Meanwhile, on the other side of the mountain, history of another sort was being made. In 1977 an all-women expedition under the leadership of Arlene Blum followed the so-called Dutch Rib, to the west of the

Herzog route, and put Irene Miller and Vera Komarkova on the summit. They were the first women and the first Americans to climb Annapurna. But the victory came at a cost: On a second summit attempt Alison Chadwick-Onyszkiewicz and Vera Watson fell 1,500 feet to their deaths.

Because of its proximity to Pokhara, reachable by bus from Kathmandu, Annapurna is a popular destination among May-to-September travelers to Nepal. For those whose adventuring doesn't require bagging a summit, the trek around the base of Annapurna or into the Sanctuary offers a breathtaking array of some of the world's most spectacular summits.

RAPPEL: *A means of descent in which the climber makes a controlled slide down a rope, governing the rate of descent by applying friction between the rope and the body or a device specially constructed for this purpose. v. To descend via rappel.*

A high-altitude Sherpa in training has big shoes to fill—and an endless curiosity about the frequent visitors from the West.

The Avalanche

FROM *Annapurna* BY MAURICE HERZOG

TRANSLATED FROM FRENCH BY NEA MORIN AND JANET ADAM SMITH

Maurice Herzog not only was the first to summit on an 8,000-meter mountain, he was also the first to write a modern mountaineering saga, in which the themes of anguish and pain are laid bare alongside those of triumph and tragedy. Although the account of the ascent of Annapurna has recently come under attack for glossing over dissension among team members and misrepresenting the role of Herzog's summit partner, Louis Lachenal, it remains a classic of the genre. In the following excerpt, Herzog describes the terror of being engulfed in an avalanche.

Lachenal was a long way behind us and every time I turned around he was sitting down in the track. He, too, was affected by snow-blindness, though not so badly as Terray and Rébuffat, and he found difficulty in seeing his way. Rébuffat went ahead by guess-work, with agony in his face, but he kept on. We crossed the couloir without incident, and I congratulated myself that we had passed the danger zone.

The sun was at its height, the weather brilliant and the colors magnificent. Never had the mountains appeared to me so majestic as in this moment of extreme danger.

All at once a crack appeared in the snow under the feet of the Sherpas, and grew longer and wider. A mad idea flashed into my head—to climb up the slope at speed and reach solid ground. Then I was lifted up by a superhuman force, and, as the Sherpas disappeared before my eyes, I went head over heels. I could not see what was happening. My head hit the ice. In spite of my efforts I could no longer breathe, and a violent blow on my left thigh caused me acute pain. I turned round and round like a puppet. In a flash I saw the blinding light of the sun through the snow which was pouring past my eyes. The rope joining me to Sarki and Aila curled round my neck—the Sherpas shooting down the slope beneath would shortly strangle me, and the pain was unbearable. Again and again I crashed into solid ice as I went hurtling from one serac to another, and the snow crushed me down. The rope tightened around my neck and brought me to a stop. Before I had recovered my wits I began to pass water, violently and uncontrollably.

I opened my eyes to find myself hanging head downwards with the rope around my neck and my left leg, in a sort of hatchway of blue ice. I put out my elbows towards the walls in an attempt to stop the unbearable pendulum motion which sent me from one side to the other, and I caught a glimpse of the last slopes of the couloir beneath me. My breathing steadied, and I blessed the rope which had stood the strain of the shock.

I simply had to try to get myself out. My feet and hands were numb, but I was able to make use of some little nicks in the wall. There was room for at least the edges of my boots. By frenzied jerky movements I succeeded in freeing my left leg from the rope, and then managed to right myself and to climb up a yard or two. After every move I stopped, convinced that I had come to the end of my physical strength, and that in a second I should have to let go.

One more desperate effort, and I gained a few inches. I pulled on the rope and felt something give at the other end—no doubt the bodies of the Sherpas. I called, but hardly a whisper issued from my lips. There was a death-like silence. Where was Rébuffat?

Conscious of a shadow, as from a passing cloud, I looked up instinctively, and lo and behold! Two scared black faces were framed against the circle of blue sky. Aila and Sarki! They were safe and sound, and at once set to work to rescue me. I was incapable of giving them the slightest advice. Aila disappeared, leaving Sarki alone at the edge of the hole; they began to pull on the rope, slowly, so as not to hurt me, and I was hauled up with a power and steadiness that gave me fresh courage. At last I was out. I collapsed on the snow.

MOUNT EVEREST

ELEVATION

29,028 feet

LOCATION

Mahalangur Himal, Nepal/Tibet

FIRST ASCENT

Sir Edmund Hillary, New Zealand; Tenzing Norgay, Nepal/India, 1953

CHINA (TIBET)

NEPAL Annapurna

Himalaya

Makalu Kangchenjunga

Everest ▲

Pauhunri

Kathmandu

Namche Bazaar

Sapt Kosi

Gangtok

BHUTAN

Darjeeling

SIKKIM

INDIA

BANGLADESH

INDIA

It is strange to have a piece of real estate on Everest named after you. But nice.

—*Thomas Hornbein, when asked how he feels about the Hornbein Couloir on Mount Everest.*

ALSO KNOWN AS •
Chomolungma: "Goddess Mother of the Earth" (Tibetan); Sagarmatha "Goddess of the Sky" (Nepalese); Peak XV(1852 British Survey)

It is not its size that makes Everest the greatest of the world's mountains; it is the richness of its history. Every step taken on its flanks and ridges resonates with the mountain's mythology—every expedition a potential new saga of triumph or defeat. Still Everest defies definition, and even its height is subject to disagreement. Identified at the time simply as Peak XV, Everest was determined to be the highest mountain in the world in 1852, when a group of British surveyors put its elevation at 29,002 feet. This number, however, was negotiated. Actual measurements, ranging from 28,990 to 29,028, reportedly averaged out at precisely 29,000 feet. Fearing that a round number would be misconstrued as an approximation, the

surveyors tacked on two extra feet to give it scientific heft. In 1954 Indian surveyors upgraded Everest to 29,028 feet, the elevation accepted today, even though that figure, too, has subsequently been disputed.

Attempts to revert to the mountain's original name have had little success. In 1865 British Surveyor General in India Andrew Waugh named the peak for his predecessor Sir George Everest. The post-colonial world eventually noticed that the mountain had a pre-Everest name—two of them, in fact: Tibetans call it Chomolungma, meaning "Goddess Mother of the Earth" and the Nepalese call it Sagarmatha, "Goddess of the Sky." But by the time consideration was given to honoring one of the mountain's original

Top: The Sherpa town of Namche Bazaar, at 12,000 feet, is the largest and most prosperous settlement in the Khumbu district.

Nepalese postage stamps bear the image of the world's highest mountain.

Top: Nepali porters, essential to
most expeditions on the mountain,
carry loads of up to sixty pounds
along the Dudh Kosi river valley
to base camp.

names, the name Everest had
accumulated too much history to
be displaced.

Everest and the surrounding
peaks would be virtually
unclimbable without the help of a
wholly unique group of people
who have lived in the shadow of
the great Himalayan peaks for
centuries. The Sherpas are a
Buddhist people of Tibetan stock
from the Khumbu district
surrounding Everest, who have
served as guides for almost every
Everest expedition from the
Nepalese side since the
1930s—generally with a loyalty
and cheerfulness that amazes and
gladdens visitors to their homeland. Because their villages are
situated above 9,000 feet in the
high valley of Khumbu Himal,
Sherpas have physiologies that are
much better suited to the rigors of
Everest than those of the climbers
they serve. They have often performed heroically at altitude, carrying loads, breaking trail, setting
up camps. But their own mountaineering achievements are less
well known. Among the many

who have made several ascents of
Everest is Ang Rita Sherpa, who
has summited on 8,000-meter
peaks a total of twelve times—six
times on Everest alone—and in all
cases without supplementary
oxygen; a feat that seems almost
superhuman by conventional
climbing standards.

Situated on the Nepal-Tibet
border in the Mahalangur
Himal, a segment of the 1,500-
mile Himalaya that contains four
of the world's fourteen 8,000-
meter peaks, Everest began to
attract mountaineering attention
right after World War I, and
attempts to climb it proved fatal

Prayer flags festoon a monument
near Everest base camp honoring
climbers and Sherpas killed on
the mountain.

almost immediately. In 1921 a
climber on the first English
reconnaissance to the mountain
died of a heart attack. A year

Tent roofs augment clotheslines for Everest trekkers caught in a downpour.

later during a second English expedition seven Sherpas were swept to their death by an avalanche. Then in 1924 the most storied fatalities in all of mountaineering took place high on Everest's Northeast Ridge.

The morning of June 8, on his third expedition to Everest, George Leigh Mallory, a thirty-eight-year-old school teacher, set out for the summit with a strong but inexperienced climbing partner, engineer Andrew Irvine. That same morning expedition geologist Noel Odell set out from a lower camp to join the pair on their return from their summit attempt. He climbed under overcast skies most of the morning. Then at around 1 PM the clouds rolled back. Odell recorded the moment in one of the most celebrated passages in mountaineering literature: "There was a sudden clearing of the atmosphere, and the entire summit ridge and final peak of Everest were unveiled. My eyes became fixed on one tiny black spot silhouetted on a small snow-crest beneath a rock-step in the ridge; the black spot moved. Another black spot became apparent and moved up the snow to join the other on the crest. The first then approached the great rock-step and shortly emerged at the top; the second did likewise. Then the whole fascinating vision vanished, enveloped in cloud once more." (From "The Mount Everest Dispatches", *The Alpine Journal*,

Top: Witness to history: this porter accompanied the 1924 British expedition in which the legendary George Mallory and Andrew Irvine perished on the Northeast Ridge.

November 1924, London).

It was the last time either Mallory or Irvine was seen alive. A Chinese mountaineer claimed to have seen the body of an Englishman at 8,100 meters (26,575 feet) on the north east ridge during a 1974 expedition, but the report was sketchy and only deepened the enduring mystery of whether either of the two had managed to summit—twenty-nine years ahead of the official first ascent in 1953.

For Mallory, Everest had been a life-long goal. But he was not the only one whose obsession proved deadly. In 1934 an Englishman named Maurice Wilson, in the belief that an ascent of Everest would somehow benefit mankind, flew a small plane to India with the intent of climbing the mountain. Denied permission to enter Tibet, he disguised himself as monk and walked 300 miles to the north side of Everest and climbed, according to a journal he kept, as high as 22,700 feet. An English party discovered Wilson's body on an approach to the North Col the following year.

In all, twelve people died on Everest before 1953 when the mountain finally was summitted by New Zealand beekeeper Edmund Hillary and Nepalese Sherpa and expedition *sirdar* Tenzing Norgay. Three years earlier access to the mountain had shifted from the north to the south, as Tibet was occupied and sealed off by the Chinese government, and Nepal opened its borders to travelers. Reconnaissance missions in 1950 and 1951 discovered a possible route up a vast amphitheater to a saddle between Everest and Lhotse, the world's fourth highest mountain, and then along a ridge to the summit. In 1952 a Swiss expedition had booked the mountain, and the Brits, to their chagrin, had to spend the season as spectators. Swiss climber Raymond Lambert accompanied by Tenzing reached to within 1,000 vertical feet of the summit when exhaustion and worsening weather forced them to retreat.

The following spring the English were back, their expedition planned with military precision by Col. John Hunt. For two and a half months, nine camps

SIRDAR: *The lead Sherpa on an expedition*

were supplied with food, fuel and oxygen. In the early darkness of May 29, Hillary and Tenzing emerged from their tent at 27,900 feet and began the final leg of their epic journey. Shortly before noon, with Hillary wondering if he had the strength to go on, there suddenly was nothing above them. All the world lay at their feet.

As Hillary and Tenzing began their return and recovery from the grueling trip, word spread quickly. The news of the pair's accomplishment reached England on the eve of Queen Elizabeth's coronation. Hillary's achievement was a victory for the Empire, and the timing was excellent. He was an instant celebrity and was subsequently knighted by the new queen. Tenzing Norgay was also a national hero, but of a slightly different nature: no one seemed to

On May 29, 1953 Edmund Hillary snapped this photo, as Sherpa Tenzing Norgay hoisted the flags of India, the United Kingdom, Nepal and the United Nations.

Because it's there.

—George Leigh Mallory, when asked why he wanted to climb Everest.

be able to decide which country he represented. India claimed him as one of their own and celebrated his triumph, as did Nepal, both hoping that he would announce personal allegiance and citizenship to one of them exclusively. He refused, saying "I was born in the womb of Nepal and raised in the lap of India." The media from India, New Zealand, the United States, Nepal and England theorized over which man actually stepped onto the summit first but got no help from either Hillary or Tenzing, who both steadfastly maintained that they summitted together.

Over the next ten years, seven more climbers would succeed to the summit—all following the Hillary-Tenzing route to

Everest's South Col and up its Southeast Ridge. On May 1, 1963, Seattle mountaineer Jim Whittaker, accompanied by Sherpa Nawang Ghumba, became the first American to reach Everest's summit—once again following the well established South Col route. Then during the following four weeks, an extraordinary new line of ascent, on Everest's West Ridge,

Sherpa Tenzing Norgay with his family on a visit to England after his triumph on Mount Everest.

Top: Chortens—cairn-like monuments—on the way in to Base Camp bear silent witness to Sherpas who have died on Everest.

was etched onto the unforgiving steepnesses of the mountain. At five in the morning of May 22, Dr. Thomas Hornbein of Seattle and Willi Unsoeld, a professor of philosophy and religion at Evergreen State College, set out from their tent high on the West Ridge over ground that had never before been touched by man. Thirteen hours later they arrived

MOUNT EVEREST, 29,028 feet

LHOTSE, 27,923 feet

NUPTSE, 25,726 feet

Hillary Step

Camp Four

South Col

Camp Four

Camp Three

Camp Three

Western Cwm

Camp Two

Camp Two

Khumbu Icefall

at the summit.

A new route had been put up on Everest, but the most dangerous part of the outing was just beginning. With no safe descent by way of the West Ridge, the pair now planned to complete a first-ever traverse of Everest by descending to the South Col, where they would join Lute Jerstad and Barry Bishop who had summited three hours earlier by the normal route. But at 6:35 PM when they departed, the hour was already desperately late. They followed Jerstad's and Bishop's footsteps until the light failed. Cloaked in blackness, they considered clearing a hole in the snow and waiting out the night, but Hornbein feared they would freeze. They called out, hoping their voices would carry to the

expedition's high camp above the col. A thin, windswept answer came back. It was Jerstad and Bishop, exhausted and near collapse and still 2,000 feet above camp. The two pairs roped together and for four and a half hours groped in the dark. At midnight they gave it up and, with no more protection from the inhuman cold than their down jackets, huddled on the rocky ridge to await the dawn. Unsoeld suffered severe frostbite that would lead to the loss of fingers and toes, but all four got through the night in what at the time the highest bivouac ever survived.

In the years since, Everest has been the scene of more heroics. In 1975 English hardman Don Whillans and Scottish super-

climber Dougal Haston forced a route up the precipitous Southwest face. In 1978 Reinhold Messner, from Italy's Tyrol, and his long-time climbing partner Peter Habeler of Austria climbed to the top of the world without supplementary oxygen, a feat many, including Hillary himself, once thought impossible. Messner was back two years later to make the first solo ascent of Everest. In 1990 the mountain was soloed again by Australian Timothy Macartney-

The vast Western Cwm is ringed by Everest (left), Lhotse (center) and Nuptse. The standard route on the mountain (and the one used by the 1953 British first ascent team) follows the Khumbu Glacier to the South Col between Everest and Lhotse and then goes up the Southeast Ridge. The West Ridge (left of and parallel to the Khumbu Glacier, climbed by Americans Tom Hornbein and Willi Unsoeld in 1963) lies on the border between Nepal and Tibet.

An outcrop of rock serves as a monument to the scores of climbers who have perished on Everest, including Jake Breitenbach, who was crushed when a wall collapsed in the Khumbu Ice Fall during the American expedition of 1963.

Snape, who, in the belief that a mountain was not truly surmounted unless the climb started at its lowest point, began the ascent at sea level in Bombay, walking the 1,500 miles (and swimming the odd river that crossed his path) to the summit of Everest.

Everest has also, unfortunately, become the scene of the world's

CWM: (pronounced "coomb") Welsh for an area surrounded by mountains; a cirque

highest garbage dump: the 26,000-foot pile of spent oxygen canisters on the South Col. Expeditions of the 1990s are finally trying to come to grips with it. Jim Whittaker's large 1990 international outing removed packloads of refuse when it left the mountain, and groups since then have at least attempted to take out what they brought in. In 1995, a clean-up climb organized by Scott Fischer and Brent Bishop, son of 1963 Everest summiter Barry Bishop, paid Sherpas a bonus for every empty canister

National Geographic photographer Barry Bishop carried out glacier and weather research with a Hillary expedition to the Everest region in 1961. Two years later he was among the first Americans to summit on the mountain.

French climber extraordinaire Benoit Chamoux, bivouacked at 24,100 feet on the north face of Everest, climbed the mountain in record time in 1988. He died in 1995 near the summit of Kangchenjunga as he was about to complete the ascent of all fourteen 8,000-meter mountains.

they carried off the mountain–a budget item that has been built into some subsequent expeditions on the mountain.

Without such programs, the garbage problem can only grow worse as larger and larger groups of climbers flock to Nepal in hopes of bagging the world's highest summit. And as these adventurers are discovering, the original Hillary route, even with the help of porters, Sherpas, professional guides and bottled oxygen, is still a worthy challenge. The South Col Route, as it is called, starts in Lukla, the last village above the Nepalese capital of Katmandu with a landing field, and ascends to Everest base camp on the Khumbu Glacier at 17,800 feet. It is customary for expeditions to stop for three to

SHERPA: *A member of a Buddhist clan that inhabits the Khumbu district of Nepal, a region south of Mount Everest generally at an elevation of 9,000 feet and higher. Because of their lifelong acclimatization to altitude, their loyalty and their ingrained hospitality to visitors to their land, the Sherpa people are a prime source of Himalayan porters, guides and base-camp workers. With a few exceptions—Tenzing Norgay, who summited on Everest with Hillary in 1953, and Nawang Gombu, with Jim Whittaker in 1963—the exploits of individual Sherpas have gone unsung, yet several have made multiple ascents of 8,000-meter peaks and are celebrities among their own people.*

Right: Aluminum ladders, carried in sections and then bolted or lashed together, bridge dark and deadly crevasses in the Khumbu Ice Fall, a broken section of glacier above Everest base camp that has had more fatalities than any other place on the mountain.

five days at high Sherpa villages for acclimatization along the way.

The initial challenge of the South Col route—and its deadliest—is the Khumbu Icefall, a stretch of broken ice below the vast Western Cwm that leads to the South Col. The icefall is riven with crevasses that descend into blackness; translucent bluish white blocks of ice the size of houses topple without warning, crushing whatever may be in their path. Current expedition practice is to place an advance base camp above the icefall, thus minimizing travel through this treacherous segment of the route. Camps 1, 2 and 3 are placed progressively higher in the Western Cwm and Camp 4 on the South Col at 26,000 feet. The push to the summit, beginning from Camp 4, gains the Southeastern Ridge by way of a couloir west of the buttress at the base of the ridge. From there the route follows the ridge over the South Summit to the Hillary Step, the thirty-foot pitch that is the final barrier to the summit.

Modern mountaineering equipment—lightweight supplemental oxygen systems, supremely efficient cold-weather apparel, well engineered boots—has put Everest within range of the rank amateur. Given proper fitness and conditioning and a modicum of technique, any determined climber with a willingness to endure intense cold, headaches, hacking coughs and profound fatigue has a shot at reaching the summit of Everest and returning to tell about it. But as evidenced during the pre-monsoon climbing season of 1996 (Himalayan mountains are generally climbed in April and May or after the monsoon season in September and October), two other factors weigh heavily in the equation. The first is the ability of the climber to adapt to altitude. Lack of sufficient acclimatization can lead, through a complex biochemical process, to a potentially fatal

Top: An aerial view of what is known as "The Roof of the World".

A climber on Everest takes a break from the intense Himalayan sun.

build-up of fluid in the brain or the lungs. It can have an equally deadly effect on judgement and mental capacity. Even experienced mountaineers have done inexplicably foolish things after sustained exposure to altitude—one of the reasons accidents happen so frequently on descent.

The other factor that can influence the course of a climb is the weather. A fine day on the mountain can become a desperate scramble for survival with a break in the weather. Most of the factors that make for violent weather on mountains are amplified on Everest by its height, its massiveness and its elevation above the surrounding peaks. Mountains make their own weather; Everest makes

How to get down.

—Nawal Gombu, when asked what he thought about when he had reached the summit of Mount Everest

more of it.

In spring 1996, as two commercially guided expeditions went for the summit on the same day, these factors came to bear with lethal effect. The summit day broke clear and bright, but with weaker clients slowing progress on narrow sections of the South Ridge, most of the climbers arrived at the summit after the 2 PM turn-around time that had been agreed upon by the head guides. Then at around 3:30 a blizzard driven by seventy m.p.h. winds engulfed the top of the mountain. By the following day three guides-Scott Fischer of Seattle, Washington, and Rob Hall and Andy Harris of New Zealand-and two clients had died of exposure. In all, there were fifteen

fatalities on Everest in 1996.

If there was a cautionary tale in the disaster of 1996, it seems to have been lost on other aspirants to the summit of Everest. There were nine deaths on the mountain in 1997, and guide services for climbing the mountain were heavily booked in 1998. People with the requisite money and ambition but without the experience are bound to swell the death roles further. Since 1984 when commercial guiding began, there have been eighty-seven fatalities on Everest—eleven for every 100 who have summited.

Such is the power of the world's highest mountain that some people will continue to find those odds acceptable.

Top: Starting in the 1990s, tons of refuse have been carted off of Everest, but meadows of plastic like this one at a 21,000-foot campsite on the Chinese side of the mountain remain, as well as mounds of discarded oxygen bottles on the South Col.

Left: The impact of trekkers and climbers from the West on Sherpa life style is a sticky issue.

The Uses of Risk

FROM "LIFE IS A MOUNTAIN: *Into Thin Air* AND BEYOND"
BY THOMAS F. HORNBEIN, M.D.

Is the risk of mountaineering worth the reward? Thomas F. Hornbein, an anesthesiologist with the University of Washington Medical Center in Seattle and one of the first Americans to summit on Mount Everest, addressed this question in view of the tragic death toll on Everest in 1996.

In the aftermath of such disasters, many questions abound. How do those who pursue such a seemingly useless, selfish activity justify to themselves and their loved ones the possible loss of life or limb? Do they have a death wish? What about those with more money than experience? Should they be able to buy their way into what for them is an even greater risk than for the more experienced and self-reliant mountaineer? Shouldn't we prevent such folk from putting themselves at risk, protect them from their own stupidity? Or can Everest be safely guided? What do we mean by "safely?" Many have referred to that tiny bit of the earth's surface that extends more than 8000 meters (about 26,000 feet) above the sea as the Death Zone. Up there the barometric pressure is so low, the air so thin, that even moving slowly is close to the limit of what most can do; climbers have little leftover with which to face the unexpected. When the chips are down, individual survival can be sorely tested, and even guides may be hard-pressed to get someone down who can no longer remain upright and at least wobble slowly downhill.

So what is risk all about? The Oxford English Dictionary defines risk as exposure "to the chance of injury or loss." Chance means uncertainty; it's the roll of the dice, not knowing the outcome ahead of time. Climbing mountains is a form of gambling, but metaphorically no more so than many other activities in our lives. Dick Emerson, for many years a professor of sociology at the University of Washington and a climbing partner, posited that uncertainty about outcome is what maximizes motivation; certainty either of failure or of success would diminish the intensity of commitment to an undertaking. He showed that individuals communicate in ways that maximize uncertainty, for example by countering optimistic or pessimistic information with that of the opposite kind, called negative feedback. Risk and its attendant uncertainty are essential to motivation.

I view risk like a drug, and, as with any drug, dose matters. Too much or too little may not be good for one's health. Dose varies from those who are risk averse, avoiding uncertain situations as much as possible, to those experiencing symptoms of withdrawal if deprived for too long of their risk fix. Between these extremes are those of us who are risk acceptors, maybe even savoring its seasoning, yet for whom the lust for a longer, fuller life is manifest by an inclination to minimize unnecessary risks. Bertrand Russell characterized such a dose this way: "A life without adventure is likely to be unsatisfying, but a life in which adventure is allowed to take whatever form it will is likely to be short."

As I present this pitch for a touch of risk in our daily lives, my mind keeps wandering back to Karkauer's account. What went wrong up there? And why? Partly I feel that at least some of those being guided up the mountain didn't belong there. They had not learned the skills and acquired the experience and judgment to take care of themselves in a crisis. But then another part of me realizes that that's what guided climbing is, whether on Mount Rainier or Mount Everest: substituting another's expertise for one's own, a way to shortcut the competence issue while lessening the risk. Guided climbing is not unlike the doctor-patient relationship, at least as I have experienced it in my own specialty. The client/patient delegates responsibility for his or her safekeeping to another, trusting that other to possess the skills and judgment to enable safe passage, whether it be through anesthesia and surgery or to the top of a mountain and back down again. Sure, the risks are greater on Everest than in the operating room, a lot greater. But as we have been, safe passage cannot be guaranteed in any setting, nor on any mountain. The difference in magnitude of risk between Everest and lesser summits is quantitative, not qualitative.

I ask myself, how do these clients differ from Tom Hornbein or Willi Unsoeld when they were climbing on Everest in 1963? While some had a fair bit of mountaineering mileage under their belts, others did not. Krakauer's observation that a few may have been stepping into crampons for the first time, gives one at least a moment's pause. But basic skills can be quickly learned, at least to some degree, and the usual route up Everest is not technically so difficult. More essential are commitment, fitness, judgment and insight regarding one's reserves to get not only up but back down again. That, in the company of a good guide, may suffice, so long as all's well. But end-of-the-day fatigue, compounded by unanticipated bad weather can suddenly change the whole complexion of things. When guides aren't there, one is left to make do on one's own resources of character and experience. When either is in short supply, safety margins are wafted off on the wind.

But noting these differences, I am struck by the similarities between now and then. Although the number of times Everest has been climbed is approaching 1000, still people are willing to risk their lives and plunk down $65,000 to try to reach the highest point on earth. Why? Exploration? Adventure? Testing personal limits? Fame? Fortune? Trophy collection? The mix of motivations seems much the same now as it did for us in 1963. Those who are bystanders have always questioned the rationality of the minority living closer to the edge, the risk acceptors. The questioning is less query than judgmental and no different now than in the past.

Risk is an ever-present part of our lives. We might wish to control the dose but, by definition, that is not completely possible. The control then that we seek is not of risk but of ourselves in living with and coping with risk, with uncertainty. For some of us, risk is more than essential to creative or decisive functioning. Risk helps define who we are, where we fit into the world around us and how we relate to and influence, for better or worse, the lives of others. I think the capacity to accept risk has helped me to be a better doctor and hopefully a better teacher, father, husband and human being. I feel blessed to have been born at a time early enough in the human relationship to Everest that the adventure could be both pioneering and lonely. Though times and the way things are done change, the needs we humans have to seek out new places in the soul to go remain the same.

GEORGE LEIGH MALLORY

1886-1924

"Have we vanquished an enemy? None but ourselves."

HOME BASE ▪ *Cheshire, England*

CLIMBING FEATS ▪ *three attempts on Mount Everest*

"It is almost unthinkable with this plan that I shan't get to the top. I can't see myself coming down defeated." By 1924, when he wrote these words, George Mallory, a thirty-eight year-old school teacher from Cheshire, England, had fallen completely under the spell of Mount Everest. He had already been to the mountain twice in 1921 and 1922, and he believed he had finally assembled the ingredients for a successful assault on the summit: a climbing partner who, though inexperienced, was magnificently fit; a rout that looked as if it would go; and—crucially—the supplemental oxygen that Mallory believed was essential to a summit attempt on Everest. The question of whether Mallory succeeded may never be answered, but the moment he and Andrew Irvine disappeared in the mists high on the North East Ridge his name became indelibly linked with Everest.

Mallory was reared in Mobberley, the son of the Cheshire rector. He began climbing as a teen—on the crumbling walls of the priory at Winchester College, which he attended—and at eighteen took his first trip to the Alps. He failed an entrance exam to the Royal Military Academy at Woolwich but then, surprisingly, was admitted to Magdalene College, Cambridge. In 1906 Mallory took a group of Cantabridgians to the rocky crags of Wales and proceeded to lead them on climbs he himself had never been on.

There he caught the eye of Geoffrey Winthrop Young, the foremost British alpinist of the day, a meeting that would determine the course of Mallory's life. Young took Mallory into his inner circle of promising climbers and sponsored him for the admission to the prestigious Alpine Club. Following graduation—with honors—Mallory became a master at Charterhouse School in Godalming where one of his students was the poet Robert Graves.

He married in 1914, had a son and two daughters, served during the Great War as a gunner in France and was invited to join the 1921 British expedition to Mount Everest. Since Nepal was closed to foreigners, the climbers approached the mountain from Tibet, and Mallory was among the first to ascend to the North Col. He also made a reconnaissance to an overlook into the Western Cwm—the route to the eventual first ascent—and declared it impracticable. In 1922 Mallory, back on the North East Ridge, was nearly killed by an avalanche that buried seven porters.

The following year, during a lecture tour in the U.S., a reporter asked Mallory why he wanted to climb Mount Everest. His enigmatic answer, "Because it's there," has been puzzled over ever since. But when, in 1924, he disappeared on the mountain that was his obsession, it became his epitaph.

Mallory, seated, far left, with the 1921 Everest reconnaissance team.

STACY ALLISON

1958–

"Only when we accept full responsibility for our lives will we have the confidence and courage to risk."

HOME BASE ▪ *Portland, Oregon*

CLIMBING FEATS ▪ *First American woman to summit Mount Everest*

At age seven, Stacy Allison learned the first axiom of climbing: getting up is only half the battle. Wandering off from a family picnic in a park near her Portland home, Stacy watched a group of boys attempting to climb a hollow in a fir tree to its lowest branch, twelve feet off the ground. When they had all failed, she tried, moving gracefully and then swinging triumphantly onto the limb. As she peered down on the envious upturned faces of the boys, however, she realized she had no idea how to reverse the moves and find her way back to the ground.

The seven-year-old had to be rescued by her father, but she was hooked. Yielding to the allure of vertical faces and steep ridges, Allison quit Oregon State University—twice—and set about becoming one of America's most formidable female climbers. In 1980 she climbed Denali by the Cassin Ridge, the most challenging of the standard routes up North America's highest mountain. Two years later she was with an all-women expedition that summited Ama Dablam, a technically demanding 22,488-foot peak in Nepal. It wasn't always an easy road, however. For a good part of her early climbing career, Stacy was also fighting some significant personal battles; she used climbing as a mechanism to find her way out of an abusive marriage and to find her own sources of personal strength.

For Stacy Allison, all of this was prelude to what she noted in her autobiography as "the one goal I could never get out of my mind." Everest, the mountaineer's Holy Grail, loomed on the horizon. Adding to her determination was the fact that no U.S. woman had yet made it to the top. In 1987 her attempt on Everest's North Face with a team headed by the late Scott Fischer ended in searing disappointment 3,000 feet below the summit as 150 mph winds made further progress impossible. A year later, Allison was back, this time on the somewhat more forgiving Hillary route up

the South Ridge. She and two men, expedition leader Jim Frush and Steve Ruoss, were on the final ascent when two Sherpas inexplicably turned around, taking with them crucial supplies of oxygen. This left only enough for one of them to continue. Stacy proposed a lottery—absolutely certain she would win it. She did: at noon on September 29, 1988, she made history as the first American woman to climb Mount Everest.

Back in the U.S., Allison was still on Kathmandu time when the phone began to ring. Talk show hosts and magazine editors wanted her story; today, so do business and trade groups, which frequently hire her for motivational speeches. Since her triumph on Everest, Stacy has turned her ambitious focus to challenges of a different nature. Instead of scaling 8,000 meter peaks, she has taken on a highly successful business career, remarried and is the mother of two boys. She can still be found, however, rock climbing around the Northwest with the same tenacity and skill that got her to the top of the world.

THOMAS HORNBEIN

1931-

"Risk is an essential dietary constituent."

HOME BASE ▪ *Bellevue, Wash.*

CLIMBING FEATS ▪ *first ascent of the West Ridge, Mount Everest*

Tom Hornbein grew up in St. Louis, surrounded by the endless expanse of the Great Plains. But at age fourteen during a trip to Colorado he climbed Signal Mountain in the northern section of the state and experienced for the first time what he called "the soaring freedom waiting at the top." At sixteen, a grainy picture of Everest in Richard Halliburton's *Book of Marvels* set his imagination on fire. Everest had placed a claim on Tom Hornbein's already considerable ambition.

While attending the University of Colorado, he fed his passion for the mountains with climbs—and some first ascents—in nearby Estes Park and on Longs Peak. He went on to medical school and interned in Seattle, where he met and teamed up with the redoubtable Cascades climber Fred Beckey. In 1960 Nick Clinch, who had helped coordinate the only U.S. first ascent of an 8,000-meter peak (Gasherbrum, 26,480 feet, in 1958), invited Hornbein to join his expedition to another Karakoram mountain, Masherbrum. Hornbein did not reach the summit, which may have been a factor in his decision to join the 1963 U.S. expedition to Everest.

It was a mammoth party—nineteen climbers, 300 porters, twenty seven tons of equipment—whose primary mission was to put an American on top of the mountain. Early on, Hornbein became the most vocal exponent of attempting the West Ridge, which if it succeeded would be the first new route on Everest. Until then, all ascents had been by way of the South Col and the Southeast

Ridge. Hornbein had to wait until Jim Whittaker summited by the established route. Then with time running out, he and his close friend Willi Unsoeld completed their daring traverse: West Ridge to summit and descent via the South Col. To this day it is considered one of the boldest exploits in Himalayan climbing history.

Back in Seattle, Hornbein focused on his medical career and eventually rose to chair of the anesthesiology department at the University of Washington Medical School. He still climbs once or twice a year—at times with his son, who works as a guide on Denali. And he still savors his moment on Everest. A key to the route, a steep gully through the rock band that defends the summit of Everest, is now called the Hornbein Couloir. "It is strange to have a piece of real estate on Everest named after you," Hornbein admitted to an interviewer. "But nice."

Death on Everest

From *Into Thin Air*,
by Jon Krakauer

In 1996, ninety-eight climbers summited Mount Everest. One of them was New Zealander Rob Hall, a highly accomplished Himalayan climber and leader of Adventure Consultants Guided Expeditions. On May 10, as other of his clients headed back to their camp on the South Col, Hall waited behind for Doug Hansen. All that is known for certain is that by 6 PM he and Hansen had descended only to the Hillary Step, not far from the summit and that when he made radio contact again at 4:43 the next morning, he was alone the South Summit. At 9:30 Hall was still alive, and two of his Sherpas left the high camp to try to bring him down.

Around 9:30 AM, Ang Dorje and Lhakpa Chhiri left Camp Four and started climbing toward the South Summit with a thermos of hot tea and two extra canisters of oxygen, intending to rescue Hall. They faced an exceedingly formidable task. As astounding and courageous as Boukreev's rescue of Sandy Pittman and Charlotte Fox had been the night before, it paled in comparison to what the two Sherpas were proposing to do now: Pittman and Fox had been a twenty-minute walk from the tents over relatively flat ground; Hall was 3,000 vertical feet above Camp Four—an exhausting eight- or nine-hour climb in the best of circumstances.

And these were surely not the best of circumstances. The wind was blowing in excess of 40 knots. Both Ang Dorje and Lhakpa were cold and wasted from climbing to the summit and back just the day before. If they did somehow manage to reach Hall, moreover, it would be late afternoon before they got there, leaving only one or two hours of daylight in which to begin the even more difficult ordeal of bringing him down. Yet their loyalty to Hall was such that the two men ignored the overwhelming odds and set out toward the South Summit as fast as they could climb.

Shortly thereafter, two Sherpas from the Mountain Madness team—Tashi Tshering and Ngawang Sya Kya (a small, trim man, graying at the temples, who is Lopsang's father)—and one Sherpa from the Taiwanese team headed up to bring down Scott Fischer and Makalu Gau. Twelve hundred feet above the South Col the trio of Sherpas found the incapacitated climbers on the ledge where Lopsang had left them. Although they tried to give Fischer oxygen, he was unresponsive. Scott was still breathing, barely, but his eyes were fixed in their sockets, and his teeth were tightly clenched. Concluding that he was beyond hope, they left him on the ledge and started descending with Gau, who, after receiving hot tea and oxygen, and with considerable assistance from the three Sherpas, was able to move down to the tents on a short-rope under his own power.

The day had started out sunny and clear, but the wind remained fierce, and by late morning the upper mountain was wrapped in thick clouds. Down at Camp Two, the IMAX team reported that the wind over the summit sounded like a squadron of 747s, even from 7,000 feet below. Meanwhile, high on the Southeast Ridge, Ang Dorje and Lhakpa Chhiri pressed on resolutely through the intensifying storm toward Hall. At 3:00 PM, however, still 700 feet below the South Summit, the wind and subzero cold proved to be too much for them, and the Sherpas could go no higher. It was a valiant effort, but it had failed—and as they turned around to descend, Hall's chances for survival all but vanished.

Throughout the day on May 11, his friends and teammates incessantly begged him to make an effort to come down under his own power. Several times Hall announced that he was preparing to descend, only to change his mind and remain immobile at the South Summit. At 3:20 PM, Cotter—who by now had walked over from his own camp beneath Pumori to the Everest Base Camp—scolded over the radio, "Rob, get moving down the ridge."

Sounding annoyed, Hall fired back, "Look, if I thought I could manage the knots on the fixed ropes with me frostbitten hands, I would have gone down six hours ago, pal. Just send a couple of the boys up with a big thermos of something hot—then I'll be fine."

"Thing is, mate, the lads who went up today encountered some high winds and had to turn around," Cotter replied, trying to convey as delicately as possible that the rescue attempt had been abandoned, "so we think your best shot is to move lower."

"I can last another night here if you send up a couple of boys with some Sherpa tea, first thing in the morning, no later than nine-thirty or ten," Rob answered.

"You're a tough man, Big Guy," said Cotter, his voice quavering. "We'll send some boys up to you in the morning."

At 6:20 PM, Cotter contacted Hall to tell him that Jan Arnold [Hall's wife] was on the satellite phone from Christchurch and was waiting to be patched through. "Give me a minute," Rob said. "Me mouth's dry. I want to eat a bit of snow before I talk to her." A little later he came back on and rasped in a slow, horribly distorted voice, "Hi, my sweetheart. I hope you're tucked up in a nice warm bed. How are you doing?"

"I can't tell you how much I'm thinking about you!" Arnold replied. "You sound so much better than I expected....Are you warm, my darling?"

"In the context of the altitude, the setting, I'm reasonably comfortable," Hall answered, doing his best not to alarm her.

"How are your feet?"

"I haven't taken my boots off to check, but I think I may have a bit of frostbite..."

"I'm looking forward to making you completely better when you come home," said Arnold. "I just know you're going to be rescued. Don't feel that you're alone. I'm sending all my positive energy your way!"

Before signing off, Hall told his wife, "I love you. Sleep well, my sweetheart. Please don't worry too much."

These would be the last words anyone would hear him speak. Attempts to make radio contact with Hall later that night and the next day went unanswered. Twelve days later, when [David] Breashears and [Ed] Viesturs climbed over the South Summit on their way to the top, they found Hall lying on his right side in a shallow ice hollow, his upper body buried beneath a drift of snow.

Sherpas on Everest

REPUBLISHED FROM *Everest Quest '96*
BY AUDREY SALKELD AND LIESL CLARK

"**Y**ou cannot be a good mountaineer, however great your ability, unless you are cheerful and have the spirit of comradeship. Friends are as important as achievement. Another is that teamwork is the one key to success and that selfishness only makes a man small. Still another is that no man, on a mountain or elsewhere, gets more out of anything than he puts into it."

—Tenzing Norgay

Sherpas have an unmatched spirit and positive outlook that has been written about the world over. From the early days of mountaineering, their prowess at high altitude has not gone unnoticed. It is generally believed that the first person to recognize the value of employing Sherpas for expeditionary work was the Aberdeen physiologist, Dr. A.M. Kellas. At the beginning of this century, he taught chemistry at Middlesex Hospital in London, and spent several months every year exploring the more remote passes and valleys of the Himalaya with trusted bands of Sherpas assisting him. General Bruce, too, appreciated the hardiness of Sherpas. For the pioneer Everest expeditions of 1922 and 1924 he engaged his porter force from among the considerable expatriate Sherpa community in Darjeeling.

These men performed so well, climbing and carrying to the highest camps, that it very soon became the custom for all Himalayan climbing expeditions to hire Sherpa help in Darjeeling. A system of registration came into force that contributed to the recognition of Sherpa "Tigers" and the creation of an elite force. Word filtered back to the Sherpa Homeland in Nepal, which was out of bounds to Westerners, and every year more Sherpas would make their way to Darjeeling to take on this kind of work. Sherpa Tenzing Norgay, hearing of the continuing British climbing expeditions to Mount Everest, came to India in 1933, hoping to be taken on for that year's expedition. He was not among those selected, but in 1935, at the age of 19, he was picked by Eric Shipton to take part in the exciting reconnaissance he was leading to the Everest area. Tenzing stayed on in Darjeeling and took part in no fewer than seven Everest expeditions, culminating in his successful first ascent of the mountain with Edmund Hillary in 1953. By that time, Nepal was opening up to outsiders, and Sherpas were hired locally and brought down to Kathmandu.

The first ascent of Everest, far from marking an end to interest in the accessibility of the highest point on Earth, opened the floodgates to hordes of other climbers, trekkers, and tourists into the Solu Khumbu region, noticeably changing the local economy and lifestyle of the Sherpa people. With the arrival of modern climbing and the desire to conquer the world's highest peaks, theirs became the gateway culture to Everest and other peaks for visitors in search of mountaineering glory.

Dr. Cynthia Beall of Case Western Reserve University and Physical Anthropology Advisor to the MacGillivray Freeman Films Everest IMAX/IWERKS film, postulates that there may be a genetic factor involved in Sherpa strength at altitude: "The Everest climbers must not only exert great physical effort to climb the mountain, but do so while under tremendous hypoxic stress. This stress is not something that can be mitigated in the way, for instance, that we would put on extra clothes when we are cold. We must adapt physiologically. How the Sherpas do this more effectively than others has been a puzzle to anthropologists and physiologists, and we don't really have the answer. There is evidence of a gene that allows their blood to carry more oxygen, but there are other factors that affect this, as well."

Sherpas have played quiet but critical roles in Everest achievements. From the beginning of their involvement with high altitude mountaineering, Sherpas have paid a disproportionately high price in life and limb. In 1922 seven Sherpa porters were buried under an avalanche on Everest's North Col. In the first seventy years of Everest activity, forty-three Sherpas were killed, more than a third of the total deaths in that period. Even this year, on the south side of Everest, two of the three evacuations from the mountain thus far— due to serious injur —were Sherpas. Because of their contribution to route fixing and ferrying supplies, they find themselves exposed to the extreme risks of high mountain climbing more frequently than their employers.

On our way up to Base Camp, we passed by a sacred site in the Khumbu valley, a testament to the Sherpas that have lost their lives on the surrounding peaks. Dozens of memorial chortens, each commemorating a death on the nearby mountains, line a ridge that looks out on a 360 degree view of snow-covered peaks. Although history has recorded their deeds as mere footnotes to greatness, it is the Sherpa contribution and effort that has been the backbone of most expeditions on Everest.

PIK KOMMUNIZMA

ELEVATION

24,590 feet

LOCATION

*Pamirs,
Republic of
Tajikistan*

FIRST ASCENT

*V.M. Abalakov,
Soviet Union,
1933*

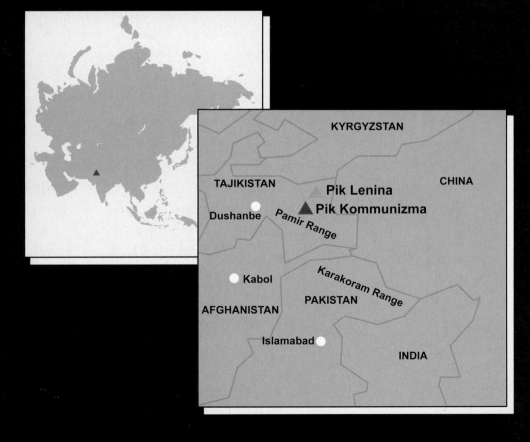

KYRGYZSTAN

TAJIKISTAN

CHINA

Pik Lenina

Pik Kommunizma

Dushanbe

Pamir Range

Karakoram Range

Kabol

PAKISTAN

AFGHANISTAN

Islamabad

INDIA

To the Vakhan people who had migrated from Persia they were the Bam-i-dunya, the "Roof of the World." Their rivers were ruled by the lord of the whirlpool; their lakes by fabulously wealthy mermaids and mermen. Later their passes provided a link in the great Silk Road between China and Rome; Marco Polo traversed their valleys. The Pamirs are suffused with myth and history, but for most of the world's mountaineers they remained a mystery.

Little was known of the Pamir Mountains—the most northwesterly of the chain of ranges stretching from central China and the coldest 7,000-meter mountains anywhere—until Russia's mid-19th century annexation of Tajikistan. In 1871 Russian geographer A. P. Fedchenko surveyed the northern mountains of the range and discovered the second highest summit in the range, now called Pik Lenin. But the highest

In summer Kirghiz herdsmen move into the high valleys of the Pamirs to graze yak, cattle and sheep.

Pamir, called Pik Stalin until he was disavowed and then Pik Kommunizma, remained uncharted until 1926. It was first climbed in 1933 by a large expedition of Russians, who forced a route up the Fedchenko Glacier from the north and east to a high camp at 22,600 feet. There, V.M. Abalakov and N. Gorbunov waited out a storm for five days and then set out for the summit. Within a few hundred feet of it, Gorbunov was overcome by altitude sickness and had to turn back, but Abalakov pushed on to make a solo first ascent.

With the exception of a German team that had joined with the Russians to climb Pik Lenin for the first time in 1928, Westerners were not invited into the Pamirs until 1962. That year the mountains were shown off to a strong team of Britons under the leadership of Sir John Hunt, who had led the 1953 first ascent of Everest. The joint expedition bagged a number of summits, including Kommunizma, but the expedition was marred by the deaths of Wilfrid Noyce and Robin Smith, two of England's

> **EXPEDITION STYLE:** *An approach to mountaineering in which climbers establish progressively higher camps and fix rope over difficult sections of the route to assist in ascent and descent.*

finest climbers, who fell 4,000 feet as they began their descent of Pik Garmo, a 21,637-foot mountain south of Kommunizma. The loss of their teammates sapped the will of the British

William Garner, left, and Randy Starrett of the U.S. return to base camp on Pik Kommunizma, the highest mountain outside of the Himalayan and Karakoram ranges.

team, though half of them elected to remain with the Soviets to make a joint ascent of Kommunizma itself. On the mountain a clash of cultures became evident. As the fit Soviet climbers fulfilled their "sports plan," the Brits, slowed by gastrointestinal problems and motivated basically by a desire not to be viewed as evidence of Western decadence, lagged

behind. Eventually both groups of climbers made the summit. An *Alpine Journal* account of the climb described it as "rarely pleasurable" but "nevertheless unforgettable."

In 1974 the Soviet Mountaineering Federation invited climbers from more than a dozen nations, including the U.S., to a sort of United Nations of mountaineering. Amid expectations that "the greatest assembly of climbers in history," as the Soviets called it, would accomplish great things, tragedy struck again. Colorado climber Gary Ullin died when he was engulfed in an avalanche on Pik 19, and eight Soviet women, trapped in a vicious blizzard on the summit of Pik Lenin, perished one by one as those who might have saved themselves refused to abandon those who were doomed.

As more Westerners have

visited the Pamirs, however, the stark beauty of the high desert plateau and rugged mountains and the hospitality of Russians and other Central Asians have become apparent. And a range that was once closed to outsiders is now one of the most accessible of any area with 20,000-foot peaks. Climbing in the Pamirs is still regulated by local climbing federations, which for the most part is a huge plus. The associations handle transportation to base camp on a high alpine meadow under the North Face of Pik Lenin. In past years this camp has had a festive international air, with the flag of each nation at the camp flying outside its group of tents. If the mountaineering is

Bottom: In the crystal clear skies over a Pamir base camp, celestial bodies trace concentric arcs around the North Star.

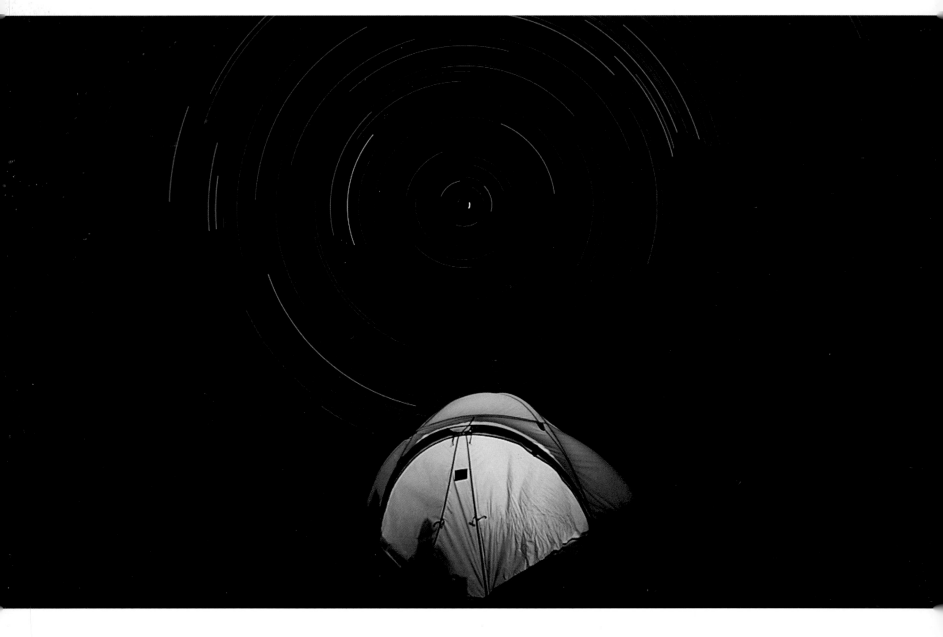

Top: An Uzbek woman visits a market in the Alai Valley, one of a network of passes and plateau lands in the Pamirs that served as a key link in the ancient trade route between China an Rome.

Right: Pik Kommunizma's northerly position makes it a magnet for heavy snow fall, which can result in immense avalanches like this in a couloir on the North Face of the mountain.

delayed by weather, climbers can bide their time with visits to yurts, the round tents that are put up by nomadic Kurds grazing their camels in high valley meadows.

Acclimatization climbs are made on surrounding peaks. Food—canned goods, sausage, dried fruit—is provided from a central commissary, but to lighten loads on the mountain some visitors stock up on freeze-dried dinners before leaving home. Then, climbers are transported by helicopter to the advance base camp of their choice. The normal route up Kommunizma, a demanding five- or six-day climb in good weather, starts in a forest glen to the side

of the Fortembek Glacier and ascends rotten rock and steep ice 5,000 feet to Camp 2. The route then traverses the seemingly endless Pamir Ice Plateau for eight miles without any gain in elevation to the base of Kommunizma's summit pyramid.

Back in base camp under Pik Lenin, there is certain to be a celebratory round of vodka, frequently poured from unlabeled bottles and indistinguishable from the grain alcohol that is kept in the camp infirmary. In such gatherings ideological and cultural differences can seem as ephemeral as snow crystals. A trip to the

Pamirs has convinced more than one climbing party that the world's conflicts could easily be ironed out at an international mountaineering camp.

Tragedy in the High Pamir

FROM *Storm and Sorrow in the High Pamirs*

BY ROBERT W. CRAIG

In 1974 the Pamirs, a range of mountains on the south central border with China that includes Pik Kommunizma and Pik Lenin, at 24,590 feet and 23,405 feet respectively the former nation's two highest mountains, were opened to Westerners for the first time. Starting in mid-July, 150 climbers from twelve nations gathered to a camp, festooned with the flags of twelve nations, on the flanks of Pik Lenin. Among them was an eight-woman Soviet team eager to demonstrate the prowess of the host country by completing a traverse of Lenin. But a violent storm hit the mountain in the first week of August and caught the Soviet women fatally ill-prepared. As the winds increased to gale force, it became increasingly clear that the women, pinned down just below Lenin's summit, were doomed.

Elvira came back on the air at 10:00 AM The roar of the wind was almost constant as she transmitted, but several standing nearest the receiver thought they could hear one of the women weeping.

"We are holding on. We cannot dig in; we are too weak. We have had almost nothing to eat or drink for two days. The three girls are going rapidly. It is very sad here where it was once so beautiful."

Her voice broke and she sobbed for the briefest moment, then regained her composure and said in a tremendously weary but steady voice, "We will carry on and talk again soon. Over."

We all asked: How could they have survived so long? 30 to 40 degrees below zero, consuming wind, no tents, no food. What keeps them going? Why do those smiling, happy, cheerful women have to die? . . .

Shataeyeva came on again at noon. One more had died. Four were dead. Two were dying. The condition of the last two we could only guess. The transmission was brief. Elvira almost seemed delirious, but she said, "We will go down, there is nothing left for us here. They are all gone now. The last asked, 'When will we see the flow-

ers again?' The others earlier asked about the children. Now it is no use. We will go down."

The mountain was totally closed in by clouds and the great wind roared across the ridges high and low. At Base we could just see across the valley, nothing above. The wind was gusting to forty miles an hour across the meadow and the temperature remained around 28 degrees. In zero visibility, with the possibility of descending to the right and over the huge east face or to the left and onto the not so precipitous, but avalanching north face, the dying Soviet women had run out of alternatives. It was only a matter of hours and, though no word was spoken, virtually every person in camp hoped they would be mercifully few.

There was no transmission at 2:00 PM from Elvira and we wondered if they were moving down or if the end had come. The receiver had been on continuously since 6:00 AM, so the batteries were changed to ensure that there was no failure either in transmission or receiving . . .

Elvira came on the air at 3:30 PM She spoke incoherently and then seemed to have lost track of time and referred to the illness of two of the women who had already died. The sound of the storm had momentarily eased and someone beside her (Valentina?) was audibly weeping. Then Elvira began to sob, "They are all dead; what will happen to us? What will happen to the children? [The two women who had youngsters had already died.] It is not fair, we did everything right."

Abalakov sat at the transmitter cutting in, trying to console Shataeyeva, "Viretska, my dear, beautiful girl, you have been very brave, all of you. Please hold on, we are trying to reach you."

Elvira came back on calmer, but distinctly weaker than she was three hours earlier. "We are sorry, we have failed you. We tried so hard. Now we are so cold."

"Elvira, don't give up. Stay awake; try to move your limbs. Kostya and Boris and others are trying to reach you. Keep calling us on the radio. We will not leave the receiver." The sad,

thin-faced lady interpreter did a brave job of keeping us informed of the conversation as, frequently on the edge of tears, she helped us understand that Abalakov was not cynically trying to raise the hopes of his doomed friends, but simply trying to make their deaths seem less forlorn. He felt that anything he could do to ease the anguish of their slow and certain dying was a merciful thing.

The transmission at 5:00 PM was garbled, but we sensed one more had died, leaving three still alive. The storm seemed to be continuing to build in intensity and for a brief moment we caught a glimpse of the clouds racing across Krylenko Pass. We estimated the wind velocity at eighty to 100 miles per hour . . . .

At 6:30 we heard several clicks of the transmitter key and then above the roar of the wind the very faint voice of Elvira, "Another has died. We cannot go through another night. I do not have the strength to hold down the transmitter button."

At this, the Russian lady interpreter burst into tears. People looked at one another in embarrassed silence. We saw Zina, the Russian camp dietitian who had been so kind to all the Americans, across the meadow with tears streaming down her face.

At 8:30 the receiver registered a few of the clicks we heard earlier and then Elvira came on in a voice almost drained of passion. "Now we are two. And now we will all die. We are very sorry. We tried but we could not . . . . Please forgive us. We love you. Goodbye."

The radio clicked off and everyone in that storm-lashed meadow knew the cheerful Soviet "girls" were gone forever. Everyone in the meadow wept unashamedly as the fact of finality was driven home by the utter silence of the radio and the unforgiving wind. The Soviet men and women wept the hardest and caused the rest of us to weep even more as they, several Russian generations removed from the Church, made the sign of the cross and with that almost forbidden gesture signified the end had come. And then there was only the wind.

MOUNT ARARAT

ELEVATION	LOCATION	FIRST ASCENT
16,945 feet	*Eastern Anatolia, Turkey*	*Friedrich Parrot, Russia, 1829*

To this day, the legend of Noah's Ark still casts its spell on Mount Ararat, the solitary volcanic summit believed to have been the site of the second creation. Though shards of evidence—an ancient timber, the sighting from a plane of a hull buried in glacial ice—show up from time to time, none has proved the presence of an ark. Still, it is not hard to imagine why Ararat remains among the holiest of holy mountains. Isolated on a plain in eastern Turkey 200 miles south of the Caucasus, its bare slopes contrasting with the green pastureland at its base, the mountain dominates the surrounding landscape. Its summit, capped with glacial ice and snow, seems to float on the horizon.

Situated just south of Turkey's border with Georgia, Ararat is now home to Kurdish herders, who set up clusters of tents on its flanks in summertime to graze their livestock. For centuries the mountain, a dormant volcano that last erupted in 1840, burying the ancient town of Ahora on its northeast flank in lava and glacial rubble, was thought to be unclimbable. So certain were the surrounding tribesmen of the mountain's invincibility that when Englishman James Brice reported his having summited in 1878, the local prelate merely smiled, saying, "No, that cannot be. No one has ever been there. It is impossible." In fact the first ascent had been achieved forty-

At the end of a hundred and fifty days the waters had abated; and in the seventh month, on the seventeenth day of the month, the ark came to rest upon the mountains of Ararat.

—*Genesis, 8:3-4*

On the way to the base of Ararat, climbers pass through high plateau settlements where Kurds pasture their horses and other livestock.

nine years earlier by Frederick Parrot, a Russian academician from St. Petersburg. Parrot had seen Ararat twenty years earlier from a summit in the Caucasus, then awaited a peace treaty between Russia and Iran to give him access to the mountain. His claim, too, was met with incredulity and only confirmed by later summiters.

From most approaches, however, the mountain requires no

Hikers getting an early start on the second day of their climb of Ararat are rewarded by a dramatic sunrise high on the summit ridge.

special skills. Trickier than the ascent itself is the procurement of a climbing permit, a process that is, after all, Byzantine. Climbers obtain a mountaineering application from a Turkish embassy, which then forwards it to the Ministry of Foreign Affairs, which in turns sends it to the Ministry of Tourism and

Culture. The process can take up to ninety days and in many cases is successfully completed only after follow-up calls to the embassy. The somewhat more cumbersome application process required of ark hunters hasn't dimmed the enthusiasm of the fundamentalists who flock to the mountain in hope of finding some remnant of the ship that

Dense volcanic boulders, this one poised above Camp 2, gleam with the glassy luster of basalt.

In the heart of Great Armenia is a very high mountain on which Noah's Ark is said to have rested. It is so broad and long that it takes more than two days to go around it. On the summit the snow lies so deep all the year round that no one can ever climb it.

-Marco Polo

rode out the Biblical flood. One of the more intense hunts was launched in 1980 by former astronaut James Irwin, who had a religious epiphany while orbiting the earth. His efforts, like those of all other ark hunters so far, came up empty.

In recent years access to the mountain has been restricted to the south through Dogubeyazit, the last major town west of the Iranian border. It is here that authorized guides, required by the Turkish government, are hired and provisions for the outing bought. A hired van takes climbers to the trailhead beyond

the Kurdish village of Eli. Camp 1, with space for about twenty two- and three-person tents, lies four hours higher at 10,500 feet. The route proceeds northeast through a series of gullies and then north to Camp 2, an exposed ridge at 13,800 feet. Since this camp has space for only ten to twelve tents, some parties have to wait a day for a site to open up. From Camp 2, it is a little more than two hours to the edge of the ice cap and another two to the summit—a time that can be reduced somewhat by climbers using crampons. From the summit, where the register is contained in a miniature wooden ark, Kucuk (little) Agri can be seen 4,000 feet lower to the east.

In the past the most popular approach to Ararat, closed in recent years because of border sensitivities with the former Soviet Union, was from the north and ascended the col between the two peaks. From there a stepped ridge leads to the

summit icefield. Were it to reopen, it would again become the mountain's preferred route. But even devoid of mountaineering challenges, Ararat will always possess a special mystique—as the place where humanity and all other living things began anew.

Aerial shots taken from NASA satellites accentuate the contrast between the snowy peak of Ararat and the arid surrounding land.

Top: Climbers, dressed for the chill winds of the summit, will strip down to shirt sleeves by the time they reach their base camp on the desert plateau.

Right: The highest mountain in Turkey, the isolated peak is to this day cloaked in an aura as the resting place of Noah's Ark.

MOUNT FUJI

ELEVATION	LOCATION	FIRST ASCENT
12,388 feet	*Honshu, Japan*	*attributed to En-no-Shokaku, Japan, 700*

The great 19th century watercolorist Hokusai painted Mount Fuji 100 times—through the stems of a bamboo tree, beyond travelers resting at a teahouse, as the reflection in a cup of sake. His countryman Hiroshige made thirty-six woodcut prints of the mountain that have become icons of Japanese art. No mountain has been more closely linked to its country and its culture than Fuji to Japan. Those who ascend the volcano's nearly perfect cone, less climbers than pilgrims, are participants in the heritage of a nation.

While there is no historical record of Fuji's first ascent, there is a detailed description of the volcano's crater in a 9th century manuscript. Dormant now, the volcano has had eighteen eruptions in recorded history, the last one, in 1707, covered Tokyo in six inches of ash. In the 12th century Matsudai Shonin, a Buddhist priest, built a

ALSO KNOWN AS • Fujiyama, Fuji-no-Yama, Fujisan

temple on the summit to honor Sengen Dainichi, the Buddhist deity of Mount Fuji. In the following 200 years a sect called Shugendo formalized worship of the mountain. Its followers, the Yamabushi, saw in its snow-peaked conical summit the concept of Zenho, a state of perfect concentration akin to the spirit in meditation, rising above the cares and passions of the material world. They built huts on the side of the mountain and guided other believers to the summit.

In the 16th century a religious visionary, Kakugyo Hasegawa, dedicated his life on Fuji and formulated a doctrine that elevated Fuji's deity to a preeminence as the supreme god of creation. Fuji-ko, as it was called, remained a minor cult until 1733 when a successor to Kakugyo, Jikigyo Moruki, starved himself to death near Fuji's summit in the belief that it would help end the famine that had devastated his country. One consequence of his martyrdom was the immediate growth of the cult into a major religious movement. By the 19th century

there were more than 100 Fuji-ko sects practicing in Japan.

Today, that number has shrunk to ten or eleven, but if religious motivation has fallen off, secular interest keeps growing. No foreigner climbed Fuji until 1860 when Sir Rutherford Alcock, the first British minister to Japan, went to the top to test an agreement guaranteeing unfettered travel to foreign envoys. Seven years later Lady Parkes, wife of the British Prime Minister, put that agreement to a more severe test: By summiting on Fuji she broke a prohibition against women climbing the mountain that had been in place since a government edict of 1558.

Fuji's summit is often marred by a shroud of smog, and many people maintain that the view from the bottom is more spiritual than the view from the top. For some the power of Fuji can be experienced at an even greater distance: its likeness on a keychain, poster, paperweight—anything will do. Paradoxically, many Japanese have an extraor-

There are two kinds of fools: the man who has never climbed Fuji, and he who climbs a second time.

—*Japanese proverb*

One of the hundred images rendered by Hokusai, the noted 19th century watercolorist.

dinary reverence for natural
things but an equal affinity for
synthetic versions thereof. Many
people, both Japanese and
otherwise, hold Mount Fuji as an
icon of serene and symmetrical
majesty even though they have
never set foot or even laid eyes

on the mountain itself.

The climbing season on
Mount Fuji begins every year on
the first of July, complete with a
ceremony at a shrine at the base of
the mountain. The ceremony is an
amalgam of Japanese culture:
with some visitors dressed in traditional garb, complete with
kimono, staff, straw hat and san-
dals, some in tee shirts and Nikes.
Thus, the stream of climbers
making their way to the top
begins. Their numbers will reach
into the hundreds of thousands
by the end of the summer—once
at the top, they can buy commem-
orative oxygen bottles, souvenir

**Traditional footwear for pilgrim-
ages to the mountain: canvas-
soled socks.**

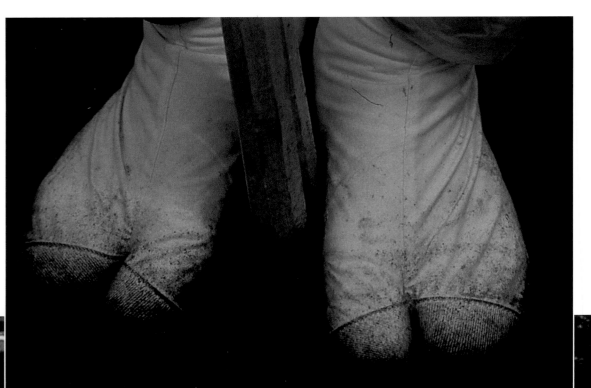

**Bottom: Served by a toll road that
reaches about half way up the
mountain, Fuji is the most climbed
mountain in the world.**

trinkets and food There are banks of telephones and huts where climbers can sleep in tiny cubicles.

Fuji presents no mountaineering challenges (though winter ascents must be prepared for heavy snows), but still the walk is no picnic. The elevation gain is 11,000 feet on the south side and 9,000 on the north. The mountain's four trails stretch in switchback after switchback for nine to fifteen miles. Many hikers take a bus on the Fuji Toll Road to its terminus 7,111 feet up the north-side Yoshida trail. From there the climb to the summit and back is an easy one-day outing. Others plan to spend the night at a hut high on the mountain, then arrive at the summit as the sun rises out of the Pacific Ocean. A walk around the crater, 700 feet deep and a mile and a half around, offers shrines, souvenir shops, a post office and stunning views: lakes, fields, towns and, after sundown, the lights of Tokyo fifty miles to the north.

For some, the biggest

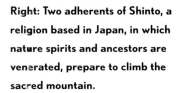

challenge, at least psychologically, is the crowds—20,000 on a typical summer weekend. One solution, since the Japanese prefer to climb the mountain in July and August when the huts are open, is to go up in June or wait for the traffic to thin out in September. Another is to set out in the late afternoon, hike through the night and arrive at the crater rim with the sun.

For others, however, the experience of Fuji is not the mountain but the procession of humanity, unbroken from base to summit, on a pilgrimage that began a millennium ago.

Top: Mount Fuji, an icon for the people of Japan, appears on this early-20th century postage stamp.

Left: The most ubiquitous landmark in all of Japan rises above the thatched roofs of Oshino.

Top: Pilgrims of all religions have been climbing Mount Fuji for hundreds of years.

Top: A hiker celebrates his moment at the highest point in Japan.

Right: The summit rim, studded with small crests, "The Eight Petals of Fuji," around its perimeter, has huts, temples, a weather station and, yes, pay phones—just in case the temporal world intrudes upon the sacred outing.

A F R I C A

Snow on the equator? Yes, and magical stands of giant ferns, groundsel, lobelia and heather below. The equatorial mountains of Africa are both a botanist's and a climber's paradise. Yet each of these mountains presents a unique personality. Kilimanjaro, Africa's highest, is serene. Kenya is fierce. Stanley, hidden in the ever-present mists of the Ruwenzori Range, is mysterious. They offer a wide range of climbing challenges, dramatic contrasts of environment, and the exotic sensation of being chilled to the bone on the Equator.

MOUNT KENYA

ELEVATION

17,058 feet

LOCATION

Kenya National Park, Kenya

FIRST ASCENT

Batian peak, 17,058 feet: Halford Mackinder, England, with Italian guides Cesar Ollier and Joseph Brocherel, 1899; Nelion Peak, 17,022 feet: Eric Shipton and Wyn Harris, England, 1922

Like Kilimanjaro, Mount Kenya occupies a revered place in the cultural memory of its people. To the Kikuyus, Kenya, the nation's tallest mountain and second only to Kilimanjaro on the entire continent of Africa, was the earthly resting place of Ngai, the god of creation. A Kikuyu fable tells how Ngai created the earth, divided it among the world's peoples and then took a man named Kikuyu to the summit of Kenya. There Ngai showed Kikuyu the splendid land at the base of the mountain he was about to receive and instructed him to return to a grove of fig trees in the center of this land. When Kikuyu did as he was bade, he discovered a wife awaiting him. They had nine daughters, each of whom became a matriarch of Kikuyu's nine tribes.

The isolated peak served as a focal point for ceremonies of initiation. Kikuyus would face

Mount Kenya, where Ngai rested, when they prayed for wisdom or prosperity or for rain. Kikuyus called their mountain Kere-Nyaga (from which the name Kenya was derived), meaning "Mountain of Brightness," and they referred to Ngai as Mwene-Nyaga, the "Possessor of Brightness." By the time the nation, once called British East Africa, gained its independence in 1963, it had taken the name of its revered mountain as its own.

Snow high on the flanks of Kenya was regarded by the Kikuyus as a supernatural substance. But when German missionary Ludwig Krapf reported seeing snow in British East Africa near the Equator in 1849, the report was dismissed back in Europe as fantastical—as had been similar sightings by his colleague Johannes Rebmann the year before. But once Scottish geographer Joseph Thomson

confirmed the existence of Mount Kenya in 1883, mountaineering expeditions began to arrive. The first successful ascent of the mountain, however, was achieved by geographer Halford Mackinder in 1899, a scientist with little climbing experience. Mackinder's party, which included six Europeans

A climber on the lower slopes of Kenya covers up as the weather closes in.

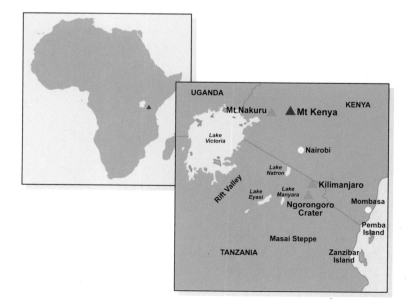

Suddenly there was a break in the clouds far up in the sky, and the next moment a dazzling white pinnacle caught the last rays of the sun, and shone with a beauty, marvelous, spirit-like and divine, cut off, as it apparently was, by immeasurable distance from all connection with the gross earth.

—*Scottish explorer Joseph Thompson, upon viewing Mount Kenya for the first time in 1873*

and 150 to 200 porters, encountered its greatest hazards not on the mountain but during the thirty-day approach from Nairobi. The team successfully warded off the charges of angry rhinoceros but lost two men to attacks by hostile tribes. After repeated attempts on Batian, the higher of Kenya's twin peaks, Mackinder and his two guides finally prevailed, etching a complex rock and snow route on the steep and technically demanding summit tower.

The mountain was not climbed again for thirty years,

For climbers wanting to avoid the difficulties of Kenya, nearby Point Lenana (16,355 feet) offers a non-technical alternative with one distinct advantage: a superb view of Mount Kenya itself.

Descent of long pitches on one of Kenya's summits is helped by joining two ropes on rappel.

Kikuyus, members of Kenya's largest tribe, graze cattle in the foothills of Mount Kenya.

when the renowned English mountaineers Eric Shipton and Wyn Harris climbed both Batian and, for the first time, Nelion Peak (17,022 feet). The most antic attempt on the mountain occurred during World War II

when three Italian POWs escaped from a nearby British camp just to relieve the boredom of incarceration, leaving a note saying they would return after they had climbed Mount Kenya. Astonishingly, they did return—with tales of skirmishes with wild animals, steep snow faces and bad weather, but no summit.

With the end of the war, interest in Kenya became intense. Dozens of routes were added, including the most difficult ice climb in Africa, the fourteen pitches of the Diamond Couloir that reaches to the col between Batian and Nelion, called Gate of the Mists. The long South Face

provides an easier route to the col, but there is no easy ascent of either of the summits. Non-technical climbers head for Kenya's third peak, Point Lenana (elevation: 16,355) with its stunning view of Nelion six-tenths of a mile to the west.

The dry seasons for Mount Kenya, like that for Africa's other

An antique Kenyan postage stamp depicting Mount Kenya.

Top: The Temple, east of the summits at the top of the Gorges Valley, drops off vertiginously to the Nithi River far below.

Left: Kenya's tortured ridges are formed from an extremely pitted volcanic syenite.

Equatorial mountains, are January to early March and July to August. Most climbers approach the mountain from Naro Moru, a town seventy-five miles northeast of Nairobi, situated on a road that circles the Kenya massif. The walk to the Mackinder campsite and Teleki Lodge at 13,500 can be done in two days—or one if a ride can be caught over the rough road to a weather outpost, called the Met Station, seventeen miles inland. From the Met Station a

Batian, Nelion and Point Lenana glow under a Kenya moon.

road (for authorized vehicles only) continues to a radio tower and then narrows to a path that climbs through a forest to a broad heath. It soon begins to climb steeply up the so-called vertical bog and then eases off along the south bank of Naro Moru River as it ascends to the campground and lodge. Most climbers spend two nights at this elevation to acclimatize—with a day of side trips to the snout of the Tyndall Glacier or to views of the Diamond Couloir and the

SCREE: *Layers of loose rocks and stones that collect in gullies and at the bases of cliffs and ledges, the ascent of which is typically frustrating and laborious.*

Gate of the Mists. The walk from Mackinder Camp to the Austrian Hut, at 15,700 feet, takes two to three hours up a steep scree slope.

The ascent of either Batian or Nelion is a serious undertaking requiring advanced rock climbing skills and a full day from one of the high camps. Those more interested in the view than the challenge of high altitude technical climbing can hike to the summit of Point Lenana, visible from the hut, which can be reached in an hour and a half by following a rocky route to the right of the Lewis Glacier. From Lenana's peak, if the morning is clear, the shimmering snows of Kilimanjaro, 120 miles to the south, seem to float on the horizon.

Lobelia still flourishes between snow-dusted rocks high on the flanks of Kenya.

MOUNT KILIMANJARO

ELEVATION	LOCATION	FIRST ASCENT
19,340 feet	*Kilimanjaro National Park, Tanzania*	*Hans Meyer, Germany; Ludwig Purtscheller, Austria, 1889*

UGANDA

Mt Nakuru

Mt Kenya

KENYA

Lake
Victoria

Nairobi

Lake
Natron

Kilimanjaro

Rift Valley

Lake
Eyasi

Lake
Manyara

Mombasa

Ngorongoro
Crater

Pemba
Island

Masai Steppe

TANZANIA

Zanzibar
Island

A Greek merchant named Diogenes, returning to his homeland from East Africa, saw them in the first century A.D. In 1848 Johannes Rebmann, German missionary to East Africa, saw them again; his report dismissed as ludicrous until confirmed by a German baron traveling in the area. There are glaciers on the equator, though curiously enough, nowhere else on the continent of Africa. The highest of these spills through a breach in the cratered dome of Kibo, Mount Kilimanjaro's major peak, where it glistens under the equatorial sun.

Kilimanjaro, Africa's highest mountain, consists of three volcanic summits (Kibo, Shira and Mawenzi) arrayed along a broad plateau and splendidly visible in every direction from a distance of more than 100 miles. Kibo's majestic summit dominates the horizon; 2,444 feet lower, Mawenzi presents a dark and shattered profile some fifteen miles to the east, while Shira, at an elevation of only 13,140 feet, hardly rises above the plateau. For centuries the mountain was revered by the Chagga people who lived in its shadow. Even after its conversion to Christianity, the clan paid its respects to the mountain by orienting church altars toward Kibo. Today, they call their land "God's backyard" and consider those who live in upland areas more blessed than those who live below.

The Chagga have a tale that explains how Kilimanjaro's two highest summits came to have such differing aspects: Kibo and Mawenzi, the story goes, were once equally proud peaks, wives of the god Ruwa. One day Mawenzi visited Kibo to borrow embers to light her fire. Arriving just before mealtime, she was, as was the Chagga custom, invited to share the repast. Presently, Mawenzi returned, explaining she had tripped and spilled the coals into a stream. Since it was again mealtime, she sat down once more at Kibo's table. But on Mawenzi's third mealtime visit, Kibo realized her hospitality was being abused and flew into a rage. She thrashed Mawenzi with a wooden paddle, leaving her with the wildly jagged

---

Left: Neve, snow that has consolidated by continual freezing and thawing, provides firm footing near the summit of Kilimanjaro.

Bottom: Fair warning: Easy access to the summit of Africa's highest mountain lures inexperienced climbers to ascend beyond their level of acclimatization. The solution: patience. Or, if signs of cerebral or pulmonary edema occur, quick descent.

Top: Southwest of the inactive crater on Kibo, the taller of the mountain's two main summits, is Point Uhuru , the true summit of Kilimanjaro.

Members of the Masai put on their finery to welcome French alpinist Christine Janin, visiting Kilimanjaro during her attempt on the Seven Summits.

and broken rim of her summit crater. Today, the Chagga people are said to regard the mists that gather around Mawenzi as an effort to hide her humiliation.

Predictably, the Europeans drawn to the mountain paid little heed to the reverence with which the Chagga regarded it. Kilimanjaro was first climbed by Leipzig geographer Hans Meyer with Austrian guide Ludwig Purtscheller in 1889, shortly after Tanzania had been annexed by Germany. Since Kilimanjaro was now the highest point in the German Empire, Meyer promptly named the topmost peak on

the crater rim Kaiser Wilhelm Spitz, in honor of the German emperor. After Tanzania gained its independence in 1963, the peak was renamed Point Uhuru (Swahili for "freedom").

Kilimanjaro's natural environment, shifting from tropical rain forest to alpine rock gardens to sloping fields of lava and glaciated ice, offers the climber unique compensations. Three of the four routes to the summit require some proficiency on ice and rock. Fortunately, the normal route, used by nine out of ten climbers, pre–

Top right: Jeremy Schmidt, who climbed Kilimanjaro with Seven Summiter Patrick Morrow, battles giant ferns on their descent via the rarely used Mkewe trail.

The Breach Wall on the west side of Kibo, two steep glaciers connected by a vertical band of crumbling rock, contains the hardest route on the continent: a permanent icicle between the two glaciers that was first climbed by Reinhold Messner in 1978.

Inside Kilimanjaro's main crater is a strange world of ice pinnacles, fumaroles, sulfur deposits and for those sufficiently acclimatized for a bivouac, a stunning dawn view of the north and east ice fields.

sents no technical difficulties. This route starts from Marangu (elevation: 5,000 feet) 500 miles north of Dar es Salaam. The first eleven miles climbs 3,700 feet through tropical terrain to Mandara, an encampment of fourteen huts (jointly built in 1975 by Norwegian mountaineers and Tanzanians from lumber imported from Scandinavia) that accommodate sixty climbers and forty guides. No

one gets lost on Kilimanjaro's normal route, but guides, included in the obligatory permits and fees of around $200 per person, can be invaluable in the slow and sustainable pace they set. Fast-drying canvas shoes are recommended on the lower sections of the climb, since afternoon rains can turn the trail into a rushing stream.

From Mandara, the second day (or the third for parties remaining in camp for a day of acclimatization) takes climbers another eleven miles to Horombo Hut at an elevation of 12,300 feet. Shortly above Mandara the trail emerges from a dense cloud forest to a vast expanse of alpine meadows and, weather permitting, the first view of ice-capped Mount Kibo. Most people spend a day or two at Horombo, sloughing off the nausea and headaches that afflict lowlanders at altitude.

The third segment of the ascent covers a little more than nine miles and rises to a height of 15,500 feet—still 3,800 vertical feet shy of the summit. Trekkers get a brief respite from

Porters settle into an easy gait as they ascend a flank of Kilimanjaro on a supply run.

their labors at the Kibo Hut and then at 2 AM are roused by the guides for the final push up a seemingly endless scree slope to the crater. Gillman's Point, where climbers from Kibo Hut make first contact with the rim, is officially recognized as a part of Kilimanjaro's summit, and anyone who has made it this far is invited to forgo a one-and-a-quarter-mile traverse of the rim to Point Uhuru, the true summit 500 feet higher; most accept. The return to Marangu generally takes two days.

Kilimanjaro has gained prominence lately as one of the seven summits, the highest mountains on each of the seven continents. But rising in isolation 17,000 feet above the surrounding plain, and through breathtaking climactic transitions, it is an awesome—and rewarding—mountain in its own right.

MOUNT STANLEY

ELEVATION	LOCATION	FIRST ASCENT
16,763 feet	*Ruwenzori Range, Uganda/Zaire*	*The Duke of Abruzzi, Italy, 1906*

"I saw a peculiar shaped cloud of a most beautiful silver color," [Stanley] wrote. Minutes later, he realized that what he was seeing was not a mirage but the mysterious peaks themselves.

Few mountains are more steeped in history—and myth. References to the Ruwenzori go back more than 2,000 years when Aristotle (some sources say Herodotus) declared that the Nile River descended from a "silver mountain." Five hundred years later the Greek geographer Ptolemy declared that the Nile arose out of a range he called Mountains of the Moon, a name that over the centuries acquired a deepening shroud of mystery. By the late-1800s, as one expedition after another failed to find the source of the great African river, the discovery of these mountains had become one of the most sought after prizes of European exploration. In 1888 British explorer Henry Stanley (who, upon finding the famous Scottish explorer in the Congo in 1871, immortalized the phrase, "Dr. Livingstone, I presume") became the first European to set eyes on the range. At first Stanley perceived only a mist-covered horizon. "I saw a peculiar shaped cloud of a most beautiful silver color," he wrote. Minutes later, he realized that what he was seeing was not a mirage but the mysterious peaks themselves.

> **ALSO KNOWN AS** · Mount Ruwenzori, Mount Ngaliema (Zaire), Mountains of the Moon

Left: A unique plant life, thriving at 10,000 feet in the Ruwenzori mountains, includes giant species of groundsel, heather and, here, lobelia.

Bottom: The summits of Mount Stanley—from left, Alexandra, Margherita and Albert—rise magically above the lacy groundsel of Ruwenzori.

At last, the Mountains of the Moon, now called the Ruwenzori Range (possibly from "runssoro," a local word meaning rainmaker), had peeked out from its veil of secrecy—but not for long. "As if offended by our scrutiny, the protecting clouds resumed their regular office, leaving us with a keener desire than ever to solve the mystery," wrote Gaetano Casati, a member of the Stanley expedition.

As subsequent visitors to the equatorial mountain range that runs seventy miles along the north south border between Uganda and Zaire have discovered, the Ruwenzori is indeed the home of exotic life forms: tall stalks of lobelia, giant groundsel and heather, tree orchids, pink-flowering balsam and wild banana trees with ten-foot leaves but no fruit. The fauna, too, are plentiful; in addition to elephants, buffalo and duiker that frequent the lower valleys, the Ruwenzori habitat supports Uganda blue monkeys, long-haired chimpanzees, horned bushbacks, Ruwenzori leopards, golden cats, servals and earthworms of extraordinary length. The luxuriant ecosystem was slightly unsettling to members of the huge Duke of Abruzzi expedition that in 1906 made first ascents of the six glaciated mountains—all of them over 15,000 feet—in the Ruwenzori range. "The impression produced was beyond words to describe," wrote Abruzzi chronicler Filippe de Filippi, "the spectacle was too improbable, too unlike all familiar images, and upon the whole brooded the same grave deadly silence."

Indeed, the Ruwenzori landscape is unlike any other on earth. Two rainy seasons, from September to December and mid-March to June, produce dense vegetation at the base of the mountains, a lush tropical rain forest at 10,000 feet and mists that almost permanently shroud the range. On lower parts of the mountain plant growth is so aggressive that whole sections of trails are shaded by a canopy of vegetation. In this lush, ethereal rain forest, ordinary bushes grow to the height of trees. There is a profusion of blossoms right up to the edge of the snow cap, which begins at 14,000 feet.

Excellent climbing—some on mixed routes demanding technical ability, some requiring little more than stamina and good route-finding skills—abounds in the Ruwenzori. For trekkers, the high valleys of the range are a botanist's paradise. For those wanting to bag a peak, Mount Speke in the central part of the range offers a straightforward glacier ascent that can be done by hikers with little climbing experience. Other summits, including the three highest peaks on Mount Stanley, the highest massif in the range, offer challenges that attract world class climbers.

BUTTRESS: *A shallow ridge projecting from a face.*

The approach to Ruwenzori from the Ugandan side is a three-day walk from the village of Bugoye (thirty-seven miles west of Fort Portal) to Lake Bujuku. From there, two principal routes lead to Stanley's highest peak: Margherita. Another, more direct route leaves from the Irene Lakes Hut (elevation, 14,750 feet), slightly northwest of Lake Bujuku. Above the hut, the route crosses the foot of the East Stanley glacier and ascends the East Ridge to the summit. The ridge is interrupted by a step requiring two pitches of difficult technical climbing but is the easiest route to follow when mist shrouds the mountain. The longer route traverses south to the Elena Hut (elevation, 14,900), above which the Elena Glacier reaches to the steeply cut saddle between Margherita and its sister peak, Alexandra. From there the terrain to either peak is straightforward.

From the Zaire side, a trail originating in the town of Mutsori, headquarters for the Virunga National Park where permits and guide services can be obtained, passes three camps

Left: Famed photographer Vittorio Sella took this picture of a camp at the base of Mount Gessi during the 1906 Abruzzi expedition to the Ruwenzori. Sella's own first ascents in the region include a mountain that would subsequently bear his name.

to the Moraine Hut at 14,430 feet. From there the route to the Margherita-Alexandra col depends on snow conditions. If it has been dry, a rock buttress leads directly to the col. When this route is snow covered, climbers generally traverse north to the Margherita Glacier, which they follow eastward to the col.

In the past, the choice of which side of the mountain to climb has been influenced by political considerations—until the end of the Idi Amin dictatorship in 1986, for instance, the Ugandan approach was out of favor. The cardinal rules of mountaineering in the Ruwenzori are to go during the dry seasons of December to February or June to August—and to bring a compass. Moist warm air from the rain forests rising to meet the cool air of the glaciated summits is a sure formula for mist, which can strand and confuse even the most experienced climbers. In the Ruwenzori, those moments in which the summits open to blue sky are treasured.

THE DUKE OF ABRUZZI

1783-1933

HOME BASE ▪ *Savoy, Italy*

CLIMBING FEATS ▪ *First ascent, St. Elias;*
first ascents, Ruwenzori Range; exploration and
mapping of K2

Prince Luigi Amedeo of Savoy, the Duke of Abruzzi, traveled in style. In 1897 during a first ascent of Mount Saint Elias on the Alaskan coast, Abruzzi had his porters carry a brass four-poster bedstead to his base camp. Yet the grandson of Italian King Victor Emanuel II could also push himself to the limit. In 1899 he lost two fingers during an expedition to within 200 miles of the North Pole, a record for proximity at the time. Seven years later he was in Africa, exploring the exotic Equatorial summits of the Ruwenzori range. His party developed excellent maps and confirmed the ancient supposition that the headwaters of the Nile trickled from the glacial melt high on the slopes of the Ruwenzori.

Abruzzi was a moderately gifted as a mountaineer—he climbed the difficult Zmutt Ridge of the Matterhorn with Alfred Mummery in his early days. But his strongest assets were a passion for adventure, a talent for picking good assistants and guides and the charisma to win their loyalty. He also possessed the organizational skills—he had been trained in the military—and the wealth to fuel his expeditionary whims. Both attributes were fully employed during his 1909 campaign in the Karakoram for which he hired 500 porters to carry nearly seven tons of equipment and supplies to the base of K2. His attempt on the world's second highest mountain fell 9,000 feet shy, but he identified the route,

now called the Abruzzi Spur, that was used on the first ascent in 1954. Again, the expedition produced outstanding environmental research, maps and the superb pictures of Vittorio Sella, Abruzzi's expedition photographer. After the attempt on K2, Abruzzi and two Swiss guides climbed to 24,600 feet on Chogolisa, just shy of its 25,110 summit but an altitude record that was not bettered until 1922 during the second British attempt on Everest.

During World War I, Abruzzi served as chief admiral of the Italian fleet in the Adriatic Sea. Thereafter, he focused his energies on the Italian colony of Eritrea, now Ethiopia, where he spent his final days.

AUSTRALASIA/ANTARCTICA

n some mountains there is no easy route to the top. On others there is no easy route to the base. For two of the mountains in this section, just getting to the mountain may be the most challenging part of the climb. Vinson Massif lies further from a commercial airport than any other mountain, and special aircraft has to be procured for the trip. Carstensz Pyramid is protected on three sides by thick tropical jungle of Irian Jaya and on the fourth by a frequently inhospitable mining company. Negotiating permission for this mountain can take more skill than an overhung jam crack. For some climbers, of course, such impediments can be an asset: there will be no queues at the base of a route on either of these mountains. Even Mt. Cook, isolated by oceans from the main climbing centers of the world, can offer both challenge and solitude. These are mountains to seek out when getting away from it all is the prime objective.

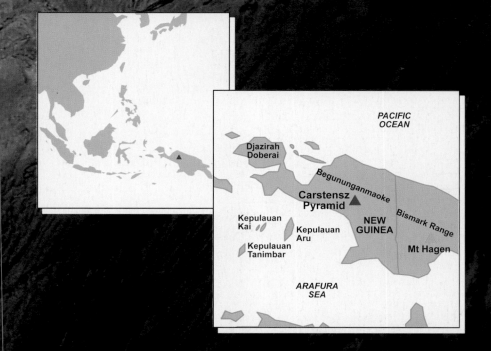

CARSTENSZ PYRAMID

ELEVATION

16,020 feet

LOCATION

Snow Mountains, Irian Jaya

FIRST ASCENT

Heinrich Harrer, Austria; Bert Huizinga, The Netherlands; Russell-Kippax, Australia; Philip Temple, New Zealand, 1962

Martyn Williams, who started up Adventure Network International to fly climbers to Antarctica, thaws out on a climb of the East Ridge of Carstensz, which—though it sports patches of ice—is never more than a few hours from the dense embrace of a tropical forest.

The highest point between the Andes and the Himalayas is hidden away in a mist-filled jungle on the island of New Guinea. Veiled by mist, rain and hail in the Indonesian state of Irian Jaya, Carstensz Pyramid is among the most remote and exotic of the world's mountains. Nevertheless, it has gained prominence as one of the Seven Summits, the highest peaks on each of the world's continents,

among those who consider Australasia rather than Australia as the true continent down under.

Carstensz Pyramid rises from the steamy mangrove swamps of Irian Jaya (formerly Dutch New Guinea), less than 5 degrees from the Equator. By noon cumulus clouds form around the mountain from the humidity that daily lifts off the jungle. Afternoon rain, sleet and snow are as predictable over Carstensz as teatime in England. The mountain itself is a fantastic uplift of limestone, sculptured by the daily runoff of rainwater that carves runnels down its sides.

Carstensz was first sighted by outsiders when English explorer and scientist A. F. R. Wallaston penetrated to the interior of the island (the earth's second largest after Greenland) in 1913. But in 1920, apparently ruing his incursion, he made an impassioned plea before his nation's Royal Geographical Society that the indigenous people of the island not be subjected to Western influence. "You have in New Guinea," he said, "the last people who have not yet been contaminated by association with the white races.... I believe that the whole of the interior of New Guinea should be kept as a vast ethnological museum, a native reserve where these people can live their own life, and work out their own destiny."

His vision was not to be realized. In the mid-1930s Dutch aircraft surveying the interior from the air discovered the largest outcrop of copper ore in the world just west of Carstensz. Mining and processing it is now the major industry in Irian Jaya. Photographs taken by the Dutch of the wildly jagged mountains in the center of the island seized the imagination of Western climbers. Heinrich Harrer—who established his place in mountaineering history with his first ascent of the Eiger Nordwand in 1938—led a first ascent of Carstensz in 1962, attacking the mountain from the North Face and the West Ridge. Interest in the mountain was renewed in the 1970 with the development of

Right: Canadian climber Patrick Morrow leads toward the summit as mists from the lush growth surrounding the mountain begin to close in. As is frequently the case on Carstensz, the summit was enveloped in cloud by the time the climbers arrived.

Indonesia University economics student Titus Pramono joined Morrow in an ascent of Carstensz Pyramid. In 1985 Morrow became the first to complete the Australasia version of Seven Summits.

summits, Carstensz version, in 1985, had to negotiate a classic catch-22 when both the government and the mine agreed to grant him passage to the mountain but only if the other agency did so first. "The crux of the Carstensz climb," Morrow later lamented, "is obtaining the right permits."

These difficulties only add to the remoteness of the mountain—and the sense that it exists in a different time and place from the rest of the world. The preferred point of embarkation is Ilaga, a town of 10,000 people, five days on foot north of Carstensz base camp. There, porters from the Dani tribe, a people at one time reputed to be cannibals, can be hired to take loads to base. They traverse the forest barefoot, some wearing shorts and tee-shirts, others nothing more than a penis gourd. They are possessed of a unique musicality, expressed from time to time in a spontaneous outburst of singing. Boston climber Mark Bowen, who traveled to Carstensz in 1997, writes that the Dani porters accompanying him, "sang themselves to sleep with ancient three- and four-part rounds."

Base camp, at 13,200 feet, sits on a meadow next to an alpine lake, whose silted bottom gives the water a turquoise hue. Below is a tropical forest; above, 2,500 feet of dolomite rock leading to the Gothic spires and towers of the Carstensz summit. Summit and return can take a strong party from dawn to nightfall. The route ascends 60-degree slabs for two pitches, then eases off for 900 feet of scrambling to a broad ledge. A traverse and then 500 feet of scree leads to the East Ridge, which provides a series of gaps and pinnacles on the way to the summit. From the ridge, mists permitting, the dark gleam of the Arafura Sea can be seen sixty miles to the north.

A young Dani, dressed only in the penis gourd that is the usual apparel for the males of this Irian Jaya tribe, mimics the odd activity of the visitors on a boulder during the walk in to Carstensz along the Baliem Valley.

numerous new lines on the North Face, a route on the East Ridge and eventually an ascent from the snow-covered South Face.

Further exploration of the mountain—and the cornucopia of promising routes on surrounding peaks—has been inhibited by the Indonesian government, which has frequently withheld permission to climb in the Sudirman Range. Parties wishing to approach the mountain from the west have had to obtain the permission of Freeport Mining, the U.S.-based corporation that controls the mine near Carstensz. Patrick Morrow, the Canadian photographer and climber who was first to complete the seven

CRUX: *The hardest pitch of a route; also the hardest move within a pitch.*

SIR EDMUND HILLARY

1920-

"Nothing venture, nothing win."

HOME BASE ▪ *Auckland, New Zealand*

CLIMBING FEATS ▪ *first ascent, Mount Everest;*
led an expedition to the South Poie

Eight years after Sir Edmund Hillary and Sherpa Tenzing Norgay set foot on the summit of Mount Everest, Hillary went back to the Solu-Khumbu region. His return rekindled a great respect and admiration for the Sherpas, an extraordinary people many of whom live in poverty, and yet exhibit an impressive generosity of spirit. Inspired by their kindness, he asked if there was something he could do for them. They answered that what they most needed was a school. It was then that the one-time beekeeper from rural New Zealand began truly to assume the greatness that had been thrust on him by his historic ascent.

Hillary began a fundraising whirlwind; he traveled the world, lecturing and touring to fund aid projects for the people of the Himalaya. The following year, 1962, Hillary established the Himalayan Trust to finance the building of schools and hospitals in the Solu-Khumbu region. Since then the trust has expanded its scope to include roads and, most recently, the establishment of the Sagarmatha National Park. In conjunction with significant efforts to arrest deforestation and plant trees, the genesis of the park, which contains much of Solu-Khumbu, has proven to be a major step in the preservation of the forests around Everest, denuded of trees in recent years by trekkers who use the wood for fuel.

Raised in a small town near Auckland, Hillary discovered the mountains during a ski trip in the north island when he was

16. He learned rockcraft from Harry Ayres, New Zealand's premier alpinist, and in 1951 had the good fortune of joining a reconnaissance of Everest with Eric Shipton, one of England's most respected mountaineers. He returned to the Himalayas with Shipton again in 1952 on an attempted first ascent of Cho Oyu (26,906 feet). Though they failed, Hillary's ability on snow and ice was sufficiently impressive that he was invited onto the Everest expedition. When Hillary and Tenzing Norgay reached the summit on May 29, 1953, he became, perhaps for all time, the world's most famous mountaineer.

After the expedition, Hillary, a quiet, unassuming man, married Louise Rose, with whom he had a son, Peter, and two daughters, Sarah and Belinda. After Louise and Belinda died tragically in a plane crash near Kathmandu in 1975, he remained a widower for fourteen years, finally remarrying in 1989—to June Mulgrew, the widow of a friend whose plane went down over Antarctica. In 1990 the Hillary saga on Everest came full circle when Peter Hillary summited, the first time the mountain had been climbed by the son of a former Everester.

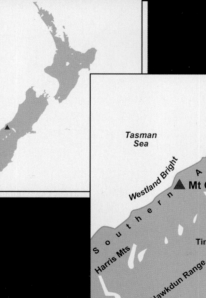

NEW ZEALAND

Tasman
Sea

Westland Bright

Southern Alps

Puketeraki Range

▲ Mt Cook

Christchurch

Harris Mts

Timaru

Canterbury Bright

Hawkdun Range

Pacific
Ocean

MOUNT COOK

ELEVATION

12,329 feet

LOCATION

Southern Alps,
New Zealand

FIRST ASCENT

Jack Clarke,
Tom Fyfe,
George Graham,
New Zealand,
1894

In the late 19th century, years after most of the mountains of Europe and North America had been climbed, the isolated mountains of New Zealand remained largely untouched. The Maoris, who had occupied the island nation for 500 years had no use for summits, and the early English settlers had had no time for them. Then in 1881 Rev. W.S. Green of Ireland arrived in New Zealand with a pair of Swiss guides to climb Mount Cook, New Zealand's highest peak. Green eventually failed, stymied by a wide crevasse within a few hundred feet of the summit—and then deteriorating weather. But not only had he pioneered a route that would later become the most popular

Glaciers on the east side of the Mount Cook Range feed into the Tasman Glacier, which opens into eerie, blue-lit crevasses.

Mount Cook Airlines, offering flights from Mount Cook village onto glaciers on either side of the mountain, can reduce the walk in to a base camp hut by a day or more.

approach to the mountain, he had awakened nationalist pride in the country's grandest mountain.

Young New Zealanders, spirited but largely untrained, began venturing onto the ridges and faces of Cook in hopes of bagging the first ascent. In 1889 a party led by Christchurch bank clerk G. E. Mannering followed Green's route up the North (sunlit, of course, in the Southern Hemisphere) Face—with precisely the same result: They were turned back by darkness within just 200 feet of the summit. Over the next five years, the competition heated

ALSO KNOWN AS • Aoraki (Maori)

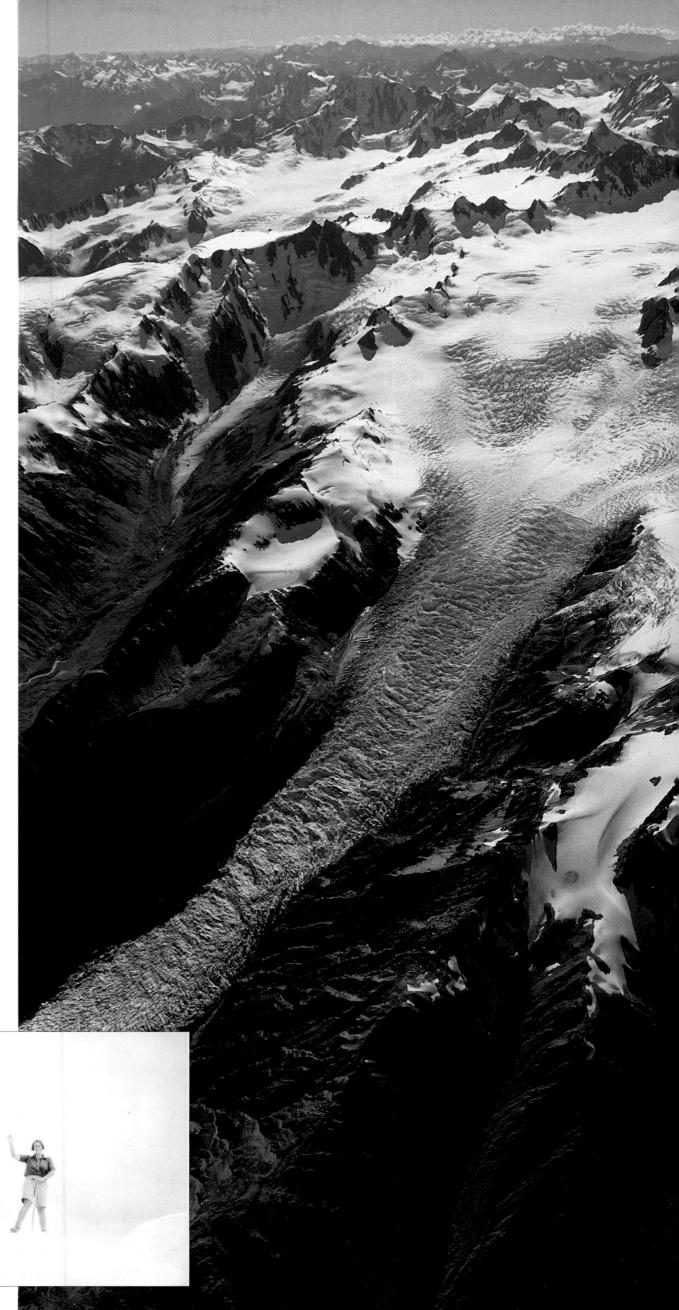

up, with one attack after another
rebuffed by the mountain's steepness, harsh weather and exposure
to rockfall and avalanche. In 1894
word reached the islands that veteran British mountaineer Edward
Fitzgerald was sailing to New
Zealand with the purpose of
bagging the first ascent of Mount
Cook. With him was guide Mattias
Zurbriggen, the superclimber from
Switzerland who had been first to
summit Aconcagua.

The news galvanized the
locals. Five attempts on the north
face all failed. Finally, with
Fitzgerald's arrival imminent,
Mannering protégés Tom Fyfe
and George Graham, joined by
nineteen-year-old Jack Clarke,
abandoned the north face for a
daring attempt on the west face
and north ridge. On Christmas
Day, the threesome, salvaging
their nation's honor, reached
Cook's summit. Their route,
exposed to avalanche and difficult
rock, is seldom repeated.
Fitzgerald, arriving shortly thereafter, was so miffed at having been
beaten to the first ascent that he
declined to climb Cook at all,
while Zurbriggen, with young
Clarke, made the first ascent of

**Right: Rivers of ice scour the valleys
in Mount Cook National Park.**

**Bottom: Guide service, still avail-
able in the Mount Cook National
Park, was going strong in the
1930s when these female alpinists
greeted prospective clients from
the head of the Tasman Glacier.**

Despite their modest elevation, the New Zealand Alps, with heavy snows feeding vast glacial systems, are a prime training ground for Himalayan climbers.

From the summit of Mount Cook it is only 12 miles to the Tasman Sea, the source of the heavy precipitation on the alpine ridges and crests.

Below the snow line melt water nourishes exotic and often delicate alpine plants, such as this Mount Cook Lilly, which is the largest member of the buttercup family.

New Zealand's second highest peak, Mount Tasman.

Today, the Southern Alps are no longer mountaineering's best-kept secret, but they can be a refreshing alternative to the sometimes crowded routes of the classic climbs in North America and Europe. Better yet for northerners, they provide a second summer (best climbing months are December, January and February) of mountaineering. Despite their modest heights, Cook and its surrounding peaks provide tough, demanding climbs—a Himalayan experience without the long, back-breaking approaches or the dangerously thin air. Storms on Cook can be monumental. It is the first landmass encountered by moisture-laden winds that come roaring in from the Tasman Sea only 15 miles to the west. Cook's glaciers

reach as low as 2,500 feet above sea level, leaving nearly 10,000 feet of ascent.

Avalanche is Cook's main event. In the summer of 1992, climbers on Cook were awakened in the middle of the night to a terrifying rumble. At first they thought it was an earthquake, but the roar didn't stop for four hours. Outside they could see the sparks of colliding rocks as the top of Cook literally slid down the East Face of the mountain. Down below the avalanche split in two. Then it roared across a mile-long flat and started climbing out of the valley before it came to a rest, four miles from its start. When it was all done, Cook had lost ten to twenty feet of elevation. Smaller versions on the snow-laden mountain occur daily, and climbers on Cook make early starts while the

snow is still consolidated when crossing faces and couloirs.

Most climbers on Cook start from the Plateau Hut on the Grand Plateau, at an elevation of 7,350 feet six hours from the road head. The normal route ascends the East Face 1,300 feet to Zurbriggens Ridge, which provides a mixture of rock and snow climbing to the Summit Rocks and then an arête to the summit. Cook's easiest—and most climbed—route is also its

> **ARÉTE:** *French for ridge. Often connotes a sharp ridge with steep sides; on rock cliffs, an outside corner.*

most dangerous. From Plateau Hut it ascends the right side of Linda Glacier, then makes a hair-raising traverse under The Gunbarrel, an unstable ice cliff on the upper Linda, to the safety of Zurbriggens Ridge.

Climbers wanting to step up the challenge a notch can try the East Ridge, a classic ice climb that ascends to Cook's Middle Peak along a knife-edge requiring very strong nerves. From Middle Peak, only 139 feet lower than High Peak, there is another half mile of icy ridge to Cook's true summit.

VINSON MASSIF

ELEVATION	LOCATION	FIRST ASCENT	
16,067 feet	*Sentinel Range, Antarctica*	*Nicholas Clinch, J. Barry Corbet, John P. Evans, Eiichi Fukushima, Charles Hollister,*	*William E. Long, Brian S. Marts, Peter K. Schoening, Samuel C. Silverstein, Richard W. Wahlstrom, 1966*

For a mountaineering outing, Vinson Massif presents more than its share of obstacles: an average temperature in the dead of summer of -20 degrees Fahrenheit; an icecap so hard that it is impossible to get ice screws to bite into it; and a remote location that only specially equipped aircraft can reach. But it also has one unique advantage: in December and January, there is light twenty four hours a day. As yet no climber has ever had to bivouac on Vinson because of darkness. Vinson has something else going for it: a stark purity like nowhere else on earth. To the north and south lies a ribbon of rock and to the east and west stretches a seemingly infinite ocean of ice.

Antarctica was first sighted in 1820, nearly a century before Norwegian explorer Roald Amundsen, in his epic duel with British naval officer Robert Scott, reached the South Pole in 1911. It would be another twenty-four years before anyone set eyes on the Sentinel Range, and then only from the air during a transcontinental flight by Lincoln Ellsworth in 1935. Once they were finally viewed from the ground by members of the International Geophysical Year explorations of 1957-58—and recognized as the highest peaks on the seventh continent—the Sentinels took the limelight. Here was an entire range of virgin peaks, hardly touched, much less climbed by any living being.

Applications to climb the Sentinels from American climbers on both coasts languished in the U.S. government for eight years before word went out to the American Alpine Club that permission—and the cooperation of the U.S. Navy—was being granted. In the fall of 1966 the climbers who would make the push to the summit were recruited, and in the first week of December a Navy C-130 transport plane deposited climbers, food and gear—including snowmobiles—on an icefield twenty miles from Vinson. "From the air the peaks had been spectacular," wrote expedition member Brian S. Marts. "Here on the plain they were overwhelming. Rising abruptly from the flat plateau, this was the most beautiful range I had ever seen."

During the next two weeks climbers pushed a route to the saddle between Vinson and Mount Shinn to the north. Then they got their first taste of Antarctic

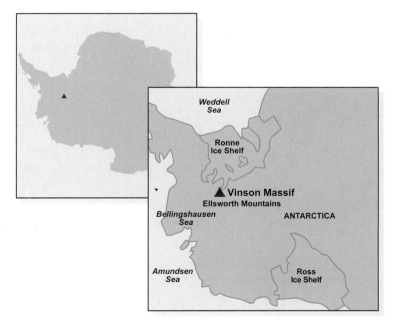

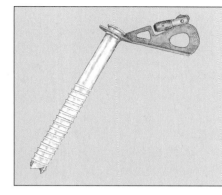

Ice screw: a hollow cylinder with a prominent thread that is screwed into ice to provide an anchor for a belay or as protection on a lead

weather. Furious storms lashed base camp for two days, tents were flattened and gear was tossed chaotically around the floor of the glacier. But the men regrouped, and on December 18 the expedition's first three climbers made it to the summit—to be followed over the next forty-eight hours by the remaining seven members of the expedition. And that was just the beginning. By the time the climbers departed for McMurdo Sound and Christchurch, New Zealand, they had done first ascents on six of the Sentinel's highest peaks.

In 1992 French alpinists barricade their camp against the winds that travel unimpeded across a continent of ice.

Given its remoteness and the expense of mounting an expedition, Vinson might not have received a lot of attention thereafter were it not for the emergence of Seven Summits fever. By the 1980s the race was on to climb the highest peak on each of the seven continents (in addition to Vinson, Everest in Asia; Aconcagua in South American; Denali in North America; Kilimanjaro in Africa; Elbrus in Europe; and either Kosciusko in Australia or the higher Carstensz Pyramid in Irian Jaya if Australasia—which includes Australia, New Zealand and the island nations of the South Pacific—is considered the true Down Under continent). In 1983 this competition brought

Dick Bass, a wealthy oilman, and climbing friend Frank Wells, then president of the Walt Disney Corporation, to Vinson with some of the best hired help available— expedition professionals Rick Ridgeway of the U.S. and Chris Bonington of England.

Top: A twin Otter ski plane, capable of landing within eighteen miles of the base of Vinson Massif, is the climbers' lifeline back to the inhabited world.

Dr. Lis Densmore, seen here fortifying her tent at Camp 3 in the col north of the summit, became the first woman to climb Vinson in 1989

The formidable powers of the mountain became apparent as less experienced climbers followed the first ascent party to Vinson. Because of its position on the 80th parallel, Vinson has an atmospheric pressure that is relatively thinner than that of mountains nearer the equator, resulting in more difficult acclimatization and oxygen absorption at the summit equivalent to that of a mountain 2,000 feet higher. The

Climbers often come away well frosted after an expedition to Antarctica's highest mountain.

summertime sun, beaming through the ozone hole over the continent, has a full spectrum of destructive ultraviolet rays. During the Bass-Wells expedition, Vinson's weather was at full throttle. Eventually, both Bass and Wells summited—as did Bonington and Ridgeway—but even Bonington had been impressed with the sudden changes of weather. On the morning of his ascent the veteran of numerous Himalayan expeditions declared, "This has to be the most fantastic day of my whole climbing career." Four hours later, as Vinson's winds gusted to sixty m.p.h. and the temperature dipped to -30 degrees Fahrenheit, his opinion had changed. Bracing himself, he shouted to Ridgeway, "These have to be the worst conditions I've ever climbed in."

Such conditions haven't dissuaded a growing number of Seven Summit aspirants. By the mid-1990s one adventure travel outfitter had put more than 100 climbers on top of Vinson. From a technical standpoint the climb via the American route is

straightforward. Most expeditions are outfitted with snowmobiles that ferry climbers and supplies from a snowfield landing strip to the base of the mountain at 7,500 feet. Climbers following the first ascent route put Camp 1 at 11,000 feet at the head of an icefall. Camp 2 goes on the Shinn-Vinson saddle at 13,000 feet. Because of the wind exposure here, some expeditions seek out an ice cave for emergency shelter in case their tents are mauled by wind. The push for the summit is usually made from a high camp at 14,000 feet, although conditions in some years have prevented the placement of a Camp 3 and the summit is attempted in one long day from Camp 2.

Take away the weather, and you have ideal climbing conditions: thick blue ice, no rockfall, no danger of being caught in darkness. And for those choosing to tackle the mountain on skis, conditions could hardly be better— as one wag put it, ten inches of powder on 5,000 inches of base.

We looked at the long horizontal line, so clear there was a fine distinction between the ice and the sky. So clear that staring at it we realized you could actually tell it curved from one end to the other. We guessed this had to be perhaps the only place on earth where you could see this phenomenon. And we realized that if the ancients had been witness to this view they would have known the earth was round.
—*Rick Ridgeway at 13,800 feet on Vinson*

EUROPE

Until the mid-19th century, any attempts on European mountains were motivated by a scientific objective. Then came the Golden Age of mountaineering. Between the ascent of the Wetterhorn by Englishman Alfred Wills in 1854 and the tragedy on the Matterhorn in 1865, there were 180 first ascents on Alpine peaks—establishing once and for all that people could scale peaks and ridges for the sheer adventure of it. Climber/writer Leslie Stephens declared the Alps "the playground of Europe," a sobriquet the Alpine communities have taken to heart with a network of ski lifts, télephériques and mountain huts second to none. To this day, this range—stretching from southern France to Slovenia and forming a natural boundary between France, Italy and Switzerland—has maintained its status as the epicenter of the sport of mountaineering.

BEN NEVIS

ELEVATION	LOCATION	FIRST ASCENT
4,406 feet	*Fort William, Scotland*	*unknown*

Despite its elevation, which barely exceeds 4,000 feet, Ben Nevis holds a towering position in the history of British mountaineering. It was on the Ben's buttresses and gullies that generations of English and Scottish climbers developed techniques that would carry them up some of the most spectacular routes in the Himalayas. A list of those who have made first ascents on the craggy ridges and gullies of the Ben reads like an honor roll of British climbing: Joe Brown, Don Whillans, Doug Scott, Dougal Haston, Robin Smith. But the renown of Ben Nevis extends well beyond a small corps of elite mountaineers. As the highest point in a nation of walkers, the summit of the dark outcrop above the Glen Nevis is one of the most climbed on earth.

There is no record of who first climbed Ben Nevis, which can be reached by an easy hiking trail from the west. But the steep Northeast Face, containing an entire encyclopedia of rock and ice climbing challenges, is now well documented. The routes that first captured the attention of the area's climbers were the Northeast Buttress and the Tower Ridge, two jagged spines of rock plastered at times with snow and ice. A description of an 1894 ascent of the Northeast Buttress by Scotsman William Brown—thought at the time to be the first—gives a flavor of the climbing technique of the day. "There are little towers," Brown wrote, "up which the leader had to scramble with such gentle impetus as could be derived from the pressure of his hobnails upon his companion's head. There are ledges (not very terrible) where it is convenient to simulate the grace of a caterpillar. A sloping slab we found, too, where the union of porphyry and Harris tweed interposed the most slender obstacle to an airy slide into the valley." Before Brown's self-effacing report was published, however, a small note in the English Alpine Journal announced that John Hopkinson and his son Bernard of Manchester, England, had climbed the buttress two years earlier. Historians of British mountaineering speculate that the fiercely competitive Scottish Mountaineering Club must have greeted this news with no small measure of chagrin.

Today, the Northeast Buttress, a moderate climb by modern standards, has the historic resonance of a famous battleground. Starting from a youth hostel on the Glen Nevis road north out of Fort William, a trail leads northwest and then west to the base of the of famous buttress. The route gains a ledge called the First Platform, ascends more steeply to the Second

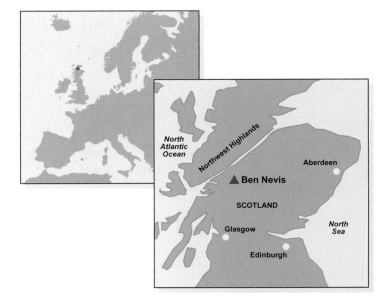

Tower Ridge, the great central buttress on Ben Nevis's north cliff, is the most popular rock route on the mountain. In winter it offers severe snow and ice ascents that, because of the Ben's northerly latitude and short days, put a premium on speed.

Platform and thence to the ten-foot overhanging Man Trap—in Brown's apt description—that is the crux of the climb. A steep open book and a chimney lead to an easier final pitch.

The Tower Ridge, at 1,900 feet the longest route on the Ben's East Face, was attempted by the Hopkinsons at one point. They also used it as a descent route after their North East Buttress ascent. But in summer, without the glaze of ice that makes winter ascents a serious outing, it, too, is accessible to climbers of moderate ability. The first of the towers, Douglas Boulder at the base of the climb, is usually circumvented by climbing a gully from the east to the Douglas Gap. A chimney regains the ridge that leads to an overhanging face and then a ledge at the base of the Little Tower,

which is surmounted on the left. A scramble ascends to the Great Tower, a tall spike that forced the Hopkinsons to retreat. A traverse left at its base leads to a large block and then easier rocks to the top of the tower. After a descent into the Great Tower Gap, the route ascends a chimney and scrambles to the summit.

The fit hiker can gain the summit of the Ben simply by following a well-worn path from the Glen Nevis Youth Hostel up switchbacks on the western flank of the mountain. From the summit, Ben Nevis commands views across Loch Linnhe to the Northwest Highlands; north to the Monadhliath Mountains, south to the Grampions, and on the rare clear day, southwest all the way out to the North Atlantic. A west-running ridge carries over Ben Nevis and a half dozen lesser peaks to a railway station twenty-five miles away. The traverse makes a long day—thirteen hours of walking according to one guide book—but the route shows off Scottish ridge walking at its finest.

Center: Winds blasting the Ben force a trio of women climbers to double up on security in order to traverse a lower flank of the mountain.

Above: The Ben rises from the gently curving meadows of Glen Nevis, just north of Ft. William in the Scottish Highlands.

Saving Face

FROM *One Man's Mountains*, WRITINGS BY TOM PATEY, COLLECTED POSTHUMOUSLY

A climber famed for his pioneering ice routes in the British Isles and a physician serving a broad swath of northwestern Scotland, Aberdonian Tom Patey (1932-1970) was a much-loved observer of the international climbing scene. He took special delight in pricking the inflated British mountaineering ego. He died when a device failed during a rappel off a Scottish sea stack.

Modern climbing is becoming fiercely competitive. Every year marks the fall of another Last Great Problem, or the fall of the Last Great Problem Climber. Amid this seething anthill, one must not overlook the importance of Staying Alive.

This is why I propose to devote a few lines to "The Art of Climbing Down Gracefully"—the long, dedicated Decline to Dignified Decrepitude.

I have had another title suggested, viz: "How to be a top climber without actually climbing." This is not only misleading—it makes a travesty of this article. One must assume that respect has been earned honorably on the field of battle and not by mere subterfuge. It is in order to maintain this respect, that one employs certain little subtleties that would ill befit a brash impostor.

In short, this is a symposium for Mountaineers—not mountebanks! ...

THE "CHOSSY CLIMB" PLOY

"Poxy," "Chossy," "Spastic" and "Rubbish" are all terms characteristically used by English and Welsh climbers to denigrate Scottish routes which they have either failed to climb or failed to find (without searching too minutely).

Eyewitness reports could in fact reveal that Spiderman made repeated attempts to overcome the crux, before he was ignominiously repulsed and left hanging in a tangle of slings and étriers, but this is completely at variance with the official Party Line, which stresses Spiderman's disgust on finding the

initial holds cloaked in greenery. His aesthetic senses had been so offended that he had instantly abandoned the climb and spent the day more profitably in a nearby hostelry. . . .

THE "SECRET CLIFF" PLOY

This dark horse is seldom seen in the Pass, but makes a belated appearance at closing time. He speaks slowly and reluctantly with a faraway look in his eyes. "We've been sizing up a new crag," he eventually admits after much probing, "amazing why nobody ever spotted it before, but then climbers don't get around much nowadays. . . . We're not giving away any details of course until we've worked it out. . . . Should be good for at least twenty more top-grade routes. . . ." etcetera.

None of these routes ever appear in print, but this too can be explained away at a later day by the Anti-Guide-Book ploy: "Why deprive others of the joys of original exploration? We don't want such a superb crag to suffer the fate of Cloggy, and become vulgarised by meaningless variations."

Evasiveness can be finely pointed.

"What route did you climb today then?"

"Dunno, we haven't named it yet!"—is perhaps one of the most spectacular.

All these ploys find their ideal medium in the "Solo Man Gambit."

THE "SOLO MAN" GAMBIT

The subtlety of this ploy is that no one, apart from Solo Man, knows how he spent the day. From the moment he disappears at the double over the first convenient hillock his movements are shrouded in mystery. He needs no accomplice, and he holds all the aces.

"Had a look at Vector today. . . . Quite thin. . . ." (Solo Man had indeed looked at Vector. He did not like what he saw.) Or: "Forgot the Guide Book. . . . No idea where I was . . . damn'd good route all the same! . . . Yes, it probably was a first ascent, but I won't be entering it. You can't expect me to remember details: one route is just the same as

another as far as I'm concerned." Or: "Found the Tension Traverse pretty tricky . . . a rope would have been quite useful. . . ."

THE "WRONG GEAR" PLOY

With a little foresight it is always an easy matter to bring the wrong equipment for the day, and then allow everyone to share your vexation. Such a man will turn up for a winter assault on Point Five Gully, wearing brand new P.A.'s

"Great God! I didn't expect to find snow on the Ben this late. Just my luck."

For a week-end's climbing at Harrison's he will have borrowed a pair of High Altitude Everest Boots.

"Just breaking them in for the Real Thing. Not much use on the small hold stuff but jolly good for the South Col."

THE "GREATER RANGES" PLOY

Historians tell us that Frank Smythe only began to function properly above 20,000 feet. This adds up to a pretty considerable handicap, when you consider how much of his life must have been spent at lower altitudes. It is all part of the mystique which surrounds The Men who are expected to Go High.

For this ploy some previous Himalayan experience is essential; it may involve a tourist weekend in Katmandu, a transcendental meditation with the Maharishi. Once the aura has formed, you can hardly go wrong. You can patrol the foot of Stanage with all the invested authority of an Everester. No one expects you to climb. It is enough that you retain a soft spot for your humble origins.

"This is all very different from South Col!" you can remark crisply, as you watch bikini-clad girls swarming over the rocks like chameleons. Any off-the-cuff comment of this nature goes down well, and gives them something to talk about after you have moved on. As I said before, nobody really expects a man who has survived the South Col to risk his neck on a paltry outcrop.

DOUGLAS SCOTT

1941-

"Without an element of danger lurking around the corner, mountaineering must lose its appeal."

HOME BASE ▪ *Cumbria, England*

CLIMBING FEATS ▪ *first ascents of Changabang, Southwest Face of Everest, North Ridge of Kangchenjunga, the Ogre*

After the pioneers, the explorers and the adventurers came the hardmen: working class British, usually from the north of England or Scotland, who valued their time in the pub next to that on the crag. There may be no harder hardman than Doug Scott. Scott's 1975 ascent of Everest with Scotsman Dougal Haston by way of the forbidding Southwest Face stands as a historic achievement in Himalayan climbing. The two survived a forced bivouac just below the summit—and without losing a single digit to frostbite.

Scott may be better known, however, for one of the most harrowing descents a climber has survived to tell about. In 1977, with a party that included countryman Mo Anthoine, Chris Bonington and Clive Rowland, he and Bonington succeeded in a first ascent of a Karakoram peak called, aptly, the Ogre. Scott, on rappel, was traversing to retrieve protection they had placed on the ascent when he suddenly lost his footing. A wild pendulum across a 100-foot span sent him careening toward an outcrop of rocks. "I just managed to get my feet up in front of me and—splat!—I

went straight into them," Scott recalled in a recent interview. "I discovered I broke both legs at the ankles."

For most climbers the loss of both legs high on a Himalayan peak could have had only one ending. But with Anthoine and Rowland setting up rappels and breaking trail, Scott literally crawled back to base camp. The ordeal, with five days of storms, lasted eight days—the final four without food. Near the end Scott had shredded not only the fabric of his trousers but the skin on his knees.

The son of a Nottingham policeman, Scott took to the crags near his home when he was twelve and by his mid-twenties was devoting his summers off from his work as a teacher to first ascents in such far-flung regions as the Sahara, Turkey, the Hindu Kush and California's Yosemite Valley. After Everest he became a leading proponent of lightweight, fast-moving alpine-style ascents-like his 1979 climb of Kanchenjunga, the first alpine-style climb of an 8,000 meter peak. "It was stepping into the unknown," Scott said of the most satisfying climb of his career.

Scott has two daughters and a son from a twenty-seven-year marriage that ended in 1989. Today he lives in northern England and makes his living lecturing and writing. He finds himself resisting the effort of each new outing, but once in the mountains, "I heave a big sigh of relief and wonder why it took me so long to get there," he once remarked. "I forget just how good it is."

SNOWDON

ELEVATION	LOCATION	FIRST ASCENT
3,559 feet	*Snowdonia Range, Wales*	*unknown*

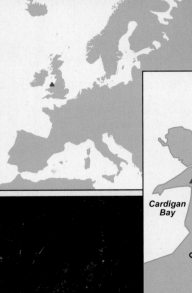

The wild and craggy ridges and the deep cwms of Snowdon, the highest peak in England and Wales, are the stuff of myth. This was the landscape of Merlin and King Arthur, who, in one version of the legend, is said to have defeated Mordred and an army of Saxons on the southern slopes of Snowdon only to be felled by a rain of arrows at the moment of his victory. It is in part the resonance of such legends that brings half a million British to this mountain annually. But it is also the stunning mountainscape: knife-edge ridges broken by sharply conical peaks and enclosing remote mountain lakes.

In summer Snowdon is accessible from every direction and provides for walkers and scramblers one of the most

Snowdon's great cirque culminates in the summit of Yr Wyddfa, rising above a Welsh cottage in Snowdonia National Park.

In the 1950s and 1960s the legendary Manchester climber Joe Brown established a level of difficulty on English and Welsh rock that is still the standard for British climbing.

rewarding outings of any mountain on earth. Its most famous route is the Snowdon Horseshoe, a seven-and-a-half-mile ridge that embraces the mountain's two major lakes. The walk starts at Pen y Pass, the storied meeting place of such legends of British mountaineering as George Leigh Mallory and Geoffrey Winthrop Young, and ascends the first of Snowdon's peaks, Crib-goch. From there the route leads westward, descending into a gap and then rising to Crib-y-ddysgl, a second peak. Between the two peaks is a bare ribbon of ridge that is airily exposed on both sides and that some prefer to traverse on footholds below the crest, using the knife edge itself for handholds. Pinnacles and towers on

**The Nant Ffrancon Pass cuts
across the rugged wilderness of
Snowdonia.**

the way to Crib-y-ddysgl can all
be climbed directly, though some
hikers may feel more comfortable
going around them on one side
or the other.

Beyond Crib-y-ddysgl the
ridge widens as it makes an arc
around the top of the horseshoe
and then climbs to Snowdon's
summit, Yr Wyddfa. This is a popular lunch spot, but climbers must
compete with tourists who have
been taken to the peak by a railroad
that once served a now defunct
mining operation on the mountain.
The descent follows the ridge
southeast into a notch, up onto
Snowdon's fourth peak, Lliwedd,
down slope to Snowdon's lower
lake, Llyn Llydaw, and finally
back to Pen y Pass.

There are a half dozen other
trails to Snowdon's summit,
most of them on ridges that
radiate to the outside of the
horseshoe. They can all be surmounted without technical
skills, but none of them, except
at the summit itself, is as heavily trafficked as the Snowdon

Horseshoe. It is this very
accessibility, together with that
of most of the other fells and
crags of the British Isles, that
led to the invention of technical
climbing. If reaching the top of
a mountain posed no real
challenge, then simply climbing
it became irrelevant. To keep
the game interesting, more difficult ways to the top had to be
sought out.

Snowdon's answer to that
challenge is winter ascents.
Ridgelines that provide fine
scrambles in the summer are
treacherous between November
and April. There are numerous
crags where generations of
British mountaineers have
learned the art and craft of step-
cutting, front-pointing and ice-
axe belay. Snowdon is one of the
principal training grounds from
which England launched its
assault on the alpine world.

STEP CUTTING: *The
practice, before the advent of
modern front-pointing crampons and ice tools, of cutting a
stairway into a snow slope to
facilitate ascent*

Mountain Music

FROM "THE MOUNTAINEER AS ARTIST,"

BY GEORGE LEIGH MALLORY, THE CLIMBERS' CLUB JOURNAL, 1914

As inventors of the game of mountaineering, Victorian gentlemen felt compelled to justify their activities in terms of their physical, moral and spiritual benefits. But for George Leigh Mallory, whose Delphic flippancy— "Because it is there"—was only dismissive, the mountains played an esthetic role. Here he is, eight years before his date with destiny high on the northeast ridge of Everest, waxing poetic as he buries a simile in an avalanche of correlations.

A day well spent in the Alps is like some great symphony. Andante, andantissimo sometimes, is the first movement—the grim, sickening plod up the moraine. But how forgotten when the blue light of dawn flickers over the hard, clean snow! The new motif is ushered in, as it were, very gently on the lesser wind instruments, hautboys and flutes, remote but melodious and infinitely hopeful, caught by the violins in the growing light, and torn out by all the bows with quivering chords as the summits, one by one, are enmeshed in the gold web of day, till at last the whole band, in triumphant accord, has seized the air and romps in magnificent frolic, because there you are at last marching, all a-tingle with warm blood, under the sun. And so throughout the day successive moods induce the symphonic whole—allegro while you break the back of an expedition and the issue is still in doubt; scherzo, perhaps, as you leap up the final rocks of the arête or cut steps in a last short slope, with the ice-chips dancing and swimming and bubbling and bounding with magic gaiety over the crisp surface in their mad glissade; and then, for the descent, sometimes again andante, because, while the summit was still to win, you forgot that the business of descending may be serious and long; but in the end scherzo once more—with the brakes on for sunset.

Expeditions in the Alps are all different, no less than symphonies are different, and each is a fresh experience. Not all are equally buoyant with hope and strength; nor is it only the proportion of grim to pleasant that varies, but no less the quality of these and other ingredients and the manner of their mixing. But every mountain adventure is emotionally complete. The spirit goes on a journey just as does the body, and this journey has a beginning and an end, and is concerned with all that happens between these extremities. You cannot say that one part of your adventure was emotional while another was not, any more than you can say of your journey that one part was travelling and another was not. You cannot subtract parts and still have the whole. Each part depends for its value upon all the other parts, and the manner in which it is related to them. The glory of sunrise in the Alps is not independent of what has passed and what's to come; without the day that is dying and the night that is to come the reverie of sunset would be less suggestive, and the deep valley-lights would lose their promise of repose. Still more, the ecstasy of the summit is conditioned by the events of getting up and the prospects of getting down.

Mountain scenes occupy the same place in our consciousness with remembered melody. It is all one whether I find myself humming the air of some great symphonic movement or gazing upon some particular configuration of rock and snow, or peak and glacier, or even more humbly upon some colour harmony of meadow and sweet pinewood in Alpine valley.

MONT BLANC

ELEVATION	LOCATION	FIRST ASCENT
15,767 feet	*Alps,* *France/Italy*	*Jacques Balmat,* *Michel Paccard,* *France, 1786*

As depicted in this 18th century print, Horace-Bénédict de Saussure, a wealthy Geneva scientist, launched a successful assault on Mont Blanc in 1787, a year after the first ascent, motivated in large part by prize money offered by Saussure, had been accomplished.

the northwest ridge climbed to an elevation of 14,000 feet before being turned back. However, one member of the expedition, a crystal hunter named Jacques Balmat, thought he had spotted a route to the top. Instead of returning with the rest of the party, Balmat stayed behind, then spent the night huddled in a snow cave. The following morning he struck out for the summit, cutting steps in a steep snowfield. He could see his way to the top of the slope, but it was too late in the day to continue. Exhausted, Balmat returned to Chamonix and immediately fell ill. Although he kept his knowledge of the promising route from the original climbing party, Balmat for some reason confided in Michel Paccard, the village doctor who had attended to him after his outing and who had himself reconnoitered the mountain. The two agreed to pair up

for another attempt. They set out, buoyed by the knowledge that Balmat had survived a night on the mountain, and on August 8, 1886, Paccard and Balmat stood on the summit of Mont Blanc. De Saussure paid the prize money and was himself led by Balmat to the top of the mountain the following year.

With the ascent of the highest mountain in the Alps, the mystery that had shrouded mountains began to fall away. Today Mont Blanc dominates a superb arena for mountaineering—magical spires of granite, terrifying blank walls, gleaming slopes of ice and snow in endless variety. More than thirty refuges are arrayed on the Mont Blanc massif in the best organized, most heavily used hut system in mountains anywhere. After World War II, skiing became the dominant recreational industry, spurring the construction of a

> CORNICE: *A cap of wind-blown snow overhanging the leeward side of a ridge. Cornices pose two kinds of hazards: They can break off, smashing into climbers moving below them, or they can give way under the weight of climbers crossing them.*

network of téléphériques that reach high up on glaciers on both the French and Italian side of the massif. While luring some climbers beyond their condition-ing or ability and contributing to a death toll on Mont Blanc (esti-mated at 6,000 to 8,000 to date) that far exceeds any other moun-tain, the téléphériques also have helped secure Mont Blanc's rep-utation as the climbing capital of the world.

In 1808 Marie Paradis, a twenty-three year-old farm girl from Chamonix, became the first woman to climb Mont Blanc. By midcentury, English gentlemen, invariably accompa-nied by a local guide, had taken over the field of play, putting up new routes on Mont Blanc and more than thirty surrounding peaks. In 1861 a party that included Leslie Stephens (father of writer Virginia Woolf) and the gifted Swiss guide Melchior Anderegg established what is today Mont Blanc's most com-monly used route, the Aiguille du Goûter.

This route, usually done in two days, requires an ice axe but

> AIGUILLE: *French for nee-dle. On a mountain, a needle-like peak; a spire or a pinnacle.*

For centuries the Alps were regarded with such fear and foreboding that people hardly had words for them. The word *alps* referred in fact not to the peaks but to the surrounding high meadows that served as pastureland in the summer. Similarly, *mont* originally designated not a mountain but a pass between mountains.

Summits were avoided or circumvented; certainly they were not climbed. In such a world it is not surprising that in a 16th-century myth Mont Blanc was viewed as a kind of maximum security prison into which the Devil was placed after having lost a battle with Saint Bernard for the possession of a mountain. But in 1761, Horace Bénédict de Saussure, a naturalist and scientist from Geneva, visited the Chamonix Valley and came under the spell of Mont Blanc. He made a determined bid to explore the mountain himself, but after several failed attempts to reach its summit offered a prize of twenty gold thalers to the first person to succeed. Starting in 1775, a series of attempts following the Glaciers des Bossons on the northern flank fell short, as did an alternative approach over the northwest ridge. In 1886, a large expedition that had divided itself between the two routes and met high on

ALSO KNOWN AS • Monte Bianco (Italian)

Crevasses and snow slopes offer an infinite variety of challenges in the Vallée Blanche, east of Mont Blanc.

Ice climbers tackle a steep wind-sculpted slope on the Mont Blanc massif.

ICE AXE: a mountaineering tool with many uses, such as to aid stability on steep snow, for cutting bivouac ledges into a snow slope, belaying or as a walking stick

September, the Goûter Hut, with bunks for seventy-five, is typically packed with 200 climbers. Those with reservations get the bunks; everyone else carries a sleeping bag and takes floor space in one of the common rooms or bivvies outside the hut.

Many climbers start out for the top at 1 or 2 AM, putting the long and monotonous trudge to the Dôme du Goûter (13,900 feet) behind them before sunup and the summit within range of a morning arrival. The route leads over the Dôme—or around it to the south—and then into a shallow col before ascending a snow slope to the Arête des Bosses, a ridge that traverses two snow-covered humps and then narrows elegantly on its way to the summit.

The normal route from the Italian side was discovered in 1890 by a party that included

---

A climber completes the final pitch on one of the Chamonix Aiguilles while his belayer gets a front-row view of Mont Blanc.

A scientist studies ice composition deep inside a glacier on Mont Blanc.

Achille Ratti, who would later become Pope Pius XI. It starts from the remote village of Val Veni, reachable by bus from Courmayeur, and ascends the Miage Glacier to the foot of the Dôme Glacier. The route continues to the southern spur of the Aiguilles Grises, then ascends northeastward up a scree-filled couloir onto a shoulder of the spur and onto the Dôme Glacier. Above, at just over 10,000 feet, lies the Gonella Hut, which is managed from mid-July to the end of August.

The 5,700 vertical feet from hut to mountaintop makes for a long summit day. The route ascends along the left side of the Dôme Glacier then exits left and ascends to the Col des Aiguilles Grises. It continues up ridge to the Col de Boinnassay on the French frontier and turns eastward to gain the Dôme du Goûter. There it takes the Arête des Bosses to the summit.

On Mont Blanc these routes are only a beginning. The mountain is so vast and varied that it can absorb several seasons and still offer new challenges. It is truly an exemplary mountain—serving both as a mainstay of alpine mountaineering and an introduction to climbing.

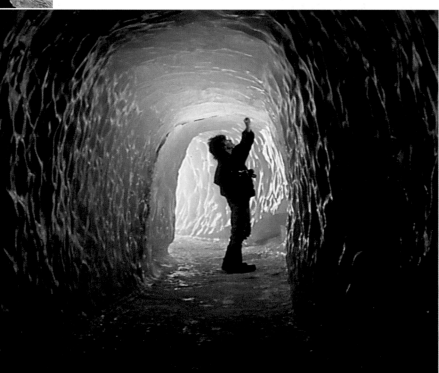

View from the top: The Aiguille Verte and the Alps from the summit of Mont Blanc.

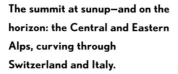

The summit at sunup—and on the horizon: the Central and Eastern Alps, curving through Switzerland and Italy.

makes no technical demands. Day one is spent climbing to the Goûter Hut at 12,500 feet, an ascent greatly facilitated by the téléphérique that runs from Les Houches in the Chamonix Valley to Bellevue and the tramway from there to Nid d'Aigle at 7,780 feet. The route then zig-zags northeast past a small hut and turns southeast past the Tête Rousse Hut toward the Aiguille du Goûter. Below the Aiguille is the trickiest section of the entire route, a steep rib of rock that requires a bit of scram-bling and vigilance for rockfall. The hut lies on a ridge just beyond the Aiguille du Goûter's summit. Open from June

The ice axes are shorter, the lad-ders longer and the belays more secure, but the essentials of crossing a crevasse, as demon-strated by these early climbers on Mont Blanc, were established a century or more ago.

ALBERT MUMMERY

1855-1895

"All mountains appear doomed to pass through three stages: an inaccessible peak, the most difficult ascent in the Alps, an easy day for a lady."

HOME BASE ▪ *Kent, England*

CLIMBING FEATS ▪ *first ascents of the Zmutt Ridge of the Matterhorn, Dychtau (Caucasus), Dent du Requin*

Growing up the son of a tannery owner in Dover, England, Albert Mummery gave little indication he would become the greatest climber of the Victorian era and a uniquely influential force for modern alpinism. As a child he was pale, sickly and severely myopic; a deformity in his spine caused back problems that would dog him his entire life. And, odd for a mountaineer, he developed an aversion to walking that may have eventually been a contributing factor in his death.

Mummery was sixteen when he visited Switzerland and was caught in the spell of the Matterhorn. His climbing skills developed gradually over the next eight years, and in 1979 he felt he was ready for the still-unclimbed Zmutt ridge of the Matterhorn. He persuaded the brilliant alpine guide Alexander Burgener, to join him—though not before Burgener had tested him on other climbs, including a severe new route on the Fletschhorn that was not repeated for fifty-three years. The Zmutt was nearly snatched from the two of them by English medical student William Penhall, who had raced to the ridge while Mummery was resting up for his attempt but was stymied high on the ridge by a notch at the base of the steep final pitch. Mummery, too, nearly turned back at the same point but was spurred on to the summit when a yodel from the Penhall team signaled that it had returned to the climb.

Mummery's signature climb came two years later on the Grépon, a peak that had already rebuffed numerous attempts. Mummery tried approaches from the south and the west and only succeeded when he discovered a wide crack, ever thereafter known as the Mummery Crack, leading out of a col on the north. Despite his successes, or perhaps because of the envy they may have aroused, Mummery's application to the august Alpine Club was blackballed. He was finally admitted eight years later.

Meanwhile Mummery, who had gotten married and had begun taking his wife on his outings, started to formulate his ideas on guideless climbing. By the early 1890s he had become the leader of a new generation of amateurs—tourists, as they were called by the guides—who pursued their adventures without professional assistance. In 1894 Mummery with fellow "tourists" Collie and Hastings completed the first guideless ascent of Mont Blanc.

The following year Collie and Hastings persuaded Mummery to join them on an expedition to the Nanga Parbat (26,568) in the Himalaya. While they clearly underestimated the magnitude of their undertaking, Mummery and a Gurkha (Gurkhas were Indians who served with the British Army in India) reached 20,000 feet on the Diamir Face before being turned back. As their time was running out, the Englishmen decided to reconnoiter the Rakhiot Face, which was separated from their camp by a long spur. Mummery, wanting to avoid the walk around the spur, elected to cross it. On August 24, 1895, he set out for the pass with two Gurkhas. They were never seen again.

On the Walker Spur

FROM *Solo Faces*,

BY JAMES SALTER

Vernon Rand, pursued by the demons of his climbing fame, sets out on a solo climb of the Walker Spur on the north face of the Grandes Jorasses. In this excerpt, Rand's first day on the classic climb has not gone well and he is preparing to bivouac. No one has better articulated how the accumulation of difficulties and fears can begin to open a crack of doubt

On top, finally, was a ledge, a good one. He paused to calm himself. It was late. If he went on, he might be caught by darkness. It was better, he decided, to bivouac here.

The stars that night were brilliant. From the ledge he gazed up at them. They were very bright—their brightness might be a warning. It could mean a change of weather. It was cold, but was it that cold? He could not be sure. He felt secure but utterly alone. Within himself, over and over again he was turning the vow to climb this pillar. The higher he went, the icier it would become.

The difficult part lay ahead. In a corner of his mind he was already abandoning the attempt. He could not allow that corner to spread. He tried to stop thinking. He could not.

In the morning it took him nearly an hour to sort out his things. It was very cold. There is a way of climbing dangerous pitches with the rope tied in a large loop and clipped to pitons along the way, but it means going back down to unclip and takes time. He tried this once or twice but found it clumsy and quit.

The rock was now glazed with ice. He had to clear the holds; even then a thin covering sometimes remained. This part of the Walker the sun did not reach. Several times he slipped. Talking to himself, reciting, cursing, he kept on, stopping to read the route

description whenever he could . . . sixty-five feet with overhang. The folds had begun to tear.

He began the overhang. The pack was pulling him backward, off the face. He was afraid, but the mountain does not recognize fear. He hammered in a piton and clipped an étrier to it. He waited, letting the venom drain from his blood, and blew on his fingertips stinging from the cold. The Gray Tower was still ahead.

The ice became worse. Things he could have done with ease were dangerous, even paralyzing. Off to the west there were clouds. He was nervous, frightened. He had begun to lose belief in the possibility of going on. The long, vertical reaches beneath him were pulling at his feet. Suddenly he saw that he could be killed, that he was only a speck. His chest was empty, he kept swallowing. He was ready to turn back. The rock was implacable; if he lost his concentration, his will, it would not allow him to remain. The wind from yesterday was blowing. He said to himself, come on, Cabot would do this. The kid at the Choucas.

At the foot of the Tower was a difficult traverse. Slight holds, icy footing, the exposure severe. There are times when height isn't bad, when it exhilarates. If you are frightened it is another story.

He was standing with one foot on a small knob. Above was a steep slab with a crack running up it. He began chopping it clean with his axe. He started up. The footholds were off to the side, no more than the rims of faint scars, sometimes only a fraction of an inch deep. He had to clear these, too. His toe kept slipping. The crack had begun to slant, forcing him out on the slab.

There was nothing to hold to. He tried to put in a piton, bits of ice hitting him in the face. There were only ten feet more, but the rock was slick and mercilessly smooth. Beneath, steeply tilted, the slab shot out into space.

His hand searched up and down. Everything was happening too fast, nothing was happening. The ice had weaknesses but he could not find them. His legs began to tremble. The secret one must keep despite everything had begun to spill, he could not prevent it. He was not going to be able to do this. He knew it. The will was draining from him.

He had the resignation of one condemned. He knew the outcome, he no longer cared, he merely wanted it to end. The wind had killed his fingers.

"You can do it," he said, "you can do it."

He was clinging to the face. Slowly his head bent forward to rest against it like a child resting against its mother. His eyes closed. "You can do it," he said.

They came up the meadow to find him. He was sitting in the sunlight in a long-sleeved undershirt and faded pants like a convalescent.

"What turned you back? Was it the weather?"

"No," he answered slowly, as if he might have forgotten. There was nothing to withhold. He waited silently

"Technical problems..." someone suggested.

He could hear the faint whirring of a camera. The microphone was being held near.

"There was ice up there, but it wasn't that." He looked at one or another of them. A summer breeze was moving the meadow grass. "I didn't prepare," he said, "that was the trouble. I wasn't ready. I lacked the courage."

It was true. Something had gone out of him.

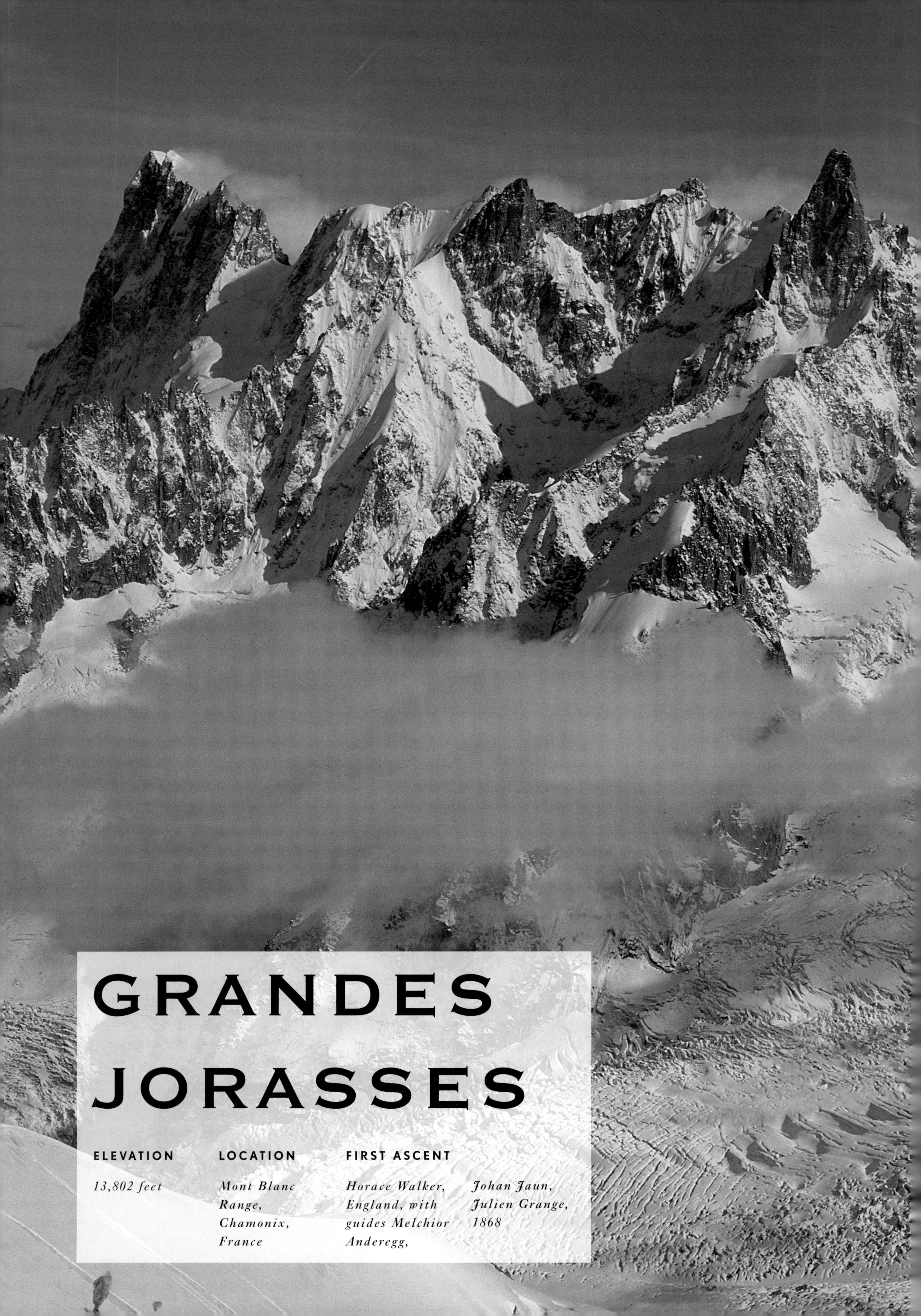

GRANDES JORASSES

ELEVATION	LOCATION	FIRST ASCENT	
13,802 feet	Mont Blanc Range, Chamonix, France	Horace Walker, England, with guides Melchior Anderegg,	Johan Jaun, Julien Grange, 1868

E ast of Mont Blanc and obscured from the sporting mecca of Chamonix by intervening peaks is the showpiece of the Alps: the immense dark granite North Face of the Grandes Jorasses. The mountain, actually a mile-long ridge that lies on the French-Italian border, has six peaks, running from Pointe Walker, the highest one, on the eastern end, to the needle sharp Pointe Young on the west. Ridges on the sun-bathed Italian side provide the easiest routes to the summit ridge, though none of them are walk ups. The remote East Face is a huge triangle rising from the heavily crevassed Frébouze Glacier. The routes on Grandes Jorasses and the men who created them constitute a virtual encyclopedia of alpine rockcraft.

It took decades for climbers to solve Grandes Jorasses's challenges—some of them wildly convoluted, some supremely elegant. It was first climbed by the redoubtable Edward Whymper in 1865, but he ascended not to the mountain's highest peak but to its second highest—now called Pointe Whymper. The first ascent to the topmost peak came with Horace Walker's climb three years later.

Daring in their time, the Whymper and Walker routes from the southern, Italian, side of the mountain are today managed by climbers of moderate proficiency. But it was on its north side that the epic history of the Grandes Jorasses would be written. The great English climber Geoffrey Winthrop Young made a reconnaissance of the North Face as early as 1907, but no one made a serious attempt to climb it until the late 1920s, when its grim dark walls began to attract the Continent's finest climbers. In 1935, after some forty attempts had failed, a route was finally established on the north side of Grandes Jorasses. German climbers Rudolf Peters and Martin Meier found a way up the Croz Spur in the middle of the face. Within days they were followed by three more pairs of climbers—including a Swiss team of Loulou Boulaz, a frail-looking but iron-willed woman, and Raymond Lambert, who in 1952 would nearly reach the summit of Mount Everest.

Still no climber had taken possession of the crown jewel of the Grandes Jorasses: the Walker Spur, a pillar that drops from the summit of Pointe Walker straight onto the Leschaux Glacier nearly 4,000 feet below. In August 1938 three Italian climbers arrived at the Requin Hut on the French side of the Mont Blanc and

A climber searches for a hold on the fine granite of the Grandes Jorasses massif.

FIRST ASCENT OF THE WALKER SPUR •
Riccardo Cassin, Gino Esposito,
Ugo Tizzoni, Italy, 1938

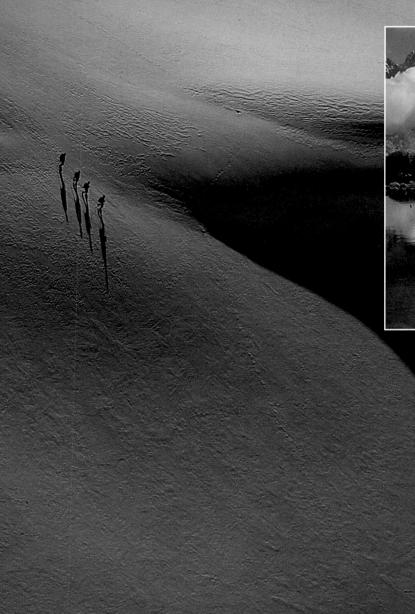

Needles form a jagged skyline south of Chamonix's Lac Blanc.

A foursome moves silently across a snowfield on their descent along the Leschaux glacier

politely asked the custodian if he could direct them to the North Face of the Grandes Jorasses. In a story told by Gaston Rébuffat, who would make the second ascent of the Walker Spur in 1945, the hut keeper dismissed the question with a vague gesture toward the wall of granite. But his amusement turned to astonishment three days later when he

learned that these same Italians had climbed the Walker Spur. The achievement was no fluke. The Walker Spur had fallen to a team led by Riccardo Cassin, who was already building a reputation as one of Italy's most distinguished climbers.

Harder and more dangerous routes—notably the Japanese route near the western end of the face that is often strafed with rockfall—were created on the north face, but the Walker Spur remains the classic testpiece of

the Mont Blanc region. Beyond the bergschrund at the head of the Leschaux Glacier the route traverses sometimes ice-covered rock to its first serious difficulty: 100 feet of high-angle slabs of rock with thin cracks their only weakness. Above this, a traverse leads to a 250-foot open book interrupted by two overhangs. The Gray Tower, midway up the spur, offers unremittingly hard climbing on steep smooth slabs. At an elevation of 13,000 feet climbers must surmount an immense step. All in all, most of the route falls within the topmost rating for difficulty.

Those seeking a less intense outing can climb to Pointe Walker from the Grandes Jorasses Hut on the south slope of the mountain, an ascent of 4,600 vertical feet that takes six to seven hours in good weather. The route ascends snow and rocky debris to a ridge between Planprincieux and Grandes Jorasses Glaciers, cuts under the foot of the ridge and continues up the eastern edge of the

Planprincieux Glacier. Above the ridge the route weaves between numerous crevasses and ascends onto the Rocher de Reposier, an extension of a sharp spur descending from Pointe Hélène. At the top of the outcrop, it traverses eastward, crossing a broad rock rib below Pointe Whymper, then ascends a gully that leads to the Pointe Walker ridge and the summit.

The view westward along the French-Italian border takes in the stars of the western Alps: Aiguille Verte, the Chamonix Aiguilles and, looming above them all, the great dome of Mont Blanc. Right under foot, however, is one of the unspoiled gems of the entire range. By its remoteness, Grandes Jorasses saves itself for true mountaineers.

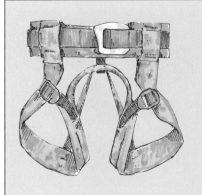

SEAT HARNESS: *a matrix of heavily stitched nylon webbing worn around the legs and the waist that provides the point of connection between climber and rope*

Right: Before the invention of SPF 15, a parasol was just the thing for a lady traversing the huge Mer de Glace that flows north of the Grandes Jorasses.

Bottom: Three climbers approach the summit of Grandes Jorasses above one of the six classic north face climbs in the Alps, the Walker Spur.

CATHERINE DESTIVELLE

1960-

*"It's very important to climb for yourself;
if you do, your enthusiasm and motivation will
allow you to progress faster than the rest."*

HOME BASE ▪ *Paris, France*

CLIMBING FEATS ▪ *Trango Tower, New route on the
West Face of the Dru, solo winter ascent of
the Eiger North Face*

At age five, Catherine Destivelle took to the boulders of
Fountainbleau outside Paris the way some girls take to the ballet
barre. By her early teens she was dancing up difficult routes on the
crags of Dijon and Verdun and commanding attention as a rock
prodigy, forget about gender. In her early twenties, she was headed
into a career as a physiotherapist, working for a women's hockey
team, when a she appeared as a contestant on TV's "Survival of the
Fittest." That led to a starring role in a documentary on rock climbing, and suddenly the world took notice.

A small woman with dark hair, green eyes and a winning smile,
Destivelle became that rare climber whose fame transcends the tight
little world of climbing. Most importantly, she had the moves of a
champion. In 1985 she entered a Bardonaccia, Italy sport-climbing
competition—a contest in which climbers try to best each other on the
same, exceedingly difficult routes—and won. A week-and-a-half later
she broke her back and pelvis in a fall into a crevasse during a climb
in the Alps, but she hardly missed a beat. In 1986, strengthened by
the weight training she had undertaken during her rehabilitation, she

won the same competition again. That, and the corporate sponsors
who flocked to her door, were enough to persuade her to turn pro.

Destivelle got top billing in subsequent competitions, but she was a
reluctant leading lady. In 1987 she took time off to appear in a documentary on the cave-dwelling Dogon people of Mali, whose climbing
is a natural adjunct to their way of life. (Her agility on their cliffs was
proof in the eyes of the Dogons that she was a witch.) In 1989 she left
the world of competition for good and committed herself to alpine
climbing. Her first big project was an ascent of Trango Tower, the
immense obelisk on the Baltoro Glacier in Pakistan, with American
Jeff Lowe. She followed that with an astonishing four hour solo of the
famous Bonatti Pillar on the Petit Dru near Chamonix—Bonatti had
taken six days on the first ascent. It is generally regarded as the
hardest solo ever done by a woman. Then she sealed her reputation
as an alpinist by creating a new route—a highly technical ten-day
climb on the Dru that was covered daily by TV newsmen shooting
footage from a
helicopter. Her
winter solo of the
Eiger Nordwand
in 1992 was
front-page news.

More than any
other woman,
Catherine
Destivelle has put
a public face on
the arcane world
of climbing.

EIGER

ELEVATION	LOCATION	FIRST ASCENT	
13,040 feet	*Bernese Alps, Switzerland*	*Dr. Charles Barrington, England, Christian Almer, Switzerland, 1858; First ascent, North*	*Face: Heinrich Harrer and Fritz Kasparek, Austria; Anderl Heckmair and W. Vorg, Germany, 1938*

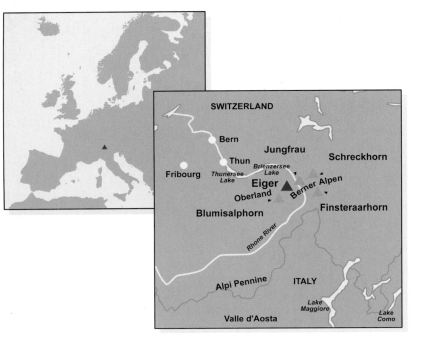

racked by storms, strafed by avalanche and rockfall and never touched by sun; there may be no more forbidding place on earth than the North Face of the Eiger. The 5,250-foot Nordwand, writes French mountaineer Gaston Rébuffat, is "hollowed out like a sick man's chest, often veiled in mist or blotted out by clouds; life up there is strangely remote from that of the flowers and animals at its feet. It stands aloof, unbeautiful, inspiring fear." Yet it remains an irresistible heart of darkness in the world of climbing.

There is one nontechnical route to the top of the Eiger: the western flank of the mountain rising from the saddle between the Eiger (German for "ogre") and the Monch ("monk") that was employed on the mountain's first ascent in 1858. In the summer the walk to the top, from the Eigergletcher train station, and return is a pleasant one-day outing. When climbers speak of the Eiger, however, it is the North Face they have in mind—the North Face and its history of malevolence toward climbers.

Starting with the initial attempt on the face in 1935, the mountain frequently killed those with the temerity to venture onto it. The first to try were Karl Mehringer and Max Sedlmeier of Munich. They had been on the face for four days when friends, checking their progress by telescope from the balcony of a hotel in the village of Kleine Scheidegg on the opposite side of the valley, spotted them on a snowfield about halfway up. Suddenly, a storm veiled the mountain. When it cleared, much of the wall was plastered with snow, and the climbers were nowhere to be seen. Days later a pilot searching the face from an

British climber Cliff Phillips takes the lead on the Eigerwand.

"Climbing!" he shouted, and continued up after leaning out and tilting his head to see where he was going to go and what he was going to do to get there. The handholds became footholds, and, as he rose, everything ahead and above was a promise fulfilled."

—*From Mark Helprin's* **A Soldier of the Great War**

airplane saw a lifeless figure frozen to a rock. That winter an avalanche hurled the body onto the scree at the base of the mountain.

In summer 1936 bad weather discouraged most climbers from attempting the ascent. But Germans Anderl Hinterstoisser and Toni Kurz, joined by Austrians Willy Angerer and Eddie Rainer, decided to press on. Hinterstoisser solved a key problem on the lower part of the climb with an upward slanting traverse—which now bears Hintersoisser's name—that joined two crack systems. The foursome took two more days to reach Mehringer's and Sedlmeier's high point, Death

TRAVERSE: *a section of a route on a steep or vertical face that is horizontal or slanting, connecting lines of weakness where upward progress can be resumed; v. to execute a traverse.*

Bivouac, as it is now called. But with the weather turning nasty and one of the climbers injured by a blow to the head by falling rock, they decided to retreat. On the morning of their fourth day on the face they reached the end of the traverse that Hinterstoisser had so brilliantly led—and made a ghastly discovery: now covered with a deadly layer of ice, it could not be reversed. The Eiger had closed the escape hatch.

Rescuers reached to within 100 yards of the stranded climbers and learned that only Kurz was still alive. Hinterstoisser had fallen; Angerer had also slipped and been strangled by the rope from

The Mitteleggi Ridge (righthand horizon) provides a serious alpine challenge but is free of the rock-fall that so imperils the North Face that it bounds on the east.

The Spider

Death Bivouac

John Harlin
Direct Route

1938 First Ascent of the North Face

Top: A sky surfer traverses the Eiger Nordwand, employing a technique that undoubtedly never occurred to early climbers on the mountain.

From the narrow summit of the Eiger, a climber gets a fine view of the Swiss Alps.

which he was still suspended; Rainer had frozen to death. The following morning the rescuers instructed Kurz to cut away Angerer and separate and rebraid the strands of the rope he had thereby salvaged. He lowered the resulting cord to the men below, who attached a new rope that Kurz was to use to lower himself to safety. Suffering from hypothermia, Kurz was barely able to tie into a rappel.

He finally started down, but the descent, too, was difficult. At one point the rope snagged on the carabiners through which it passed; at another he was hit by an avalanche. Two body lengths from his rescuers, Kurz could endure no more and died.

By early in the climbing season of 1938, the Eiger had claimed two more lives—Italians who had become lost in a storm—and still no one had reached beyond Death Bivouac. Then in late July Austrians Heinrich Harrer and Fritz Kasparek and Germans Anderl Heckmair and W. Vorg finally succeeded on the fourth day of their attempt, after nearly having been swept off a high icefield— called The Spider—by an avalanche.

Since then numerous other routes have been put up on the famously inhospitable face, notably a direct line created by American John Harlin II that eliminated several traverses of the first ascent. In 1966 Harlin, who had established a climbing school in Leysin, Switzerland, and had become so closely identified with the mountain that a postcard addressed "Eiger John, Switzerland" made its way to him, tried to solve the Eigerwand's last great problem: a winter ascent. Harlin was regaining his high point, having been driven off the face by

CLIMBING ROPE: a kern-mantle rope, typically 150 to 165 feet long and .44 inches in diameter, composed of continuous strands of nylon (the kern) enclosed in a braided nylon sheath (the mantle) and sufficiently elastic to absorb the energy of a falling climber

deteriorating weather, when the rope he was ascending broke, sending him hurtling down the face to the talus 4,000 feet below. England's Dougal Haston, one of Harlin's climbing partners, helped complete the route.

Eleven years later Haston was skiing in Leysin, where he had taken over Harlin's school, when he died in an avalanche.

Since then the face has been the theater of some amazing feats of daring. In 1988 French superclimber Jean Marc Boivin, using a helicopter to ferry himself from one base to another, climbed the north faces of the Matterhorn, the Grandes Jorasses and the Eiger in a single twenty-four-hour period. In 1992 Catherine Destivelle, also

of France, became the first woman to solo the Eiger Nordwand. She did it in winter—in just over sixteen hours.

The intensity of the Eiger borders on the surreal: in the heart of the historic Swiss Alps and very much encroached on by the development therein, its North Face remains nightmarish and almost untouchable, even in a sea of wildflowers and quaint hostels. There is even a rail station inside the mountain itself, whose windows face out onto the Nordwand. Luckily for many, there is a door—always unlocked—near where the standard route passes, into the train

tunnel. Climbers have used it to escape storms or fatigue; and at least one has had to press himself against the tunnel wall to avoid being flattened by oncoming trains.

The North Face of the Eiger no longer ranks among the world's hardest technical climbs: It has long since been surpassed in steepness, length and overall difficulty. But given its nasty weather, its rockfall and its history—the Eigerwand will always be a classic test.

Climber-cinematographer Eric Jones makes a delicate move on the infamous Hinterstoisser Traverse, the key to the upper two-thirds of the North Face climb. When Anderl Hinterstoisser, who discovered the traverse in 1936, could not reverse it during an attempted retreat, he and his three climbing partners perished.

REINHOLD MESSNER

1944-

"Nature for man is only truly manifest where danger, challenge and exposure have not been shut out."

HOME BASE ▪ *Staben, Italy*

CLIMBING FEATS ▪ *first ascent of Everest without supplementary oxygen; solo ascent of Nanga Parbat; first person to summit all fourteen 8,000-meter peaks*

As a boy growing up in the South Tyrolean town of Brixen, Reinhold Messner started to climb, he says "to see where the clouds came from and where they went." He has never stopped searching. In one of the most extraordinary climbing careers of any era, Messner has astonished even seasoned veterans with the audacity of his ambition and the purity of his execution.

A naturally gifted climber with a rangy build and a steely determination, Messner pretty much exhausted the classic testpieces of the Alps before he was twenty-five. In 1969 he moved on to high-altitude climbing in the Andes and, in the following year, the Karakoram. Almost from the start, his exploits were marked by drama. In 1970 he and his brother Günther climbed the Rupal Face to the summit of Nanga Parbat and then succeeded in an epic descent of the unexplored Diamir Face. Their bold venture ended in tragedy as Günther was buried in an avalanche near the base of the mountain.

The devastating loss of Günther, far from inhibiting Messner's climbing, seemed to spur him on. In 1972 he joined a Tyrolean expedition to Nepal to climb Manaslu, at 26,781 the world's seventh highest peak. Although he summited, the only climber to do so, two of his team members died during the descent and the undertaking soured him on expeditions. With the exception of an unsuccessful 1975 Italian expedition to Lhotse (27,923 feet, Everest's neighbor to the south and the world's fourth tallest mountain), Messner's projects have all been done in alpine style, many of them solo.

In 1974 he teamed up with Austrian Peter Habeler to climb the Eiger North Face in an utterly unprecedented ten hours—the previous record had been three days. For an encore, he soloed the huge south face of Aconcagua. Then in 1975, after the retreat from Lhotse, he and Habeler introduced alpine style to the Himalaya with a new route on the north face of Gasherbrum I (a Karakoram peak on the Pakistan-China border that at 26,470 is the eleventh highest mountain). It was a historic achievement that would have a profound impact on Himalayan climbing. But Messner was just getting started. In 1978 he and Habeler shed what was long considered an essential component of any climb on Everest when they summited the world's highest mountain without supplementary oxygen. In 1980 he pulled off the ultimate climb: a solo, bottled oxygen-free ascent of Everest. Then with his 1986 climb up the west face of Lhotse, Messner became the first man to summit on all fourteen 8,000-meter peaks.

Today, Messner, whose only marriage ended in divorce in 1977 and who has had three children with two other women, lives in a castle in the South Tyrol and campaigns for a mountain wilderness free of human manipulation. "Every single time anyone achieves success in the mountains by artificial means it adds to the over all damage," wrote Messner recently. "Let's give the mountains back their mythology and make a fresh start."

At One With the Mountain

FROM THE INTRODUCTION TO *Starlight and Storm: The Ascent of Six Great North Faces of the Alps*

BY GASTON RÉBUFFAT, TRANSLATED FROM FRENCH BY WILFRID NOYCE AND SIR JOHN HUNT

Gaston Rébuffat, one of France's top-climbers, was a 20th century mountaineer with the soul of a 19th century romantic. Here, he explains his love affair with the mountains

In this modern age, very little remains that is real. Night has been banished, so have the cold, the wind and the stars. They have all been neutralized: the rhythm of life itself is obscured. Everything goes so fast and makes so much noise, and men hurry by without heeding the grass by the roadside, its colour, its smell and the way it shimmers when the wind caresses it. What a strange encounter then is that between man and the high places of his planet! Up there he is surrounded by the silence of forgetfulness. If there is a slope of snow steep as a glass window, he climbs it, leaving behind him a strange trail. If there is a rock perfect as an obelisk, he defies gravity and proves that he can get up anywhere.

I come from Marseilles, and it was in my native Provence, on the hills of the Sainte Baume and the Luberon, and on the sea cliffs of the Calanques [A line of limestone cliffs near Marseilles: a well-known training ground of rock-climbers.], that I learned to love wind and wide spaces, starlight and storm, flowers and forests, the taste and smell of all these.

In 1950 I was with the French expedition to the Himalaya. On Annapurna [26,493 feet. The summit was reached on 3rd June. The descent involved a night in a crevasse and severe frost-bite. See Maurice Herzog, *Annapurna* (Jonathan Cape Ltd., 1952).] as on the Ecrins or the Jorasses, we were guided by the same dream. At first we felt a pleasing sense of awe, face to face with these gigantic peaks; then we entered into their secret places. We walked, we explored, we climbed, and every evening we slept the sleep of happiness under the sky of Asia. Wood fires, camps in the valleys, camps on the glaciers in the Himalaya, evenings and sunsets in Alpine huts—these nights in the mountains are among the fairest memories of a climber's life. But the most lasting and often the best are the bivouacs on the earth itself, under the stars.

To succeed in scaling the great north faces, the pioneers had to climb for two or three days and spend at least one night clinging to the face. Nowadays, despite our knowledge of the routes, you still very often have to bivouac on some of them. But this is no drawback. At the end of the day the mountaineer looks for a ledge, lays down his sack, hammers in a piton and attaches himself to it. After the hard, acrobatic effort of the climb he is lost—like the poet—in contemplation; but to a greater degree than the poet he can be a part of the hills around. The man who bivouacs becomes one with the mountain. On his bed of stone, leaning against the great wall, facing empty space which has become his friend, he watches the sun fade over the horizon on his left, while on his right the sky spreads its mantle of stars. At first he is wakeful, then, if he can, he sleeps; then wakes again, watches the stars and sleeps again; then at last he stays awake and watches. On his right the sun will return, having made its great voyage below this shield of scattered diamonds.

This evening, as I write these lines, the desire seizes me to breathe the night air for a few minutes. It is winter, and cold. Hemmed in between two black masses of houses, fringed by the roofs of my narrow street, the stars seem to be moving slowly as I advance.

'It's cold,' I say to myself, 'that's a good sign. The snow will be hard.'

How stupid of me! Am I not in Paris, in the Rue des Grands-Augustins? But my street leads on to the quays where the Seine, with its sentinel trees, and the quiet night combine to recall nature, even in the heart of the great city. It is both early and late. It is the hour when mountaineers go out on to the hut terrace to scan the sky, test the wind and the snow. It is cold, and cold nights mean a fine day. It is the time to light the lantern and start out. . . .

Here in Paris I dream of high hills.

JUNGFRAU

ELEVATION	LOCATION	FIRST ASCENT	
13,638 feet	*Bernese Alps, Switzerland*	*Hieronymus Meyer, Johan Rudolf Meyer, Joseph Bortes,*	*Aloys Volker, Switzerland, 1811*

The mountain range was named not for the peaks, but for the high meadows, like this wildflower blanketed alp near the Jungfrau.

The first winter ascent of the Jungfrau was an aid climb. American mountaineer Meta Brevoort made it to the summit in January 1872—transported to a snowfield below the summit pyramid on a sledge hauled by six Swiss guides. She went the rest of the way on foot accompanied not only by her nephew W.A.B. Coolidge but also by Coolidge's pet beagle Tschingel, which eventually achieved canine fame with thirty Alpine ascents. It is hard to imagine that an outing of such aplomb could have occurred anywhere but in the heart of the Alps, the original mountaineering playground of ladies and gentlemen of leisure. A sleigh is no longer needed for assistance onto Jungfrau's lower slopes. But the Jungfrau (so named because its huge northern slope, viewed from a distance, looks like a maiden's veil) still represents a classic melding of Alpine mountaineering and continental civility.

To Swiss herdsmen grazing their goats or cows in the hills above their alpine villages, the word alp refers not to a mountain but to the meadowland surrounding it. For them the Alps are less mountains than a way of life. But their familiarity with the local terrain would become a valued asset as alpinists gathered to the Alps with summit aspirations. For an August 1811 attempt on the Jungfrau brothers Johan Rudolf and Hieronymus Meyer, sons of a well known cartographer, recruited chamois hunters Joseph Bortes and Aloys Volker. The climb, up a southwestern flank of the mountain, was still an ordeal entailing some unorthodox technique. On their third day they encountered a ridge so narrow that they had to climb it a cheval, their hands and feet gripping the slope on either

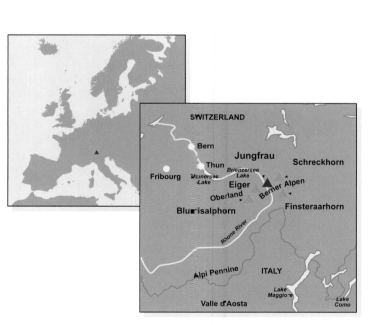

HELMET: *a safety device specially designed to protect climbers' heads from falling rock and ice. Climbing helmets must be light, strong and comfortable; some are equipped with headlamp mounts, most have ventilation holes and adjustable exterior and interior straps.*

AID CLIMBING: *A rock climbing technique in which such equipment as pitons, chocks or bolts are used not simply for protection but to support the weight of the climber. Typically, aid is employed where free climbing techniques appear to be unavailing. Many aid routes have later been freed by subsequent climbers.*

side. Though their account of a successful first ascent is accepted today, at the time there was speculation that it had been fabricated—certain details were vague—so Johan Rudolf's son Gottlieb took it upon himself to defend the family honor. The following year—again with Bortes and Volker in attendance—he climbed Jungfrau from the southeast, joining his father's route on the final ridge between the Rottalhorn and Jungfrau's

Left: An observatory, photographed in 1957, on the 11,398-foot summit of the Jungfraujoch, a smaller peak which rises from the col between Eiger and Jungfrau, opens to a smog-free view of the heavens.

A CHEVAL: *French for on horseback, a technique in which a narrow ridge is climbed with legs straddled to either side.*

summit. This time the party hoisted a flag that could be seen in the valley below.

Gottlieb's approach is now the normal route for the mountain. Today, a train from Grindelwald, the elegant resort town opposite the Eiger and northeast of Jungfrau, takes climbers to the Jungfraujoch station on the col between the Jungfrau and the Mönch, which at 11,719 feet is Europe's highest railroad station. Only World War I deflected the

A room with a bar, where the ice is outside the glass as well as in it, has been carved sixty-five feet deep into the Guggigletscher, a glacier that descends from the Jungfraujoch.

A great alpine ridge seen end on and at close quarters presents one of the ghastliest pictures of utter inaccessibility imaginable . . . .Those who have never mountaineered will never know that a hard climb in the High Alps is one of the most soul-stirring experiences that a man can undergo.

—*Charles Francis Meade following his descent of the Jungfrau's Northeast Ridge.*

Adventurous skiers at the summit of Jungfrau prepare for a rapid descent.

The west face of the Jungfrau dominates the alpine village of Winteregg near Murren in the Bernese Oberland.

railroad's owners from their plan to build a track all the way to Jungfrau's summit. Once construction was interrupted, it was never resumed. As it is, easy access to the mountain has made the Jungfrau one of the more dangerous peaks in the Alps. In good conditions, the summit is a three-hour climb from the station. But lured high by the railway, inexperienced and insufficiently acclimatized climbers all too often have gotten into trouble on the steeply rising traverse to the summit ridge where falls have proven fatal.

The recommended way to climb Jungfrau is to take the train to the col the day before the climb, then spend the evening partaking of the wine and geniality of the Mönchsjoch Hut an hour's walk from the station (125 beds, open in spring and summer). No need for an alarm clock. The clatter and hubbub rouses everyone for an "alpine start" well before dawn the next morning. From the hut the route returns to Jungfraujoch, then ascends a broad snow field in a southerly arc to a rocky spur descending from the Rottalhorn, a subsidiary peak south of Jungfrau. The route rounds the base of this ridge and then ascends it, climbing a steep sixty-five-foot step by way of a crack. Farther up the ridge, the route traverses the northeast face of the Rottalhorn to its col with the Jungfrau. The final ridge, a combination of steep rock and moderately angled snow, requires technical ability and the protection of a rope.

The summit puts climbers at the center of the Central Alps, with 4,000-meter peaks to the north, east and south and foothills that ripple down to Lake Geneva on the west. Climbing the Jungfrau is the quintessential Alpine experience.

MATTERHORN

ELEVATION

LOCATION

FIRST ASCENT

14,870 feet

Pennine Alps, Switzerland/ Italy

Francis Douglas, Douglas Hadow, Charles Hudson, Edward Whymper, England;

Michael Croz, France; Peter Taugwalder, Peter Taugwalder Jr., Switzerland, 1865

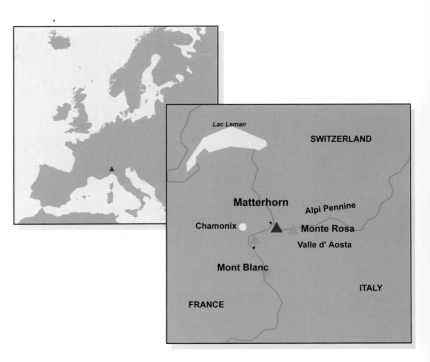

Displayed with antique ice axes and old pitons in a small museum in Zermatt, Switzerland, is a short strand of cord: frayed, insignificant looking and the most famous piece of rope in all of mountaineering. It is the rope that snapped, sending four of the seven men on the first ascent party of the Matterhorn hurtling down the east face to their deaths. The tragic accident is now mountaineering legend and a part of the mystique that makes the Matterhorn perhaps the most coveted summit in the world.

The rest of the mystique is provided by the mountain itself. As viewed from the north and east, it seems to have come out of

a storybook—a finely wrought pyramid, its solitary peak piercing the alpine sky. Four sharp ridges ascend steeply to two peaks, which are joined by a knife-edge arête. The Matterhorn's North Face, a nearly perfect triangle, is one of the six great north faces of the Alps. Of all the Alpine 4,000-meter peaks, the Matterhorn is the most difficult to climb.

The beauty of the mountain was not lost on the early mountaineers. For some of them, notably renowned English alpinist Edward Whymper, it became an obsession. Whymper first saw the Matterhorn in 1861. During the following three years he and stonemason-turned-guide Jean Antoine Carrel made numerous attempts on the Matterhorn from the Italian side, all of which failed. In 1865, after an early season of climbing had taken him to summits throughout the Alps—

ALSO KNOWN AS • Cervino "The Stag" (Italian), Cervin (French)

At nine in the evening we stepped out on to the final crest: a fine finish to the day. Alone up here we had the benefit of the sun's last light. Down there our fellow men were already in darkness, and a line of lights picked out the main street of Zermatt. At our feet the great slope dropped sharply away. The north face! What disagreeable climbing, and yet what a splendid climb!
—*Gaston Rébuffat on the Matterhorn*

including the Aiguille Verte, the Grandes Jorasses, La Ruinette and the Dent Blanche, which he later deemed to have been his most difficult climb ever— Whymper returned to the Matterhorn. He had planned to engage Carrel, but the Italian, claiming a scheduling conflict, was suddenly unavailable. When Whymper learned that Carrel was in fact headed for the Matterhorn with a team of Italians, he became enraged.

While Whymper stewed over the heist of his long sought-after first ascent, Lord Francis Douglas, a young English mountaineer happened into the village where he was staying, and Whymper persuaded him to join in the chase for the Matterhorn. They set out for Zermatt to attempt the rarely tried Hörnli Ridge from the north, and encountered Whymper's favorite Chamonix guide, Michel Croz, who with the accomplished English climber Reverend Charles Hudson and the novice Douglas Hadow was also planning an attempt on the Matterhorn. They agreed to join

As vividly demonstrated in this engraving of the *Matterhorn's Morning Pass*, Edward Whymper's artistry was as bold as his mountaineering.

Top: A walkway provides visitors who may never have heard of a traverse or a pendulum access to the vertical world of the Gorner Gorge of the Matter-Visp near Zermatt.

Left: Surrounded on three sides by 4,000-meter peaks at the southern end of the Valais, Zermatt has preserved its character as the quintessential alpine resort.

forces, adding Taugwalder father and son, Zermatt guides, to make a party of seven.

On July 14, racing against the Italians, Whymper's group reached the summit with surprisingly little resistance at 1:40 in the afternoon. Whymper rushed to the western lip of the summit and, to his relief and satisfaction, saw the Carrel party still far below. Whymper and Croz shouted at them and, in an intemperate show of triumph, tossed rocks in their direction to make sure the Italians knew they had been beaten.

Though victorious, the English party was too large and essentially without a leader, and therein lay the seeds of the most famous disaster in mountaineering history. Not far below the summit, with the entire team roped together, Hadow slipped, knocking over Croz and pulling Douglas and Hudson with him. The elder Taugwalder, fifth in line, braced for the shock, but the rope connecting him to Hudson, a

BACK ROPE: *An auxiliary rope that prevents the second climber from an uncontrolled pendulum in case he or she falls on traverse. The back rope, tied into the second climber and run through protection at the start of the traverse, is paid out by the belayer while the main rope is gathered in. After completeing the traverse, the climber unties from the back rope, which is then pulled through the protection at the beginning of the traverse.*

Top: An antique Swiss postage stamp

Right: An 1898 poster issued by the Visp-Zermatt Railroad entices tourists to the land of the Matterhorn. Even today, the railroad is the only way to get to Zermatt, which prohibits cars and trucks except for service personnel.

Climbers shake off the chill of a bivouac on the Matterhorn.

spare one in poor condition, broke, and the four men plummeted to their deaths 4,000 feet below.

It was a tragedy from which Whymper never fully recovered. But in no way did it inhibit further attempts on the mountain. Three days later Carrel led a successful ascent on the Italian ridge from the south. Within three years both the towns of Zermatt to the north and Cervinia to the south began attracting tourists. The Zmutt Ridge, a long arcing arête on the northwest considered the finest route on the mountain, fell to Albert Mummery in 1879. The north face, 3,600 feet of steep ice and friable rock, resisted all attempts until 1931, when it was climbed by Franz and Toni Schmid, engineering students from Munich who survived a standing bivouac and a violent thunder and lightning storm during thirty-four hours on the face. (At the Los Angeles Olympics the following year, the brothers were awarded gold medals in recognition of their bold ascent.)

More recently, the Matterhorn has been a stage for speed ascents, hang gliding descents and other hyper-climbing stunts, but not surprisingly, perhaps, most of the more than 500 deaths on the mountain have occurred on the easiest route on the mountain, the Hörnli Ridge. A pleasant though crowded outing on a clear summer day can turn into a rout if the weather breaks. Falls and fatal hypothermia are too often the result among climbers ill-prepared to deal with adversity.

To reach the base of the Hörnli Ridge, climbers start from Zermatt, itself reachable only by train (none but workers' cars are allowed in the village) from Tasche, the next town to the

north. A cable car and a two-hour walk (or a five-hour walk from Zermatt) leads to Hörnli Hut, a perpetually overcrowded facility that sleeps fifty and is open from mid-June to mid-September. The route from the hut leads to a step at the base of the ridge. From there, it loops onto the East Face, regains the ridge for 300 vertical feet and then swings onto the East Face once again until just below the steep rock that ascends to the Solvay Hut, an emergency shelter a little more than halfway up. Above the hut, the route leads up the blocky ridge to the Red Tower, turning it on the left, and then up to the snow- and ice-covered Shoulder (it was here that the Whymper tragedy occurred). The route follows the ridge to the steep summit block, where fixed ropes aid the final pitch.

For accomplished climbers the greatest difficulty of the Hörnli Ridge is its congestion—a problem that can be ameliorated by starting late, and then side-stepping descending climbers. For some an even nicer option is the more challenging Italian Ridge which starts above Cervinia. Because of the longer approach to huts at the base of the climb and the more strenuous pitches on the climb itself, this route is less frequented than the Hörnli Ridge. As on the Hörnli, the steepest sections are aided by fixed rope.

Even on a summer day when the peak becomes so congested that queues form below the summit block, the Matterhorn casts its spell. There is no other peak that so alluringly combines classic architecture, imperious aloofness and notorious history.

Descent of the Matterhorn

FROM *Scrambles Amongst the Alps*
BY EDWARD WHYMPER

In the most famous passage in mountaineer-ing literature, Edward Whymper relates with admirable objectivity the accident that has had a greater influence on the public's perception of mountaineering than any other single event.

Hudson and I again consulted as to the best and safest arrangement of the party. We agreed that it would be best for Croz to go first, and Hadow second; Hudson, who was almost equal to a born mountaineer in sure-ness of foot, wished to be third; Lord F. Douglas was placed next, and old Peter, the strongest of the remainder, after him. I sug-gested to Hudson that we should attach a rope to the rocks on our arrival at the difficult bit, and hold it as we descended, as an additional protection. He approved the idea, but it was not definitely settled that it should be done. The party was being arranged in the above order whilst I was sketching the summit, and they had finished, and were waiting for me to be tied in line, when someone remembered that our names had not been left in a bottle. They requested me to write them down, and moved off while it was being done.

A few minutes afterwards I tied myself to young Peter, ran down after the others, and caught them just as they were commencing the descent of the difficult part. Great care was being taken. Only one man was moving at a time; when he was firmly planted the next advanced, and so on. They had not, however, attached the additional rope to rocks, and nothing was said about it. The suggestion was not made for my own sake, and I am not sure that it even occurred to me again. For some little distance we two followed the others, detached from them, and should have contin-ued to had not Lord Francis Douglas asked me, about 3 p.m., to tie on to old Peter, as he feared, he said, that Taugwalder would not be able to hold his ground if a slip occurred.

A few minutes later, a sharp-eyed lad ran into the Monte Rosa Hotel, to Seiler, saying that he had seen an avalanche fall from the summit of the Matterhorn on to the Matterhorn Glacier. The boy was reproved for telling idle stories; he was right, nevertheless, and this was what he saw.

Michel Croz had laid aside his axe, and in order to give Mr. Hadow greater security, was absolutely taking hold of his legs and putting his feet, one by one, into their proper positions. As far as I know, no one was actually descending. I cannot speak with certainty, because the two leading men were partially hidden from my sight by an intervening mass of rock, but it is my belief, from the move-ments of their shoulders, that Croz, having done as I have said, was in the act of turning round, to go down a step or two himself; at this moment Mr. Hadow slipped, fell against him, and knocked him over. I heard one startled exclamation from Croz, then saw him and Mr. Hadow flying downwards; in another moment Hudson was dragged from his steps, and Lord F. Douglas immediately after him. At the moment of the accident, Croz, Hadow and Hudson were all close together. Between Hudson and Lord F. Douglas the rope was all but taut, and the same between all the others who were above. Croz was standing by the side of a rock which afforded good hold, and if he had been aware, or had suspected that anything was about to occur, he might and would have gripped it, and would have prevented any mischief. He was taken totally by surprise. Mr. Hadow slipped off his feet on to his back, his feet struck Croz in the small of the back and knocked him right over, head first. Croz's axe was out of his reach, and without it he managed to get his head upper-most before he disappeared from our sight. If it had been in his hand I have no doubt that he would have stopped himself and Mr. Hadow.

Mr. Hadow, at the moment of the slip, was not occupying a bad position. He could have moved either up or down, and could touch with his hand the rock of which I have spoke. Hudson was not so well placed, but he had lib-erty of motion. The rope was not taut from him to Hadow, and the two men fell ten or twelve feet before the jerk came upon him. Lord F. Douglas was not favourably placed, and could neither move up nor down. Old Peter was firmly planted, and stood just beneath a large rock which he hugged with both arms. I enter into these details to make it more apparent that the position occupied by the party at the moment of the accident was not by any means excessively trying. We were compelled to pass over the exact spot where the slip occurred, and we found—even with shaken nerves—that it was not a difficult place to pass. I have described the slope generally as difficult, and it is so undoubtedly to most persons; but it must be distinctly understood that Mr. Hadow slipped at a comparatively easy part.

All this was the work of a moment. Immediately we heard Croz's exclamation, old Peter and I planted ourselves as firmly as the rocks would permit: the rope was taut between us, and the jerk came on us both as on one man. We held; but the rope broke midway between Taugwalder and Lord Francis Douglas. For a few seconds we saw our unfortunate companions sliding downwards on their backs, and spreading out their hands, endeavoring to save themselves. They passed from our sight uninjured, disap-peared one by one, and fell from precipice to precipice on to the Matterhorn Glacier below, a distance of nearly 4,000 feet in height. From the moment the rope broke it was impossible to help them.

So perished our comrades!

EDWARD WHYMPER

1840-1911

"Climb if you will, but remember that courage and strength are nought without prudence, and that a momentary negligence may destroy the happiness of a lifetime. Do nothing in haste; look well to each step; and from the beginning think what may be the end."

HOME BASE ▪ *London, England*

CLIMBING FEATS ▪ *First ascents of Mont Dolent, Aiguille Verte, Pointe Whymper of the Grandes Jorasses, Matterhorn, Chimborazo*

Born in London, the second of eleven children, Edward Whymper may never have met a mountain had he not followed his father into a career as an artist. He was twenty in 1860 when publisher William Longman, a member of England's recently established Alpine Club, commissioned him to produce a series of engravings of the European Alps. His sketches of mountain landscapes in the Oberland, Valais, Mont Blanc and Dauphiné so impressed Longman that the publisher sent him back to the Continent the following year.

This time Whymper was smitten. His career as an artist became firmly enmeshed with his ambitions as a mountaineer. Without any previous experience, he soon became one of the most celebrated climbers in the Alps with a dozen major first ascents in 1864 and 1865. Seeking both summits and fame, Whymper set his sights on what was then the highest unclimbed peak in Europe: the Matterhorn. But in July 1865 his dream turned to nightmare when his triumph on the Matterhorn was almost instantly followed by the most famous accident in the annals of mountaineering.

The immense furor over the death of four members of Whymper's party eventually died out, while Whymper's celebrity increased. He earned a comfortable living from lectures and articles. His *Scrambles Amongst the Alps*, which ends with a description of the Matterhorn tragedy, was published in 1871 to great acclaim.

With a couple of exceptions—one of them an ascent of the Matterhorn with his former rival, Jean-Antoine Carrel—Whymper did not climb in the Alps again. But he was not finished with the mountains. In the 1881, he and Carrel went to South America, where they did first ascents of Cotopaxi, Cayambe and Chimborazo, then the highest mountain ever climbed. The tour yielded a second Whymper classic: *Travels Amongst the Great Andes of the Equator.* In 1901 he was greeted with deference and respect on a trip to the Canadian Rockies, though at age sixty-one, he passed up some of the major peaks still awaiting a first ascent. On a third visit to Canada in 1909 he finally signaled his retirement by offering his equipment for sale to help fund a clubhouse.

In September 1911 he was on one of his regular visits to Chamonix, France, the scene of so many of his early triumphs, when he repaired to his room saying he didn't feel well. Four days later he suddenly and quite unexpectedly died. He was buried in a Chamonix graveyard, where his tombstone has been a shrine of sorts for visiting climbers ever since.

PIZ BERNINA

ELEVATION

13,281 feet

LOCATION

Bernina Alps,
Switzerland/
Italy

FIRST ASCENT

Johann Coaz,
Jon Tscharner,
Lorenz Ragut
Tscharner,
Switzerland,
1850

The Biancograt, an exquisitely sculptured arc of snow and ice swooping northward from the summit and held to be the finest ridge climb in Europe, is reason enough to visit Piz Bernina. But the highest mountain in the Bernina Alps—heavily glaciated and crevassed, with vast snow faces, steep sections of exposed rock, and fields of knife-edged névé—provides outstanding climbing from every direction.

An east-west range on the Swiss-Italian Border, the Bernina Alps rise out of the Engadine, a long valley anchored by the resort town of Pontresina in eastern Switzerland. They are lower than

the Pennine Alps around Chamonix and Zermatt but, mantled in a thick layer of ice and snow, no less impressive. Tucked away in southeastern Switzerland (where the heavily Latinate language of Romansh is still spoken), they are somewhat less frequented by tourists than the more famous peaks to the west but great favorites of climbers wanting to escape the high-fashion, high-octane scene around Chamonix.

Piz Bernina was first climbed by Johann Coaz, a Swiss surveyor, with brothers Jon and Lorenz Ragut Tscharner in September 1850. The team plotted a labyrinthine route

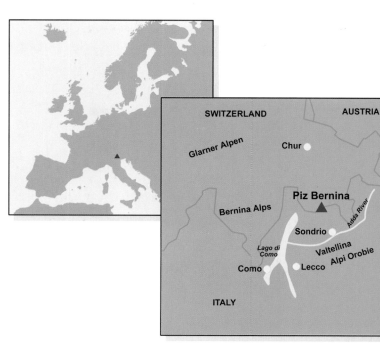

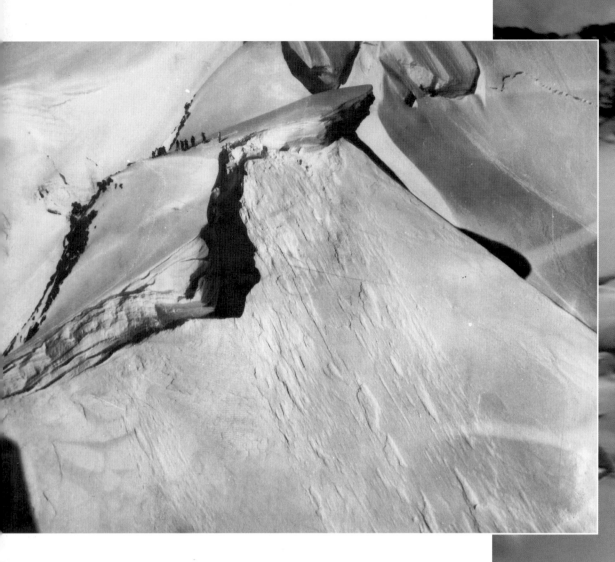

Top left: Piz Palu, just east of Bernina, was the scene of a horrendous climbing accident in June 1957 when a summit cornice broke away, plunging nine Italian climbers to their death.

Left: A Swiss rescue copter lands at Marco-e-Rosa Hut, which serves as base camp for a climb of Piz Bernina by the normal route.

among the crevasses of the north sloping Morteratsch Glacier to Piz Bernina's East Ridge and thence to the summit. A longer but less dangerous approach to the summit, skirting most of the Morteratsch crevasses, is now Piz Bernina's standard route. Established in 1866 by Englishman Francis Fox Tuckett, this route leads southward out of the Engadine, passing either the Boval Hut or the Diovolezzo

Huts, then ascends to the Fortezzagrat, a north-south ridge that lies to the east of the Morteratsch. The ridge narrows and steepens as it reaches a terrace under the splendid Bellavista summits east of Piz Bernina. From here the route turns west, parallel to the Bellavistas, and then descends steeply, threading huge crevasses near the top of the Morteratsch Glacier, to the Marco-e-Rosa

Hut at 11,800 feet on the Italian side of the mountain. From valley to hut is a seven- to eight-hour climb. The route from the Marco-e-Rosa (which sleeps sixty but tends to be crowded in season) heads northward up a snow slope to the crest of the Spallagrat, Piz Bernina's south ridge. The route from here, magnificently exposed and narrowing in places to a catwalk, leads straight to the summit.

Climbers, with the summit of Piz Bernina at their back, descend the Spallagrat toward the subsidiary peaks of Argient and Zupo.

The jewel of Piz Bernina, however, is its North Ridge: the Biancongrat is a strenuous climb, of medium difficulty (Assez Difficile, in the French grading system) and with sections of up to 45 degrees of steepness. It has a purity of line that can be found nowhere else in the Alps. The usual point of departure for the route is the Tschierva Hut, two hours from the trailhead in the Roseg Valley south of Pontresina. The route ascends southward on a lateral moraine of the Tschierva Glacier and cuts below the southwestern slopes of 12,300-foot Piz Morteratsch. It then goes up a snowfield to the foot of the Biancograt and traverses an outcrop onto the ridge itself. A predawn start puts climbers on the Biancograt as the first light of day defines a sinuous line between two curved planes: the soft white glow of snowfields descending to the east and the dark blue-gray shadow cloaking steeper slopes to the west.

The long, graceful curve of Biancograt, corniced at times, reaches to Bernina's subsidiary summit, Piz Bianco (13,104). From there an arête connecting the peaks descends past gendarmes to a saddle with two deep notches. The first, requiring deft downclimbing or a rappel, is separated from the second by a tower that can be turned on either side. Beyond the second gap is a steep ascent on snow to the summit. Most parties descend by way of the Spallagrat to complete what many regard as a true classic and the finest traverse in Europe.

MORAINE: *The rocks and soil pushed along the path of a glacier and deposited along its sides, a lateral moraine; along its center, a medial moraine; or at its snout, a terminal moraine.*

Climbers tread a narrow corridor on the summit ridge of Piz Bernina.

RAPPEL: *A means of descent in which the climber makes a controlled slide down a rope, governing the rate of descent by applying friction between the rope and the body or a device specially constructed for this purpose. v. To descend via rappel.*

MONTE ROSA

ELEVATION

15,199 feet

LOCATION

*Pennine Alps
Switzerland/
Italy*

FIRST ASCENT

*John Birkbeck,
Charles Hudson,
brothers
Christopher and
James Grenville
Smyth, Edward
John Stevenson,*

*England; with
Swiss guides
Ulrich Lauener,
Johann and
Matthias
Zumtaugwald,
1855*

Mont Blanc is higher by 568 feet, but Monte Rosa, western Europe's second tallest mountain, is mightier. It stretches in a majestic north-south arc of peaks, ten of which exceed 4,000 meters (13,120 feet), and provides one of the finest Alpine traverses on earth. The most massive mountain in the Alps is said to have impressed none other than Leonardo da Vinci, who viewed it from a peak to the east during an outing in the late 1600s.

Monte Rosa was the object of intense interest for almost a decade before its highest peak was climbed in 1855. In 1847 two Frenchmen climbed to Silbersattel, a col at the head of the Monte Rosa Glacier that is less than 300 vertical feet below Dufourspitze, the main summit. By 1854 the Ostspitze—a satellite peak just to the east of Dufourspitze—was climbed four times, possibly in the belief that it was the mountain's highest point—in fact it is barely fifteen feet lower. The following year a large party led by Reverend Charles Hudson set out for Dufourspitze and finally completed the true first ascent, despite a change of heart by most of the guides, who elected to repeat the known route to the Ostspitze rather than take on the more daunting exploration of an unclimbed peak. Hudson (who fell to his death in the famous accident on the Matterhorn ten years later) and his fellow Englishmen—ironically, leading their guides—solved the problems of the airily exposed West Ridge to the summit of Dufourspitze.

Even by today's standards, this route presents some interesting technical difficulties. It starts at the Monte Rosa Hut (9,167 feet), six hours hike from Zermatt, Switzerland, or a little more than two hours above Rotenboden Station of the Gornergrat railway from Zermatt. The hut, which sleeps 128 and is managed from March to September, comes alive at 3 AM as climbers prepare to take on the long slog up the Monte Rosa Glacier before daybreak. The route moves past two outcrops of rocks, then weaves through a crevasse system and ascends a shoulder before turning

Leaving the Gnifetti Hut at dawn, a group of climbers will cross eight peaks on the way to Dufourspitze, Monte Rosa's main summit.

Top: The Margherita Hut, situated on the Swiss-Italian border and at about the midpoint of Monte Rosa's summit ridge, is ideally located for a bivouac during a two-day traverse of the mountain.

Left: With the Matterhorn on the horizon, skiers get an early start on an ascent of Monte Rosa.

Monte Rosa, with ten summits that reach above 4,000 meters, is the highest massif in Western Europe. For climbers, like this duo on the summit ridge, the Monte Rosa traverse is one of the most rewarding—and strenuous—outings in the Alps.

south to a 14,300 foot high col west of the summit, called the Sattel. From here the windblown West Ridge begins steeply over firm snow. A flat section of rock leads to a notch, beyond which a series of boulders and a troublesome iced up chimney must be surmounted. A final knife edge to the summit commands the climber's full attention.

The true glory of Monte Rosa, however, is contained not so much in its highest summit but in the variety of its offerings. The remote Nordend summit, north of all of Monte Rosa's major peaks, offers a rewarding combination of route finding and technical rock problems. The usual route to Nordend

CHIMNEY: *n. A crack in a rock cliff wide enough for a climber to enter and ascend by means of applying pressure to the opposing walls. v. To ascend a chimney.*

starts from the Monte Rosa Hut and follows the trail to Dufourspitze until it turns off toward the Sattel. Another Nordend route pushes steeply up to a col on the main north-south ridge called the Silbersattel (14,800 feet), then follows the ridge northward. The route ascends the ridge on its west side, remaining below its prominent cornices. Two or three pitches of steep rock lie just below the summit.

Instead of reversing the ascent route, accomplished parties can continue southward from Silbersattel, traversing Grenzgipfel and Zumsteinspitze to the Margherita Hut just south of Signalkukppe. The internationally renowned traverse of Monte Rosa's remaining 4,000-meter summits can be completed on the following day with a second night spent at the Gnifetti Hut below Vincent Pyramide, the most southerly of the peaks.

Monte Rosa's most spectacu-

BERGSCHRUND: *Also simply 'schrund. A broad crevasse or series of crevasses occurring at the head of a glacier where moving ice separates from static ice or rock.*

lar ascents lie on its massive East Wall, 6,500 feet high and more than six miles long. Climbers starting from the Marinelli Hut on the Italian side must surmount wildly exposed 60 degree ice on the way to the Silbersattel. The opening of a route on the East Wall by Swiss guide Ferdinand Imseng, hired by English climbers in 1873, established him as among the finest guides in Europe, and this face remains a testpiece of Alpine climbing. There is no walk-up anywhere on the huge massif, so its summits will never swarm with weekend hikers, but for variety of terrain and the quality of mountaineering challenges, Monte Rosa is unexcelled.

CIMA GRANDE

ELEVATION	LOCATION	FIRST ASCENT
9,836 feet	*Dolomites, Italy*	*Paul Grohmann, Peter Salcher with guide Franz Innerkofler, Austria, 1869*

You don't have to be a climber to be enchanted by the Dolomites. Extraordinary limestone towers with striations of yellow and purple rising from pedestals of gleaming white scree, they bombard the senses. Set apart from the main arc of the Alps in northeastern Italy, the Dollies rise from a tangled maze of valleys covered in riotous meadows of wildflowers. The herby scent of pine and larch from high valley forests hangs in the air. Best of all, most of the peaks are accessible by mountain roads that reach to within a few minutes walk of the superb trail system that wends among the spires of rock from hut to hut.

Still, the Dolomites are also a technical climber's paradise. While mountaineers in the Central Alps were learning to cope with snow covered ridges and glaciated faces, climbers in the warmer, lower Dolomites could focus exclusively on rock.

Consequently, the strange obelisks of limestone became Europe's laboratory for the development of rock climbing technique and equipment. Nowhere were these skills more severely tested than on the famed Cima Grande, the middle peak of the astonishing Tre Cimi di Lavaredo. Starting in the mid-1850s the Dolomite peaks fell one by one, but the summit of the Cima Grande, long considered unreachable, held out. In August 1869, Viennese surveyor Paul Grohmann, a founder of the Austrian Alpine Club who had already done a number of first ascents in the range, finally worked out a route on the southern flank of Cima Grande and summited with Paul Salcher, a friend, and guide Franz Immerkolfler. Today, the ordinary route, starting some 225 feet south of the col between Cima Grande and Cima Piccola, follows their line. The route climbs a gully then zigzags up

the face to a notch behind a tower. Face climbing and another gully reaches to the scree-covered lower terrace that cuts across the entire south face. From there the route follows a combination of ridges and chimneys with a sixty-five-foot smooth-sided chimney near the top that is the crux of the climb. This route, offering a modicum of difficulty but a maximum of exposure, is the most popular climb in the Dolomites.

In the decades following the Grohmann climb, attention gradually shifted to the ridges and faces of the range. Once again, the Cima Grande provided the hardest test: the grotesquely steep and seemingly unclimbable North Face. The dead vertical upper two thirds of the face was bad enough, but the first 700 feet defied reason. It was so overhung that a dime dropped from the top of this section would land sixty feet from base of the climb.

The Dolomites offer spectacular views and an excellent trail system for climbers and mountain bikers alike.

In 1933 the North Face of Cima Grande was climbed, ushering in the age of "super-alpinism," climbing beyond the vertical. The ascent, by Trieste climber Emilio Comici, required equally a leap of imagination and a deftness with what came to be called "aid." The key to the Comici ascent was the piton, which Comici used to anchor a series of ladders reaching between otherwise unclimbable sections of rock. Comici and his climbing partners, Cortina guides Giuseppe and Angelo Dimai, even hung from pitons for a night's bivouac on the face. Sixth-class climbing, as this use of aid was called, would soon open up a whole new arena of rock, as Dolomiters fanned out to demonstrate their piton-craft on faces throughout the Alps. By

Climbers use chalk on their hands to absorb perspiration and enhance grip.

1937 Comici had become so adept on extreme rock that he soloed his climb on the Cima Grande north face in a stunning three hours and forty-five minutes. The route is now a classic, joining the north faces of the Matterhorn, the Eiger, Grandes Jorasses, the Petit Dru near Chamonix and Piz Badile in the Bernina Alps as one of the six great north faces of the Alps.

Mountaineering continued in the Dolomites, but for strategic reasons. Once a part of the Austro-Hungarian Empire, the Südtirol in which the Dolomites are situated was sharply contested by Austrian and Italian troops in World War I. At one point the Italians hauled a big, hand-cranked spotlight to the summit of the Cima Grande, then turned it on to expose the Austrian position during a night attack. The Treaty of Versailles, turning the Dolomites over to Italy, was amended by a 1947 edict giving semi-autonomy to the district and proclaiming both German and Italian as official languages. The detritus of the war—boots, mess kits and gun positions hewed into the limestone—can still be found in parts of the Dolomites. As late as 1958 a team of climbers putting in a new route on Cima Grande's north face encountered a remnant of barbed wire high on the wall.

A happier legacy of the Great War is the trail system originated by the Italian army to facilitate the transport of munitions within the range and now maintained for walkers. A particularly popular trail starts at the Rifugio Auronzo, less than an hour's drive from Cortina d'Ampezza, circles the Tre Cimi and returns trekkers to the starting point in time for an afternoon picnic at the pine-ringed Lake Misurina. But hikers need not hurry back to the valley. They can continue from rifugio to rifugio, sampling the Italian and Tyrolean culinary specialties in huts throughout the Dolomites—and taking in the most dramatic mountain scenery in all of Europe.

I always focus on a sense of balance when I climb. It's my most valuable tool and a real source of inspiration. The closer I am to a balanced body and mind, the more efficient I am across the rock. And that's the ultimate experience.

—Ron Kauk

The Northeast Face of the Cima Grande glows in the waning late-afternoon sun.

CLEAN CLIMBING: *Rock climbing that abstains from the use of pitons in favor of protection that does not deface the rock.*

A Passing of the Torch

FROM *A Soldier of the Great War*
BY MARK HELPRIN

In an epic tale that pivots around Italy and the Dolomites during World War I, a novelist describes a young man's discovery of the world of the Alps and the empowering joy that comes from the mastery of its steep rock faces and spires.

When he had tied himself to the tree, pulled up the slack in the rope, and passed the rope around his body into the belay position, he called out to Rafi: "Climb!"

The minute Rafi's hands touched the rock, he knew that everything had changed. The sun had come around the cliff now and the air was warmer, even hot. He could smell pine resin on the updrafts that brought the sound of the steadily thundering waterfall. The world and the blue sky were behind him, and he walked up the crack as if it had been a ladder. A shock ran through him and he feared to trust what he felt so strongly. He had not been born, it seemed, to be either a butcher or a lawyer, but to do this. The length of his arms and legs, the strength of his hands and fingers, and his extraordinary and newly discovered balance saw him up the first pitch.

When he wedged himself in to knock out Alessandro's well placed pins he did not shiver or shake the way new climbers often do, and he was happy all the way up. He didn't ask for advice, he needed no tension on the rope, he climbed twice as fast as Alessandro had expected, and at the stretch below the tree he absolutely astounded his teacher.

Instead of using the étrier and abandoning it on the piton, he knocked out the piton, racked it, and looked up.

"Now what are you going to do?" Alessandro asked. "I'll have to pull you up."

"No," Rafi said as he began to climb, using an almost imperceptible handhold. When his hands had moved as high as they could inside the narrow crack, he began to bring up his feet. Soon he had formed himself into a bow, with his hands and feet sharing the same nearly impossible hold. "No tension," he said as Alessandro looked on in amazement. Then, just as Alessandro had done, Rafi stood up, but in the inhospitable crack rather than in a solidly anchored étrier.

He began to fall, but as he did he caught the bent tree with his fingertips, and soon thereafter he, too, was sitting on the ledge.

In ten days the pupil had begun to outdistance the teacher and was leading the most difficult and precipitous pitches, the ones that had to be climbed artificially because they offered not a single hold. These were the walls upon which climbers developed their immense strength, driving fifty bolts into the rock in an afternoon.

Five hundred meters in the air, with nothing beneath him, Rafi felt entirely at ease and would peg his way up an impossible hairline crack, never seeming to tire.

They rappelled off many a spire, almost flying, spending a whole day's hard climb in one joyous hour. They climbed ice and snow and reached the top of peaks where the light was doubled by reflection. They accomplished several extraordinary glissades, skiing without skis for kilometers and kilometers down couloirs of untouched powder.

Though they ate prodigiously, they lost weight as the altitude and exercise whittled them down. They were asleep before dark and up before the light. Just as the sun was beginning to set and they had come in from a climb, they would wash, devour a few packets of biscuits, cheese, and dried meat, and surrender to oblivion. They slept without dreams, and jumped up every morning, when the moon was sinking into Switzerland, full of energy, stronger than they had ever been, able to run up the steep meadows in the half light and push themselves eagerly into the vertical world where, by midday, hawks glided in dizzying circles below them.

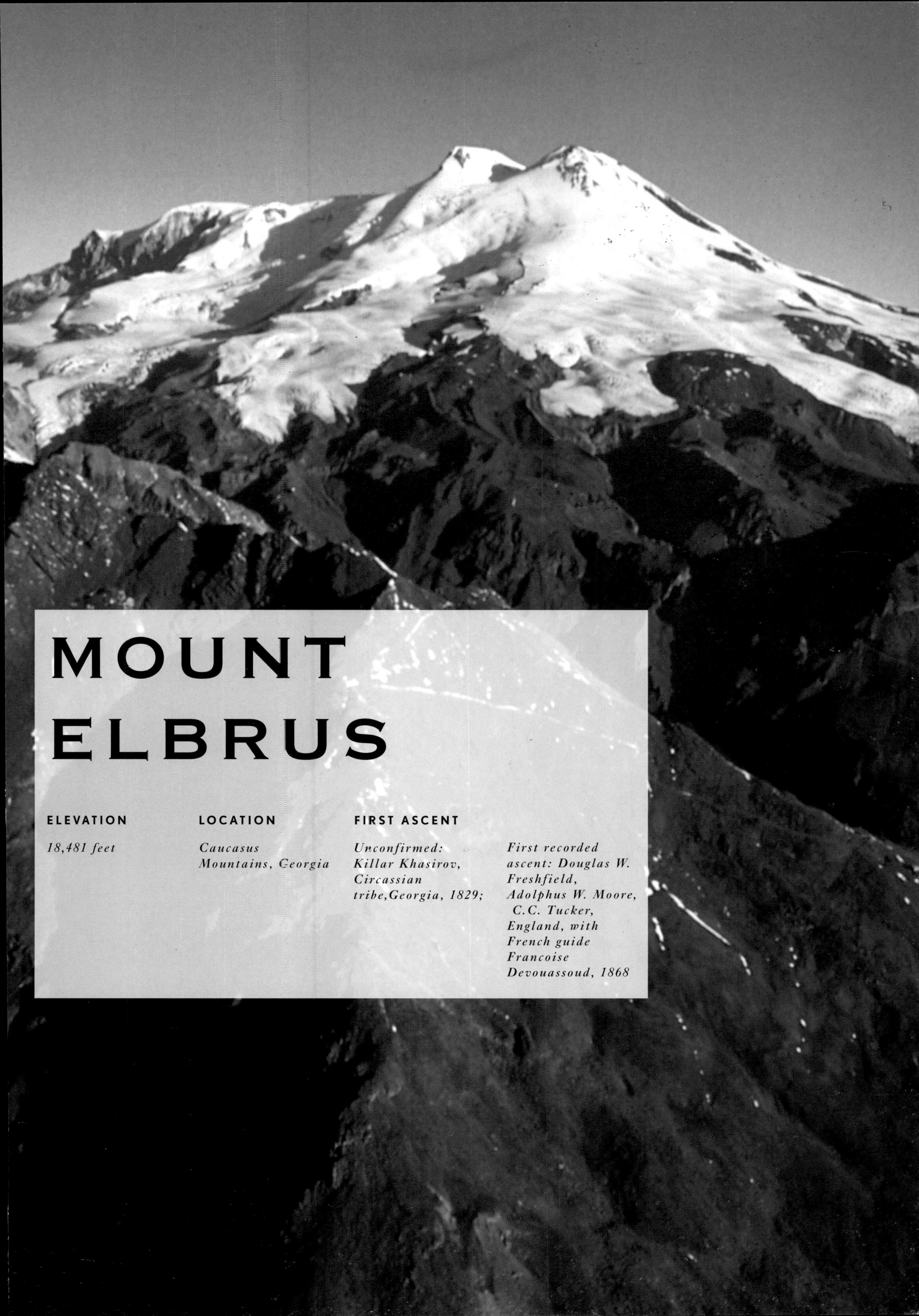

MOUNT
ELBRUS

ELEVATION

18,481 feet

LOCATION

*Caucasus
Mountains, Georgia*

FIRST ASCENT

*Unconfirmed:
Killar Khasirov,
Circassian
tribe,Georgia, 1829;*

*First recorded
ascent: Douglas W.
Freshfield,
Adolphus W. Moore,
 C.C. Tucker,
England, with
French guide
Francoise
Devouassoud, 1868*

To the ancient Greeks, the Caucasus Mountains lay at the edge of the known world. In punishment for his theft of fire, Prometheus was chained to a rock on what is thought to be Kazbek, the second highest peak of the range. Jason sought the Golden Fleece on the slopes of Colchis, another of the Caucasus peaks. But to the mountaineers of Victorian England, the Caucasus represented a renewal of the sport. With the ascent of the Matterhorn in 1865, most of the major peaks of the Alps had been bagged by the gentlemen climbers of the Alpine Club. The game needed fresh summits, and some of the players began looking eastward—to the virgin peaks of the Caucasus. They were astonished at what they saw lying between the Black and Caspian Seas: a 600-mile-long range with no fewer than twelve peaks higher than Mont Blanc. The Caucasus, said explorer Clinton Dent, "are the finest chain of ice mountains that Europe can claim."

The highest of them is Mount Elbrus, situated twelve miles north of the watershed separating Europe and Asia and thereby Europe's tallest mountain. As such it has drawn the attention of the Seven Summits aspirants, peak baggers whose objective is to climb the highest mountain on each of the earth's seven continents. But Elbrus, a vast dome with a double summit, has fascinated mountaineers for a century and a half, and it is perhaps the most popular mountain of all for large-scale assaults by Russian and Georgian alpine clubs. Better yet, the Central Caucasus, of which Elbrus is the western anchor, contains a half dozen great mountains—among them Dych-Tau, Shkhara and Kazbek, all of which exceed 17,000 feet, and the fiercely difficult Ushba, generally considered the most

Top: A ruined hut on the saddle between the twin peaks of Elbrus is a vestige of a once ambitious hut system on the mountain. Today, most climbers use the large Refuge of the Eleven hut at the base of the mountain.

A villager stirs the coals of her outdoor oven in a Caucasus town near the foot of Elbrus.

beautiful mountain in the range.

In 1868 Alpine Club member Douglas Freshfield traveled to the Caucasus on an exploration that would become his life's work: in 1896 he published *The Exploration of the Caucasus*, an impressive two-volume compendium of mountaineering history and physical science, illustrated by the preeminent mountaineering photographer of the day, Vittorio Sella. During his first summer, in the company of fellow Englishmen Adolphus W. Moore and C. C. Tucker, Freshfield climbed Kazbek and then the East Peak of Elbrus. The view was impressive. "The Pennines from Mont Blanc look puny in comparison with Koschtantau and his neighbors," Freshfield wrote. Freshfield's claim of a first ascent of Elbrus was disputed by Russian historians, who hold that the honor should go to Killar Khasirov, a porter who had accompanied a team of Russian surveyors to the mountain in 1829. Whoever was first on Elbrus, most first ascents of the other peaks in the range—starting with the West Peak of Elbrus, which, though both are recognized as summits, is slightly higher than the East Peak—went to the British. By the turn of the century, all of the significant mountains of the Caucasus had been summited.

For much of the 20th century access to the Caucasus was limited, first by the Soviet Union's struggles to control independent-minded Georgia and then by cold war hostilities with the West. By the 1970s, however, the Soviet desire for hard currency overrode a perceived need for internal security and both the Caucasus and the Pamirs were opened to Western climbers. Today Elbrus is easily reached from the Georgian city of Mineralye Vody via a four-hour bus ride along the Baksan River to the Baksan Valley at the

An American and a Russian conduct their own East-West summit at the Caucasus pass of Domguseron, where Europe and Asia meet.

Top: A climber ascends to the top of Europe.

ALSO KNOWN AS • Mount Elborus

foot of the mountain.

The mountain's main summits are gently sloping domes—Freshfield said the east peak looked like an inverted teacup—but Elbrus can still be a severe test. Moist air rising off the Black Sea fuels blizzards that can cut visibility almost to zero. A crystal clear sky at 1 or 2 AM when most parties start for the summit has been known to turn to gale force winds and snow within minutes of daybreak. Midsummer temperatures of minus 25 degrees Fahrenheit at the summit are not unusual. This weather has produced a bewildering array of glaciers and an ice cap, hundreds of feet deep in places, that covers fifty-six square miles.

The traditional ascent of Elbrus starts from Terskol on the

west side of the mountain and follows a trail five to six hours to the Refuge of the Eleven Hut at 14,775 feet—a three-story structure with a kitchen and accommodations for 200 people. Most climbers eliminate the walk-in by taking a cable car and chairlift, constructed in the 1980s, that reaches the hut from Azau Alm. From the hut the route ascends the Azau Glacier toward the East Peak, goes between two prominent outcroppings of rock, then curves westward to the deep saddle between the mountain's twin domes. From the saddle, five or six hours from the hut, either of the two peaks can be reached in an hour or two up steep snow and ice slopes. Climbers will need ice axes and crampons and should be prepared for suddenly deteriorating weather.

An alpine club sign shows the way into a Caucasus cirque.

If the skies remain clear, however, the mountains visible from the summit of Elbrus are impressive. Douglas Freshfield thought them superior to anything he had seen in Western Europe. "The Caucasian groups are finer, and the peaks sharper," he said, "and there was a suggestion of unseen depth in the trenches separating them, that I never noticed so forcibly in any Alpine view."

NORTH AMERICA

From the vast glacial systems of the Alaska-Yukon Range to the ancient and deeply forested White Mountains of New England, North America contains an astonishingly varied mountain landscape. The Canadian Rockies offer 500 miles of stunning ridges and peaks that rise from a seemingly endless expanse of evergreen dotted with brilliant turquoise glacial lakes. In the U.S. Northwest, great volcanic domes sparkle in cloaks of ice, eternally renewed by coastal storms. Colorado has such a profusion of 14,000-foot peaks that it took ninety-six years for mountaineers to summit them all. Yosemite has the world's best Big Walls and the big Californian sun. North America is a continent with a mountain for every ability and every inclination.

DENALI

ELEVATION	LOCATION	FIRST ASCENT
20,320 feet	*Denali National Park, Alaska*	*Hudson Stuck, Walter Harper, Henry Karstens, Robert Tatum, U.S., 1913*

Dall sheep, native to the lowlands around Denali, were a prime source of food for the first ascent team in 1913. "Why should anyone haul canned pemmican hundreds of miles into the greatest game country in the world," wrote Hudson Stuck, leader of the expedition.

Denali is the classic American mountain: tall, brawny, larger than life in every way. It is a mountain that goes to extremes; the highest in North America, the farthest north of all the world's major peaks and the mountain with the greatest expanse of snow and ice—stretching from the summit to 4,600 feet above sea level. The Tanaina, an Athapaskan-speaking group native to the area, have a legend that explains how the mountain was formed: Raven, an ancient mythological figure, was being threatened by huge waves rolling in from the sea, and to defend himself he threw his harpoon at them. When his weapon found its mark, the wall of water became solid, forming the vast Alaska Range. The largest, most powerful wave became Denali.

A word about the name: the mountain was called Bolshaia

Climbers prepare to cross the tundra and some two dozen channels of the McKinley River on their approach to the mountain from the north.

Gora by early Russian traders; Traleika by coastal Indians and Denali by the Tanaina—all of them meaning in essence "The Great One." The name McKinley was bestowed by staunch Republican William Dickey, a young Princetonian who sighted the mountain while prospecting for gold in 1896, in honor of his party's Presidential nominee that year, William McKinley. Although McKinley remains the official designation, most climbers favor Denali in recognition of the natives' reverence for their land. In fact, neither name is particularly appropriate. The Alaska Indians had little interest in mountains, and a horror of glacier ice, while

McKinley never set foot anywhere near Alaska. In a Solomon-like decision, however, the government has recently renamed the land surrounding the mountain. What was once McKinley National Park is now officially Denali National Park.

Although most climbers fly to a base camp on the Kahiltna Glacier, those who walk in will have to deal with the presence of grizzly bears—and some of the world's most voracious mosquitoes. Most of all, Denali climbers have to deal with the cold. During the first winter ascent in February 1967 three climbers were pinned down on McKinley Pass at 18,200 feet in a wind chill that worked out to minus 148 degrees Fahrenheit. But even the normal climbing months of June to August have featured a killing combination of wind, whiteout and inhumanly low temperatures. "It's colder," wrote world-class Austrian mountaineer Peter Habeler, "than all the peaks I have attempted in the Himalaya."

In 1908 explorer Frederick Cook came down from Denali, claiming to have reached the summit. He presented extensive journals describing his arduous trek to the top, along with maps and photographs—many of which were published in *Harper's* shortly after the climb. But even before Cook had returned to his Brooklyn home, his claims were being questioned—and with good reason. His journals were shot full of inconsistencies and climbing rates impossible to achieve. The photo that supposedly depicts Cook's climbing partner, Edward Barrill, on the summit is now widely believed to show a place called Fake Peak, a nice blip on the horizon, 5,260 feet high and nineteen miles from Denali.

The 1913 party did not create such controversy. They mounted an honest effort to summit with the utmost respect for the demanding conditions found on Denali: Among their supplies, hauled onto the mountain by dogsled, was a twenty-five-pound wolf fur blanket. The expedition

"I shall never forget the notable moment when the rope became taut with a nervous pull, and we crept impatiently over the heaven-scraped granite toward the top."

—Dr. Frederick Cook describing his "first ascent" of Denali in 1906.

Single-engine planes carry climbers to the Kahiltna Glacier from Talkeetna. Wind, storms and the varying consistency of the glacier snow make nearly every flight an adventure.

At 11,000 feet on the West Buttress route, the world is blanketed in a pristine covering of snow.

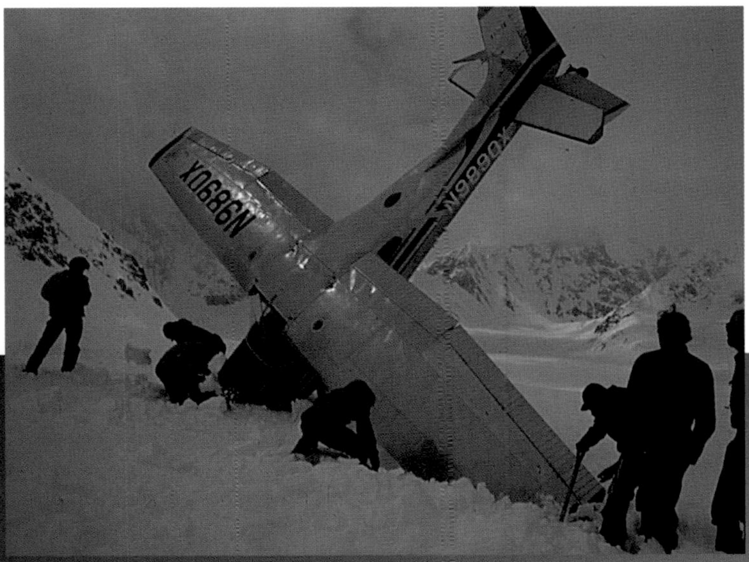

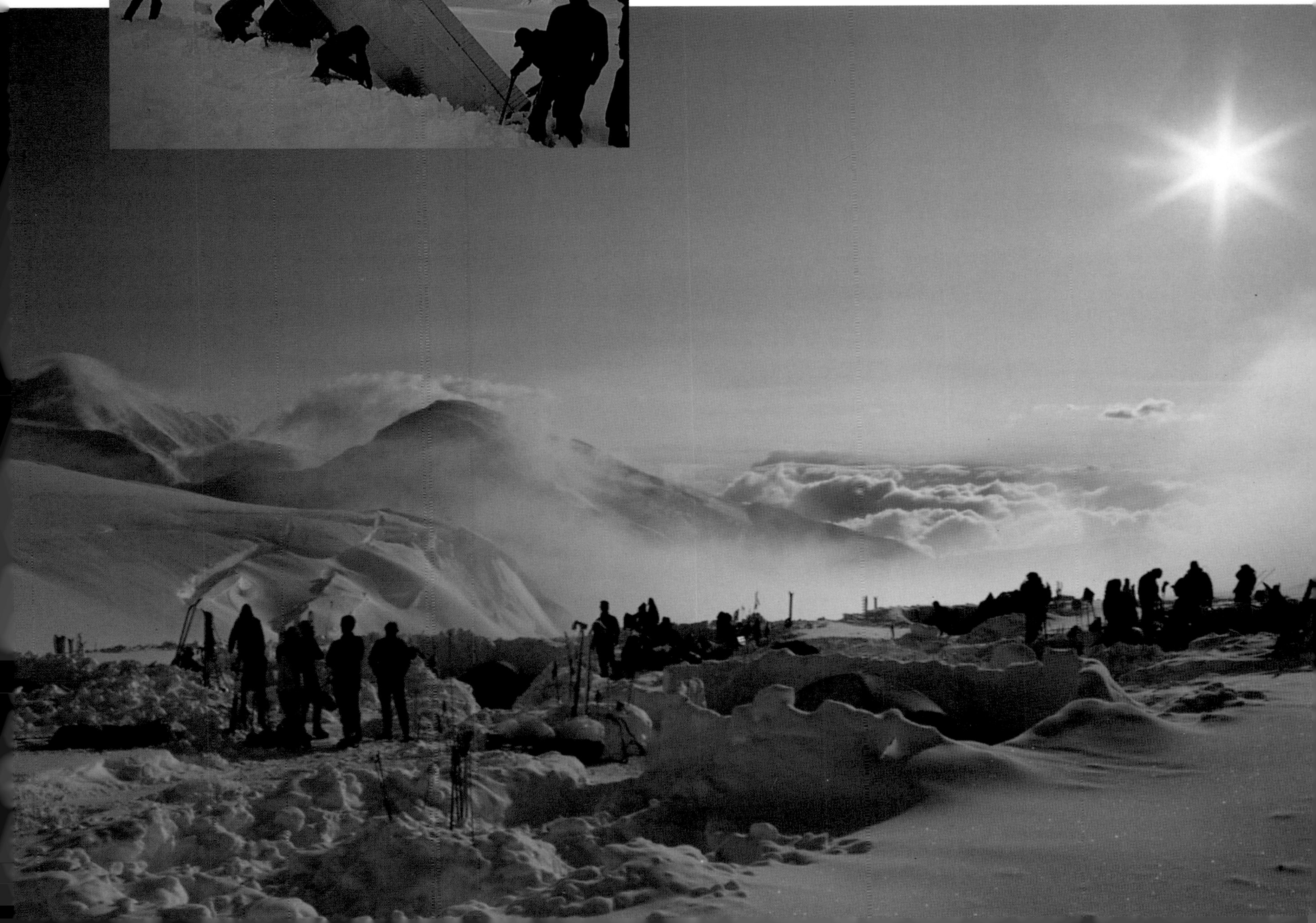

Mechanical ascenders, designed to slide up a rope but grip it when pulled downward, are useful for crossing a crevasse via a Tyrolean traverse, in which a rope is firmly anchored on either side of the crevasse.

was led by Hudson Stuck, then a forty-nine-year-old archdeacon of the Yukon whose travels into central Alaska to minister to the Episcopalian faithful first introduced him to Denali. He was accompanied by three other adventurers: Henry Karstens, who had traversed the mountain's foothills running mail between

Fairbanks and Kantishna; Walter Harper, son of a prominent Alaska pioneer, and Robert Tatum, a young deacon in training. They reached the summit, after eighty-two days on the mountain, on June 7.

Stuck's route up the west-running Hudson Glacier is vulnerable to avalanches, and is now considered unnecessarily risky. Today, the normal route up Denali starts on the Kahiltna Glacier on the south side of the mountain and follows the West Buttress to a saddle between the mountain's north and south peaks. Established in 1951 by a party led by Washburn, the route is favored by three quarters of the climbers who attempt the mountain. "Some people call the West Buttress a walk-up," writes Glenn Randall, author of *Mount McKinley Climber's Handbook*. "Usually, those people have never been on the route."

Flights from Talkeetna, sixty

Bottom: Ascenders can be a climber's best friend when extricating oneself from a fall into a crevasse.

miles south of the mountain, put climbers on a broad, level section of the Kahiltna Glacier, 7,100 feet above sea level. Most start off from here, creating a season-long village of multicolored tents with the attendant urban characteristics of overcrowding and waste disposal problems. The impromptu community that has popped up at "Kahiltna International Airport" is extensive: The glacier is home to a full-time medical center, a dispatch tent and a variety of communal facilities designed to accommodate the needs of climbers while minimizing the impact on the mountain. From here the route descends 350 feet down Heartbreak Hill (so named for the pain of ascending it at the end of the expedition) and then turns north fives miles up glacier where Camp 1 is normally established. Most climbers hump the 100 pounds of food and equipment for the two to three weeks they will be on the mountain in two carries—or by using sleds to pull large loads. Camp 2 is normally situated at an elevation of 10,000 feet just below Kahiltna pass another three miles up glacier. A third camp is established at 11,000 feet.

Since the route above begins to get seriously steep, teams that have brought sleds and skis usually stash them here. An ascent of a short headwall leads to a ridge whose north side drops giddily to a glacier 2,000 feet below. At 12,200 feet the route arrives at the foot of the West Buttress proper, at a place aptly named Windy Corner. Camp 4 is situated up ridge in the Ice Bowl at 14,300 feet. From there the route ascends at a heart-pumping 45 degrees to the final camp at 17,200 feet. In 1951 Washburn cut an 800-foot staircase into the steep hard ice starting at 15,000 feet and secured

PROBE: *A long wand used in avalanche rescue to feel for bodies that may be buried in snow.*

Herds of caribou roam the meadows of Denali National Park.

a rope alongside it to assist climbers burdened with heavy backpacks. Today this section of the ascent often has fixed ropes, though climbers should test them before putting any weight on them and then use them only for protection. The final camp is generally placed on a saucer shaped plateau called The Crow's Nest, at the top of the West Buttress about 3,100 feet below the cone of the south summit. A fit party can complete the ascent from the high camp in six to ten hours, making it back to The Crow's Nest in two to four hours. From there it is a day or two back to Heartbreak Hill and Base Camp.

In 1989, 1,009 gathered to the flanks of Denali, pushing the number of climbers to four figures for first time in any single year. However, climbers seeking a road less traveled can start from Wonder Lake, north of the summit. This route encounters the McKinley River at a stretch in which it splits into twenty-five or thirty shallow channels—a tricky crossing that benefits from a staff picked up from the forest floor. South of the river, the route encounters tundra and then ascends to McGonagall Pass, where most climbers put down a base camp. From there they pick up the Muldrow Glacier and beyond that Karstens Ridge (named for the first in Hudson Stuck's party to reach the actual peak of the mountain), which opens to the broad summit cone.

Karstens Ridge was the route employed by a party led by Belmore Browne, who attempted an ascent of Denali a year before Hudson Stuck. Browne and three other men reached a spot within

A climber ascends a snow slope on the Muldrow Glacier, a route that was pioneered by the first ascent team.

simply incapable of ingesting any more of it and descended, beaten and exhausted on the second day.

Climbers on Denali have been buffeted by cold, wind and whiteout, but since then none have been driven off the mountain by pemmican.

Top: Igloos built from slabs of consolidated snow provide base camp shelter on the Kahiltna Glacier.

Bottom: Ski mountaineers side-step up the Ruth Glacier, which, flanked by mile-high cliffs, is the most spectacular glacier on the mountain.

With all of North America at their feet, two climbers contemplate a swift descent.

they were pinned down by a wind-driven snowstorm that did not permit them even to crawl to the top of the mountain. They returned to their high camp to wait for a turn in the weather, but were done in by a miscalculation made at the outset of the expedition. The only food they had brought above base camp was pemmican, a high-energy mixture of dried fruit, lean meat and fat. But its high fat content, they learned to their great physical distress, was not digestible in the thin air above 15,000 feet. Although they had a six-day supply at their high camp, they were

FRONT POINTING: *A climbing technique in which the front two points of the crampon, which project forward rather than down, are kicked into snow or ice to provide purchase for ascent or descent of steep or vertical slopes.*

A U.S. postage stamp issued in the early 20th century depicting Denali.

BRADFORD WASHBURN

1910-

"My generation was lucky to be able to do wonderful virgin climbs that were pretty damn safe."

HOME BASE ▪ *Lexington, Massachusetts*

CLIMBING FEATS ▪ *first ascents of Mount Hayes, Mount Lucania, Mount Marcus Baker, Mount Crillon and the West Buttress route of Denali*

There is no Super Bowl, no World Cup, no gold medal. But mountaineering at the highest level of performance is intensely competitive. Witness the race for a first ascent, the sometimes desperate effort to become the author of a new route. That is what makes Bradford Washburn such a rare player of the game. His major contributions to mountaineering history have come not from what he has done but from the exquisitely wrought information he has shared.

Not that Washburn's CV is devoid of climbing accomplishments. He put up a number of first ascents in Alaska and Canada, notably Mount Crillon in 1933, Mount Lucania in 1937 and Mount Hayes in 1941. Lucania became irresistible when Canadian climber Walter Wood, having seen it from the summit of neighboring Mount Steele, declared it that it was too inaccessible to be climbed. Washburn's plan was to be flown onto a glacier to the east of the mountain and then to be met by the plane after he and his party had summited. Washburn and climbing partner Bob Bates, an English teacher at Phillips Exeter Academy in New Hampshire, were deposited at the base of the mountain, but the snow was too soft to hazard another landing and takeoff. The two men climbed Lucania, traversed Steele and then began the 100-mile trek out of the wilderness. In the end they were subsisting on mushrooms and the occasional squirrel to stay alive.

Washburn's true contribution to mountaineering, however, has been his meticulously detailed aerial photographs and maps of Denali and Everest. A generation of climbers in the 1960s, inspired and informed by Washburn's work, put up dozens of new routes on Denali and other Alaska peaks. "I got an enormous amount of vicarious pleasure in taking pictures from the air and locating routes I would have liked to climb if I were twenty years younger," said Washburn. "Then I would write an article for the American Alpine Journal and sit back and see what would happen."

Washburn himself was introduced to climbing when he discovered that hikes into the White Mountains of New Hampshire relieved his hay fever. He studied and taught geography at Harvard University and was for forty-one years director of the Boston Museum of Science. His skills as a gifted cartographer were reconfirmed in 1988 with the publication of his superb maps of Mount Everest and the Presidential Range of the White Mountains. "Some people have asked me why I'm still doing this," he remarked. "I tell them I like to be on the cutting edge of the twilight of life."

Bradford and Barbara Washburn in 1998

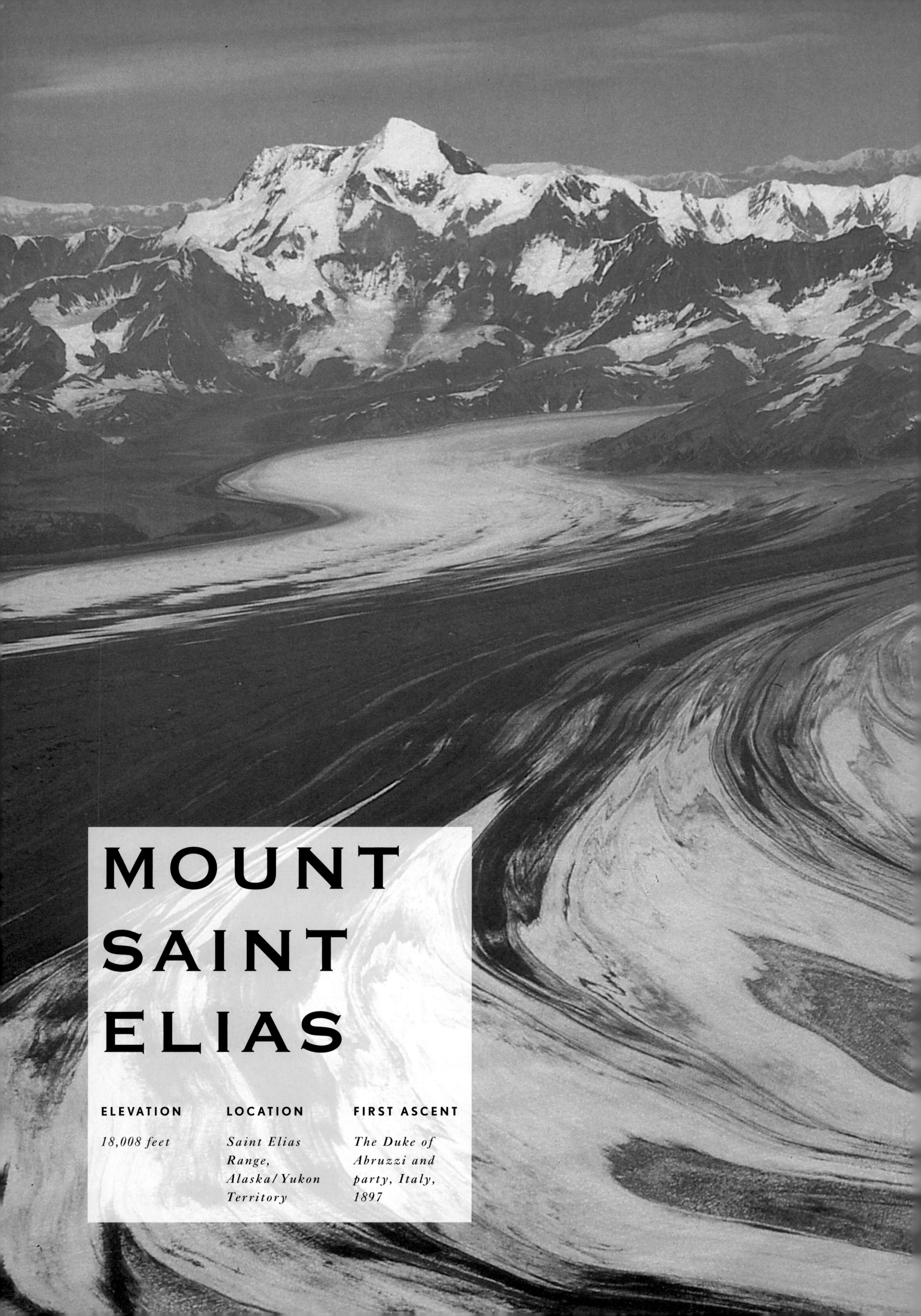

MOUNT SAINT ELIAS

ELEVATION

18,008 feet

LOCATION

Saint Elias Range, Alaska/Yukon Territory

FIRST ASCENT

The Duke of Abruzzi and party, Italy, 1897

Members of the American Alpine Institute camp out in the St. Elias Mountains to practice camping and rescue skills—and they set a nice table.

The summit of Mount Saint Elias lies two miles below the top of Everest, but measured by its elevation above its base, it would be the world's highest mountain. The Saint Elias Range contains the loftiest coastal mountains anywhere—a condition that accounts for both their drama and their danger. Moist air, blowing inland from the Gulf of Alaska just thirty-five miles to the west, frequently is transformed into vicious snowstorms as it carries high up into the frigid heights of the coastal mountains—ten feet of snow has fallen on the upper reaches of Saint Elias in a single week. The environment that accounts for some of the world's cruelest weather also creates vast cathedrals of ice. When haze obscures the lower slopes, wrote an early coastal traveler, "These peaks, high in the crystal clear atmosphere above, are sometimes still to be seen, a line of magnificent icebergs floating on the denser air."

Danish navigator Vitus Bering claimed the first recorded sighting of the Saint Elias Range in 1741, on his third voyage through the waters that were later to bear his name. On July 20, Bering anchored off a cape reaching down to the ocean from the mountains and named it for the patron saint of the day, Saint Elias. When Captain James Cook explored the area in 1778, he attached the cape's name to the highest peak on the inland horizon. Near the end of the 19th century, in fact, Saint Elias gained a brief reputation as the highest mountain in North America. Interest in climbing it soon followed. The first party to attempt an ascent, in 1886, sponsored by the *New York Times*, encountered worrisome crevasses

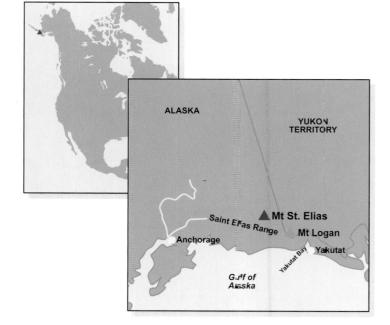

on a glacier to the south and, declaring that approach to be impassable, turned back at 7,200 feet. A second expedition two years later stopped at 11,460 feet. Weather frustrated attempts led by Israel Russell, a University of Michigan geologist, in 1890 and 1891. "The white snow surface could not be distinguished from the vapor-filled air," Russell wrote. "There was no earth and no sky; we seemed to be suspended in a white, translucent medium, which surrounded us like a shroud."

Russell was able to carve out a route up the east-running Newton Glacier to a 12,280-foot saddle (now called Russell Col) between Saint Elias and Mount Newton. From there he climbed to an elevation of 14,500 feet before he was stopped by wind and heavy snowfall. Nevertheless, he had found the key to the summit.

A hiker on the Tana Glacier inspects a *moulin*, a cylindrical opening in a glacier that is scoured by the melt water that pours into it.

Russell's maps and route descriptions were obtained by the Duke of Abruzzi when the twenty-four-year-old adventurer arrived in the Pacific Northwest to expand the scope of his alpinism. A mediocre climber, Abruzzi had the financial resources to assemble an expedition in the grand style. Among the supplies Abruzzi's porters carried by sled on the approach to the mountain were several brass bedsteads. On July 1, 1897, the Italian team started inland from Yakutat Bay, southeast of Saint Elias, along the Malaspina and Seward Glaciers and within two weeks put down a base camp on the Newton Glacier. From there the party wended its way up the heavily crevassed glacier, finally gaining Russell Col after fifteen days of tortuous route finding. The 31st broke cold and clear, and the climbers set out along what is now known as the Abruzzi Ridge for the summit. Shortly before noon the guides in front, follow-ing the protocol of the day, stepped back and allowed their expedition leader to be the first to plant his boot on the summit.

Because of its isolation and perhaps because it soon lost its distinction as the highest North American peak, Saint Elias was not climbed a second time until 1946, when an expedition under the aegis of the American Alpine Club fought its way to the sum-mit against 30 m.p.h. winds in 0 degrees Fahrenheit temperatures. Since then a few new routes have been established, but most parties still climb the mountain via the Abruzzi Ridge. Today's climbers can make use of an air service from Yakutat Bay to ferry sup-plies to Oily Lake, south of the mountain. From there the Newton Glacier of the Russell-Abruzzi route is reached from a 3,700-foot col at Samovar Hills and a traverse of the Agassiz Glacier. Some published guides to Saint Elias recommend climb-ing to the Russell Col in the dead of night to minimize avalanche exposure. The route from col to summit is long and steep in places, but the principal hazards come not from the terrain but the sky—in the form of Saint Elias's world famous bad weather.

The white snow surface could not be distinguished from the vapor-filled air. There was no earth and no sky; we seemed to be sus-pended in a white, translucent medium, which surrounded us like a shroud.

—*Israel Russel, describing his 1890 attempt on Saint Elias*

FRONT POINTING: *A climbing technique in which the front two points of the crampon, which project forward rather than down, are kicked into snow or ice to provide purchase for ascent or descent of steep or vertical slopes.*

A tentbound hiker checks out the weather.

Unique among the world's mountains, the glaciers of the Saint Elias range calf directly into the Pacific Ocean. Here, the Hubbard Glacier snakes its way toward the Gulf of Alaska.

Weather

FROM *On Mountains: Thinking about Terrain*

BY JOHN JEROME

In the end, the thing that most distinguishes mountains from the rest of the world is their weather. It can make all the difference between a sublime adventure and a deadly epic. Here is a brief explanation of why mountain weather goes to extremes.

Mountain climbing's principal danger is not the height but the weather that surrounds those heights. Mountain weather is awful. If there is a redeeming feature to it, it is that the weather is often awful in the literal sense of the term: awe-full. Awesome. Fine weather in the mountains can be finer than it ever is anywhere else—hot, bright days and cool, clear nights. But when it turns bad, as it does rather more often than anywhere else, it can do so in ways that are positively alarming. It has the capacity to strike terror into the hearts of its observers. Whatever else it may be, mountain weather is not boring. . . .

At high altitudes the thinner air has less carbon dioxide, less water vapor, and less dust, as well as less oxygen than at sea level. There is much greater insolation—the amount of the sun's energy absorbed by the ground—at altitude. The thinner air reflects less of the sun's heat back into space and absorbs less in the form of raised air temperature; the ground surface gets a great deal more of that energy and therefore heats up more rapidly and intensely than at lower levels. When the sun goes down, the ground cools again just as rapidly and intensely, without a thick blanket of atmosphere to insulate it. On a normal bright day at altitude, exposed ground surface may vary by as much as fifty degrees Fahrenheit between sun and shade. Sizable, rapid variations in temperature make for weather instability.

(While 75 percent of the radiant energy from the sun penetrates the earth's atmosphere to 6,000 feet, only about 50 percent makes it to sea level. The intensity of that radiation on Mont Blanc is estimated to be 26 percent greater than that which reaches Paris, four hundred miles away—and 15,500 feet lower. There are some other interesting effects besides broad temperature ranges from the more intense radiation. High altitude sun is also richer in the ultraviolet end of the spectrum, and often falls on mountainsides tilted at angles so they receive the rays of the sun as directly as does the equator. One result of this is phenomenal if sporadic growth of plants in summer; another is excruciating sunburns on careless skiers in winter.)

Because mountain air heats up rapidly in daytime and cools rapidly at night, mountain atmosphere is required to carry on an eternal balancing act, flowing from cold to hot, from high pressure to low. (It's the same balancing act that goes on everywhere else, but intensified by the mountains.) All that rushing about makes wind—and weather. The temperature imbalance is exaggerated by a general decrease in air temperature with altitude. Rising air does cool off, simply because the decreasing pressure allows the molecules of air to spread out and therefore to bounce off each other less frequently. (Air temperature is primarily a product of this friction; severe cold is simply a lack of kinetic energy in the air.) . . .

Add a fairly high variation in ambient temperature between mountain peak and valley to the already sharply varied sun-versus-shade and day-versus-night temperatures, and the result is going to be weather. Wind, for starters; precipitation as the inevitable follow-up.

When the exposed upper slopes of a mountain are heated in daytime, the air over those slopes gets warmer than air at the same altitude over nearby valleys. The result is a convection current, in which air is propelled up the mountain in a thermal upslope wind during the daytime. The upslope wind starts with the first heating of the peak at daybreak, gradually increases in intensity during the day, and dies down to calm at sunset. Then it reverses direction and turns into a downslope wind for the night, as the cooling, heavier air heads for the valley.

Precipitation happens when a mass of air cools below the dew point—the point at which water vapor starts forming into clouds. Radiation cooling, as on a still, clear night, can generate low fog, but it can't make rain. The only dependable way to get rain is to get an air mass moving upward.

Mountain-related precipitation results when prevailing winds force an air mass upward along the rising slope of a mountain, cooling it sufficiently to condense the moisture out of it as rain or snow. Thus mountains do "rake" or "sweep" rainfall out of passing clouds, just as the folklore would have it.

Water vapor tends to gather largely in the lower layers of the atmosphere. Pushing those layers against mountains, forcing their ascent, makes for heavy rainfall. Highland areas almost always have greater annual precipitation than surrounding lowlands. Orographic precipitation is responsible for all greenery on the occasional isolated mountain in the midst of barren desert. More commonly it makes the windward side of a mountain range much more heavily vegetated than the lee. That's what's responsible for the great forests on the western slopes of the Cascades of the Pacific Northwest, where prevailing winds pick up great quantities of moisture from the nearby ocean, then dump it on the mountains as they sweep east. Similar conditions prevail along Madagascar's east coast and India's west coast; mountain-generated upslope winds provide a boost to normal seashore wind conditions in both places. A miniaturized freshwater version occurs in Vermont's Green Mountains, where prevailing winds sweep across Lake Champlain before being bounced upward to unload their moisture in the hills.

Mountain regions collect precipitation by other means than this forced ascent. When lower air conditions are unstable, contact with even a minor slope can trigger condensation; thereafter the added heat released by that condensation sets up a convection cell, which generates rain on its own. The very turbulence associated with mountain air (where vegetationless peaks have little ground friction to help damp out gusts) can cause otherwise layered air masses to mix and grow unstable. Mountains also function as weather barriers, delaying the passage of cyclonic systems—which means that those systems have more time to dump precipitation on the mountains before they move on.

Hence the frustration to mountain visitors. Early mornings can often be clear and fine, but once the mountain weather phenomena go into operation, cloudiness and rain develop quickly. Even when the general mountain weather stays clear, the peaks themselves gather clouds more often than not. Upslope winds can put a cumulus cloud right over the peak . . . .

The problem with orographic precipitation is that what goes up must come down, and in the case of moving masses of air the phenomenon reverses itself. After passing a mountain summit the air mass expands rapidly down the lee slope, drying out and heating up in the process. (The dry adiabatic rate of 5.5 degrees per thousand feet holds for descending air as well, heating it up instead of cooling it off.) A mountain range with a consistent prevailing wind will have a rain shadow extending—sometimes for hundreds of miles—from its downwind side: an area of extremely sparse rainfall, often desert-like. California's Sierra Nevada gets fifty or more inches of precipitation per year. Nevada means snow-covered, and winter storms there dump snowfalls that can literally be measured in feet of accumulation per hour; Death Valley, tucked immediately against the eastern edge of the Sierra and thus well within its rain shadow, gets only about four inches of rain per year. The high, dry plains of eastern Oregon and Washington, similarly shadowed by the Cascade Range, suffer from a climate produced by the same natural mechanism. . . .

Not to be discounted in any consideration of mountain weather and climate is the quality of the air itself. If mountain air seems to hold more snow, rain, fog, and sheer, miserable coldness, it also holds fewer pollutants, fewer unpleasant smells, fewer of all the characteristics that give postindustrial air a bad name. The air quality indices published daily in the cities are in effect measurements of how un-mountainlike their air is. For all the possible measurements taken by scientific gadgetry in the mountains, and for all the respiratory rehabilitation centers located there, I suspect that one's response to mountain air must remain purely subjective. It feels better. It smells and tastes better than the low-altitude stuff. Language fails in the face of its sensual qualities. Breathing it is like drinking from a crystalline, tumbling, bedrock mountain brook. I know it is subjective, and I can't prove any of this, but here's my advice. It is worthwhile, in the high mountains, to spend some time simply sitting still, breathing the air, paying attention to it. Feeling it flow in and out. (If you've exerted yourself at altitude, you won't have to search out the opportunity, believe me.) It silver-plates your lungs. It carbonates your blood. Don't give me any of that guff about the fickle miseries of mountain weather. Altitude is its own reward.

MOUNT HOOD

ELEVATION

11,239 feet

LOCATION

Location: Cascade Range, Oregon

FIRST ASCENT

T.A. Wood, W. Lyman Chittenden, Wilbur Cornell, H.L. Pittock, U.S., 1857

M ount Hood offers variety on all sides: the Columbia River Gorge to the north, a great ocean of high desert juniper and sagebrush, orchards and lush valleys to the south and the Portland metropolitan area to the west. Situated less than sixty miles from Portland, the peak has been adopted by Oregonians as something of an icon—its image can be found everywhere from murals in downtown Portland to labels on beer bottles from a number of the area's notable microbreweries. Beyond its role as a picturesque backdrop for the city or as a marketing tool, the mountain has been integrated into life in northwest

Mount Hood looms above Portland. The flight path from the east into Portland International Airport goes directly over the mountain, offering travelers an unforgettable view.

Oregon. It is the home of a variety of vacation communities, the site of world-class music festivals, the focal point of year-round ski and snowboard camps, and a recreation area for hikers, mountain bikers, camping enthusiasts and climbers alike.

The Cayuse believed that Mount Hood was the source of fire and volatile spirits—other tribes tell of evil spirits in the mountain, and a valiant chief who desperately tried to save his

It's unfortunate that mountaineering lingers on the fine edge of tragedy, but it does.... I've always felt that a person who lived a little bit close to the edge lived a little bit more aware.

—*Jim Whittaker*

people and their land from an angry spirit. The great chief battled the demon inside the mountain, but to no avail; his people fled and the land was left charred and desolate. The chief was so heartbroken that he turned to stone—legend has it that his profile, looming huge and striking, can still be seen on the north side of Mount Hood.

Like other mountains situated near coastal waters, Hood had a momentary fling with fame as the "world's highest mountain." In 1792 British Royal Navy Captain George Vancouver, on his historic exploration of the Pacific Northwest, estimated that Hood soared to a height of 25,000. He sent a crew up the Columbia

BRAKE HAND: *In a belay, the hand that holds the dead end of the rope (rather than the end of the rope that runs toward the climber, i.e. the live end), and is used to lock the rope against the body or a belay device in case of a fall.*

Not all climbs on Mount Hood are walk-ups. An ice climber tackles the tough Eliot Glacier.

Illumination Rock provides high-caliber mixed climbing.

Mount Hood at sunset.

River for closer inspection. The officer in charge, Lieutenant William R. Broughton, was impressed. The river passes only twenty-four miles north of Hood, the view of which is unimpeded by intervening peaks. He named the lofty summit for Lord Samuel Hood, the British Admiralty member who had sponsored the Vancouver expedition.

Early climbers of the mountain were only slightly less impressed. In 1867 Reverend H.K. Hines, in an article in England's Alpine Journal, opined that Hood was higher than any peak in Europe or North America. Thomas Dryer, publisher of the *Oregonian*, put the mountain at above 18,000 feet, based on his claimed first ascent in 1854. (That account was later disputed by Hood historians, who credit the 1875 claim of a team led by Reverend T.A. Wood as authentic.) Surveyor Josiah Whitney, who put Hood at 11,700 feet, finally cut the mountain down to close to its actual height.

What Hood lacks in elevation, however, it makes up for in accessibility. The mountain is thought to have been the most-climbed glaciated peak in North America, though that distinction may have been eclipsed by Mount Saint Helens after its spectacular eruption in 1980. The Mazamas, a

Crevasses, like this one on the Eliot Glacier, glow with a blue all their own.

a local hiking club, was formed one summer day in 1894 when 193 climbers congregated on Hood's summit. The normal route on Hood's south slope has been completed by dogs, children, disabled people and, according to one account, by a woman wearing high heels.

Not surprisingly, such under-estimation of the mountain has had disastrous consequences. Hood is the target of sudden changes of weather, sometimes trapping climbers in a sea of whiteout. The characteristically wet Pacific Northwest weather does not ignore Mount Hood. Huge storms inundate the mountain with heavy, wet snow, which is highly prone to avalanches, the most significant danger to climbers on this particular peak.

Inexperience can be deadly—in 1956, eighteen youths, all tied to a single rope, were descending when one of them stumbled and pulled the entire party 200 feet down the mountain. One of them died, and thirteen others had to be taken off the mountain in litters in the largest rescue operation in Cascades history. Fatalities unfortunately are a familiar occurrence on Hood; people at every level of mountaineering experience die almost every year on this magnif-icent and unpredictable peak.

> **SELF ARREST:** *A tech-nique for decelerating and then stopping a falling slide on a snow slope, in which the climber rolls onto his or her ice axe and twists the pick so that it gouges a furrow into the snow and thereby acts to brake the descent.*

Ahead of the crowds, a climber has the summit of Mount Hood all to himself.

The normal route on Hood starts at Timberline Lodge 6,000 feet up the southern flank of the mountain. Ski lifts service the lower section of the snowfield but begin operation too late in the day to be of use to most climbers. The route heads directly north, keeping to the east of a prominent outcrop known as Crater Rock and then up a steep gully to the summit. Expect to spend six hours on the ascent, four on the descent, or less if you have cached a pair of skis at the top of the snowfield above Timberline Lodge (a stunning, historic lodge built by the Federal Works Project Administration in 1936, whose exterior was featured in the 1980 film *The Shining*).

Climbers seeking less congested routes start off from Cloud Cap Inn, reachable by a Forest Service road on Hood's northeast side. The popular Sunshine Route, so named for its all-day exposure to sunlight, ascends the Eliot Glacier, keeping right of a crevassed area, to Cathedral Ridge on the west side of Hood. The climb takes six to eight hours. A more direct, four-to six-hour ascent follows Cooper Spur to the middle of the North Face and then snow slopes as steep as 50 degrees to the summit. On both routes crampons and an ice

Historic Preservation USA 14

axe are necessary equipment.

If Hood's challenges seem tame, bear in mind that it is a not quite entirely dormant volcano. Although geologists have seen little activity since 1907, many believe that an eruption is coming—some think sooner rather than later. Hood is right in the middle of the surprisingly active Cascade Range, a line of picturesque, snow-capped volcanic cones that stretches from Canada to Northern California. The 1980 eruption of one of Hood's closest neighbors to the northeast, Mount Saint Helens, prompted much speculation as to which would be next, and Mount Hood has been the most common answer.

MOUNT RAINIER

ELEVATION

14,410 feet

LOCATION

Cascade Range,
Washington

FIRST ASCENT

Philemon Van
Trump, Hazard
Stevens, U.S.,
1870

No mountain in the American West offers the variety of Rainier. It has rock, snow, ice, wind, volcanic fumaroles—and a weather system all its own. Mount Rainier is an enormous mountain—impressive in its circumference as well as its height—which can be seen for hundreds of miles in every direction. Located in the picturesque North Cascades, Rainier is the patriarch of the most important and active range of volcanoes in the United States. Famous for its wildflowers, fantastic day hiking trails and proximity to the

extremely outdoorsy Seattle population, Rainier can be easily recognized: it even appears on the license plate for the state of Washington.

Mount Rainier figures largely in a variety of Native American myths; a descendant of the great Chief Seattle related a legend where "the great changer of things," having finished with the creation of the Northwest, sat on the summit of Rainier to rest and named it Takkobad: caretaker and water provider for all of the surrounding land. Another section of the Puyallup tribe calls the mountain Takhoma, which means "breast of the milk-white waters," while to the east, the Yakima and the Klickitat use the name Tahoma, which translates to "the great thunder-giver near the skies". While there are a multitude of names for Rainier, there are as many creation stories that explain the origin of the mountain, all of which describe a connection between Rainier, a creator figure and the great waters of the

For climbers on the Emmons Glacier, Little Tahoma at 11,138 feet serves as a benchmark for the elevation remaining to Ranier's 14,410-foot summit.

Below: A time-lapse photo records the light trails of headlamps as climbers leave Camp Muir for a midnight start to the summit of Rainier.

The first thing we learn as guides is that the client will probably try and kill himself. The second thing is that he'll probably try and kill you because you're roped to him. You really learn how to watch what's going on.

—*Jim Whittaker*

Pacific Northwest—a connection that endures today.

It dominates the landscape all the way to the Pacific Ocean 100 miles west and seems to have a magnetic pull on the entire population of the Seattle metropolitan area. No matter which route you take, you can expect company on the summit. About half of the 8,000 people who attempt the mighty Rainier, the highest volcano in the lower forty-eight states, each year make it. With

A climber greets the morning from his camp high on Mount Rainier.

such large numbers of people on the mountain, there are bound to be accidents. Even the 1879 first ascent was believed to have ended in tragedy: Philemon Van Trump and Hazard Stevens spent a night inside the summit crater and were thought to be ghosts by their Native American guide when they returned to camp the next day. Since then, more than seventy people have died on the mountain.

Many of those miscalculated the power of Rainier's weather. Moist air carried off the Pacific colliding with Rainier's sub-zero temperatures has dumped world-record snowfalls on Rainier—ninety-three and a half feet in 1971-72. Even by early summer in some years, snow has so buried Paradise Inn, a Mount Rainier National Park facility at the southern base of the mountain, that visitors have to enter the

lodge through a tunnel. Lenticular cloud halos are often seen girdling the summit of the mountain while the surrounding horizon remains sky blue. Vicious storms can develop with little warning.

For the uninitiated, the most prudent way to the summit is via the Disappointment Cleaver Route. It is approached from the east, starting at Paradise Inn and

Rainier is widely reputed to offer the most challenging ice climbing in the lower forty-eight-as evidenced by this awkward off-width chimney, requiring a strenuous stemming maneuver.

proceeds along well trod trails to the Muir snowfield (named for the naturalist whose philosophy of wilderness preservation was

A Tyrolean traverse carries a climber across a mammoth crevasse in the Emmons Glacier.

A climber emerges from her camp on the Kautz Glacier (climbed to an elevation of 13,000 feet by Lieutenant August Kautz in 1857), which was the most popular way up the mountain until the Disappointment Cleaver Route was established.

As early as the 1920s, when this contingent of Swiss climbers gathered to the base of the mountain, Rainier has attracted climbers from around the world.

Getting away from the crowds, a climber celebrates his scramble up a spire with Rainier just a blip on the horizon.

manifested in his founding of the Sierra Club in 1892). It leads at an elevation of 10,000 feet to Camp Muir, whose shelter and tent sites are limited by the Park Service to 100 visitors per night–first come, first served, no reservations permitted.

Disappointment Cleaver, a route used by 1,200 climbers a year led by guides from Rainier Mountaineering, Inc. (the dominant guide service on the mountain), traverses the top of Cowlitz Glacier and ascends the cleaver by a snow-filled gap to Ingraham Glacier. From there, the route heads straight for the east rim of the summit crater.

The ascent and return to Muir will take six to eight hours.

The routes leading out of Muir are as different to most of Rainier's other routes, writes Rainier guide book author Jeff Smoot, "as modern freeways are to country roads." Those with mountaineering skills preferring a less congested trip might consider Liberty Ridge, deemed by some the finest route on the mountain. This route is approached from the roadhead at Sunrise northeast of the summit. The Glacier Basin Trail to St. Elmo's Pass and thence across the Carbon Glacier leads to the foot of Liberty Ridge, a prominent escarpment on the west side of the notoriously dangerous Willis Wall. The route ascends the rocky crest of Liberty Ridge—or the ice slopes just to the west of it—to Thumb Rock,

the campsite for most parties. The gully above Thumb Rock leads to ice slopes and then to the crux of the route: the bergschrund of the Liberty Cap Glacier. In some years the bergschrund can be circumvented; in some, it presents a pitch or two of vertical ice. Snowfields lead to Liberty Cap north of the summit and then the summit rim itself. The first ascent of the Liberty Ridge was achieved in 1935, but it was not seconded for twenty years. Today it is a classic.

BERGSCHRUND: *Also simply 'schrund. A broad crevasse or series of crevasses occurring at the head of a glacier where moving ice separates from static ice or rock.*

An antique postage stamp depicting Mount Rainier.

A World War II American Mountain Trooper emerges from a snow cave during a 1942 training session on Mount Rainier.

LONGS PEAK

ELEVATION

14,225 feet

LOCATION

Front Range,
Colorado

FIRST ASCENT

John Wesley
Powell, William
Byers, L.W.
Keplinger, U.S.,
1868

JAMES W. WHITTAKER

1929-

"If there's an ocean, we cross it. If there's a disease, we cure it. If there's a record, we break it. If there's a mountain, we climb it."

HOME BASE ▪ *Seattle, Washington*

CLIMBING FEATS ▪ *Mount Everest, 1963; Expedition leader, first American ascent of K2, 1978, Mount Everest, 1990*

The three Whittaker kids, Jim, his twin brother Lou and Barney, had just completed a frighteningly exposed ascent of a Cascade mountain called the Tooth, and they weren't looking forward to the descent. "The three of us said, 'God, if we get off this mountain, we'll never climb again,' " Jim recalled in a recent interview. Two decades later Jim Whittaker was standing on the summit of Mount Everest, the first American to climb the world's highest mountain. So much for vows proffered in moments of panic.

That day on the Tooth, in fact, may have been the last time Whittaker displayed any failure of confidence. In psychological testing of the nineteen climbers who went with the 1963 American expedition to Everest, he was the only one who said unequivocally, "Yes, I will get to the summit." In 1978 he led the expedition that put the first Americans on K2 and in 1990 headed a mammoth international assault on Everest in which

twenty climbers summited.

Whittaker's executive skills found an outlet in the business world as well. In 1955 he was hired as the sole employee of a small Seattle retailer of climbing gear called Recreational Equipment, Inc. By the 1960s he was its president, and when he left in 1980, REI had grown to a $200 million company. Whittaker also helped build the guide service he started with his brother Lou into a dominant force on Mount Rainier. (His sixty-six ascents of Rainier prior to the Everest trip made him one of the strongest climbers of the expedition.) In 1966, Whittaker guided Senator Robert Kennedy, a novice climber, to the summit of Mount Kennedy (named in honor of his slain brother) and remained a friend and confidante. He ran Kennedy's Presidential campaign in Washington State and was with him when he was gunned down in Los Angeles in 1968.

The father of five sons and now a goodwill ambassador to the great outdoors, Whittaker maintains that challenge is a mainspring of human behavior: "If there's an ocean, we cross it. If there's a disease, we cure it. If there's a record, we break it. If there's a mountain, we climb it."

Bill Dunaway, Jim and Lou Whittaker

Stephen H. Long first sighted the Front Range as he headed toward Colorado on a scientific expedition in 1820. It was so enormous that, as a botanist in his party noted, "for some time we were unable to decide whether what we saw were mountains, or banks of cumulous clouds skirting the horizon." A dramatically pyramidal mountain that towers over its neighbors, Longs gained early fame—it was the site Jules Verne chose for a fictional observatory in his 1866 sci-fi novel *From the Earth to the Moon.* Consequently, it was one of the first summits targeted by the explorers of the day. But the mountain rebuffed numerous attempts—more than one party declaring it unclimbable—until John Wesley Powell, who would go on to explore the Grand Canyon, arrived in Colorado in August 1868. Powell, who had lost an arm fighting in the Civil War, was a geology professor from the Midwest with a university grant to explore the Colorado River. Camped south of Longs and hoping to obtain an overview of the system of streams that fed the Colorado, Powell mounted an attempt on the summit. The party ascended to 11,000 feet, camped out for the night and summited the next

morning, celebrating with a toast from a bottle of wine one of the climbers had the foresight to bring along.

Climbers have been toasting Longs ever since. The highest peak in Rocky Mountain National Park and the jewel of a spectacular constellation of peaks arrayed to either side of the world's highest continuous paved road, Longs has more than 100 routes, some of them Colorado classics. Today, the summit can be a crowded place—a midday summer weekend congregation of 100 climbers is not uncommon, and 4,000 make it to the top annually. The mountain's most popular route is the Keyhole, a circuitous, fifteen mile trek that requires no technical skills but provides airy exposures and world-class views in every direction. The route starts at Longs Peak Campground and Ranger Station (elevation 9,000 feet) ten miles south of Estes Park. The first stretch, which gains 3,000 feet over about six miles, leads via East Longs Peak Trail to the aptly named Boulder Field. A scramble up the boulders leads to the signature formation of the route, a keyhole-like opening on the northwest ridge formed by a large overhanging rock. Beyond the Keyhole, the route is exposed to winds from the

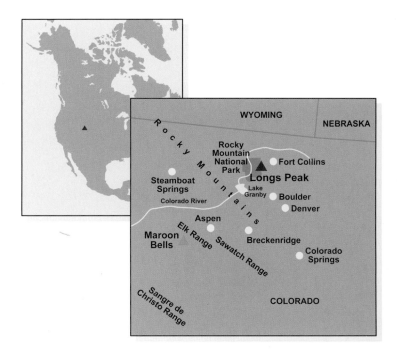

west, and if the weather looks dubious, this is the place to turn back.

From here, the route ascends via ledges on the west side of Longs to the top of a long couloir called the Trough, a cleft in the rock that ascends steeply 550 feet to the west ridge. To exit the Trough, a slightly dicey maneuver is required to get past a large chockstone wedged into the cleft near the top. The climb, almost complete now, presents one more obstacle: cliffs rising from a platform at the top of the Trough. These are surmounted by traversing southward along an exposed ledge, the Narrows, that leads finally to the Homestretch, a sloped slab with a convenient system of cracks that end at the summit.

If the congestion on this ascent is not your idea of a wilderness outing, Longs offers dozens of alternatives, all of them harder than Keyhole. Particularly noteworthy is Kieners, widely considered the finest mountain route in the state, which begins on the East Longs Peak trail but then cuts southward to the base of the mountain's vast East Face at Chasm Lake. The trail ascends Mills Glacier to a couloir named Lamb's Slide, which rises to a ledge system called Broadway. Broadway leads airily across the center of the East Face to a block on the narrowest section of the ledge, requiring a delicate traverse. Many parties rope up here.

Shortly thereafter the route

CHOCKSTONES:
Naturally occurring rocks or stones jammed into chimneys and cracks, sometimes a barrier to ascent, sometimes useful for handholds or placement of protection.

A climber, carefully coiling rope to avoid snags, prepares to lead a pitch on the East Face.

Top: The Keyhole route, possibly the most popular route in Colorado, ascends via the northwest ridge (right hand horizon of photo). Longs' hardest route, unclimbed until 1960, lies in the Diamond at the top of the East Face.

A hiker on Longs digs out the foul-weather gear as potential rain clouds gather.

Family outing: The East Longs Peak Trail leads to Chasm Lake in a spectacular basin walled in by the mountain's awesome East Face and neighboring Mount Meeker's North face.

slants upward into the Notch Couloir, providing two rope lengths of nearly vertical rock. A scramble leads to a spectacular view down onto the notorious Diamond, a sheer section of the East Face that remained

unclimbed until 1960 and contains some of the hardest climbing in the West. Kieners continues up talus to the summit—and blessedly level ground under foot. Most climbers descend either via Keyhole or the Cables Route on the west side of the mountain.

In the 1870s, Longs's first professional guide, Reverend Elkanah J. Lamb, liked to say of his clients, "If they would not pay for spiritual guidance, I compelled them to pay for material eleva-

tion." On a clear summer day, a climber standing on the summit of Longs with Rocky Mountain peaks rippling across the horizon gets material and spiritual elevation simultaneously.

MAROON PEAK

ELEVATION	LOCATION	FIRST ASCENT
14,156 feet	*Maroon Bells-Snowmass Wilderness Area, Elk Range, Colorado*	*Percy Hagerman, U.S., 1908*

Try to find a calendar showing the natural beauties of Colorado that does not include a photograph of the Maroon Bells. During one climbing trip, guidebook writer Gerry Roach recalls seeing a picture of the exquisitely matched peaks on the wall of a small restaurant—in a remote valley in Peru. Indeed, the Maroons, elegant pyramids rising above the chattery hush of quick silver groves of Aspens, possess a kind of perfect beauty.

Their beauty, however, can be deadly. Without notice, these peaks can lead the unwary climber onto a teetering pile of sedimentary rock or suddenly to the edge of a precipice. Maroon Peak and North Maroon (which is actually a sub-peak on the north ridge) would provide a wealth of technically challenging routes were their cliffs and ledges more stable. Loose rock, complex routes and sudden changes of weather can have fatal consequences. In one particularly disastrous stretch—July 1965 to April 1966—an Outward Bound instructor was killed when he was knocked off a ledge by rock fall; three scientists from Los Alamos, New Mexico, perished when they lost their footing and tumbled from a steep snow field; and two college students, attempting a moon-lit descent, fell to their deaths in a couloir.

In June 1971 mountaineer Fritz Stammberger made news of a different sort. He climbed North Maroon checking for snow covered gullies on the ascent and then at the summit strapped on a pair of skis and returned to the valley down the north face in an outlandish forty-eight minutes.

The Elk Range was explored extensively by U.S. Department of the Interior surveyors in the 1870s, and was very near the epicenter of the silver mining boom at the end of the 19th century. Maroon Peak is believed to have been climbed in the 1880s or 1890s, but there is no record of a first ascent until Percy Hagerman, a thirty-nine-year-old businessman, made a solo ascent in August 1908. Just ten miles west of the arts and sporting mecca of Aspen, the Maroon Bells have been much-climbed ever since. South Ridge, the most popular route up Maroon Peak (sometimes called South Maroon), starts at Maroon Lake Campground (9,600 feet), climbs gently past Crater Lake and

COULOIR: *French for gully. A cleft in the side of a mountain that rises to a ledge, a ridge or the summit itself. Since couloirs can serve as funnels for loose rock and avalanches, they pose a special danger to climbers.*

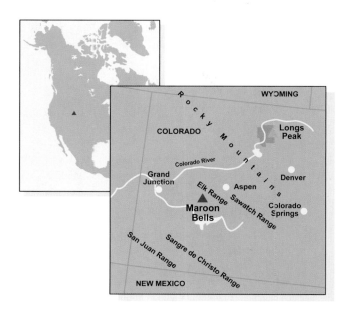

The Maroon Bells-Snowmass Wilderness area is popular among outdoor enthusiasts of all kinds; here, backpackers circumnavigate Maroon Lake.

The much favored North Face Route up North Maroon is best done in late spring after snow on the face has consolidated but before it starts to get mushy under the June sun. Once the snow has gone, climbers must contend with ledge after ledge of rotten rock–conventional rock climbing is not feasible here. This route also starts at the campground but continues west at Crater Lake, crosses a creek and then angles southwest to the foot of the North Face. A traverse south leads to a couloir rising steeply to the west and thence onto a ridge ascending southwesterly. A large crack at the top points the way across a narrow catwalk to the summit. Climbers can descend the way they came, a seven-and-a-half mile round trip, or to make a classic day of it traverse the two peaks, then descend by the couloir between them.

If at the end you want to show your friends where you've been, send them a picture postcard of the Maroons. Every gift shop in Colorado has one.

Skiing, cultural festivals and some of the most beautiful mountains in the West have transformed Aspen, once a hardscrabble mining town, into a playground of the rich and famous.

bends southward, traversing the foot of the peaks' ledgy east faces. Then the trail arcs westward to gain the South Ridge in an unrelentingly steep climb of 2,800 feet. From there the summit lies only 850 feet higher, but the ridge is filled with breakable rock and straying off route can lead the climber onto technically demanding pitches. To the summit and back is a ten-mile round trip.

GRAND TETON

ELEVATION

13,766 feet

LOCATION

Grand Teton
National Park,
Wyoming

FIRST ASCENT

William O.
Owen, Frank
Peterson, John
Shive, Franklin
Spalding, U.S.,
1898

The Tetons are America's Alps. Reaching jaggedly above the wild-flowered meadows of Jackson Hole, Wyoming, the granite peaks present a tableau of raw power. In some ways the mountains are too beautiful for their own good.

Neighboring Jackson Hole, once an ordinary cowtown, is now a tourist destination serving the 3.5 million visitors annually to the Grand Teton National Park alone. World-class skiing, picturesque ranches, and kitschy western theme bars draw extraordinary numbers of people to

an area that, 100 years ago, saw more moose than people. Too late, it would seem, environmentalists have begun to debate the wisdom of expanding transportation facilities into the area.

But before the Winnebagos and the trail bikes, the motels and the boutiques, before there was a 310,000-acre national park, there were the mountains. Geologists call the Tetons a trap-door block: a range where a fault runs along one side the mountains are tilted like a trap door, with one very steep side facing down on the fault and a gentle slope on the other side. The result is an almost vertical wall of rock, snow and ice that is the delight of mountaineers, hikers and skiers from all over the world.

At first The Tetons were simply landmarks for trappers working the valleys east of the range. The European Golden Age of mountaineering was long past

Climbers scope out routes on the Grand Teton from Signal Mountain.

Opposite: With the Grand piercing the skyline, a rancher punches cattle on pastureland on the east side of the Snake River.

before anyone thought of climbing the them. In July 1872, a large party under the leadership of James Stevenson of the Hayden Society mounted a concerted campaign to reach the summit of the mightiest of the Tetons. Eventually all but two turned back, but Stevenson and Nathaniel Langford continued on

CHOCKSTONES:
Naturally occurring rocks or stones jammed into chimneys and cracks, sometimes a barrier to ascent, sometimes useful for handholds or placement of protection.

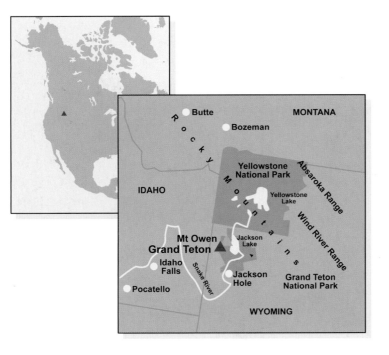

Kris Ericson gets the snarls out of his rope in preparation for a rappel on the Owen-Spalding, the route of the first ascent in 1898.

DIHEDRAL: *A vertical section of a cliff in which two slabs meet to form a more-or-less right angle. Also called a diedre (French): an inside corner or an open book.*

and claimed, in Langford's account, to have "stepped upon the highest point of the Grand Teton." The claim remained uncontested until 1898 when William O. Owen, after numerous failures, finally reached the summit in the company of Reverend Franklin Spalding, Frank Peterson and John Shive. Finding no cairn, the Hayden Society's traditional summit marker, or any other sign of a previous human presence, Owen rancorously refuted Langford's claim. While the dispute has never been conclusively settled, most histories of the mountain accord the first ascent to Owen's team.

The Owen-Spalding is now by far the most popular route to the summit of the Grand. The approach, beginning in the Lupine Meadow parking area east of the mountain, follows Garnet

Canyon Trail to a broad saddle between the Grand and Middle Tetons. From there a pathway leads through fragile tundra past a dark stripe in the rock, called the Black Dike, to a series of prominent landmarks—a tower, called The Needle; a tunnel formed by a boulder, called the Eye of the Needle; and Wall Street, a ramp that leads eastward to the Exum Ridge. Owen-Spalding continues northward to the Upper Saddle, a sharp cleft in the West Ridge between the summit and a spur with a mysterious circular pile of rocks assumed to have been placed there by Native Americans. Most parties rope up here for protection past the Bellyroll, the Crawl and the Catwalk and a scramble up a chimney and a right-angle dihedral to the summit, where the fortunate will find an awe-inspiring view of the

Yellowstone National Park to the north, the Bighorn Mountains to the east and the Wind River Range to the southeast. Return is via the ascent route, though climbers wishing to bypass the exposed and awkward Bellyroll and Crawl sections can rappel to the Upper Saddle.

For twenty-one years every ascent of the Grand followed the Owen-Spalding. Then in 1929 Harvard philosophy professor Robert Underhill arrived in the West with an arsenal of climbing techniques he had learned during a season of alpinism in Chamonix, France, which he employed to put in a new route on the Grand's East Face. That climb, however, was just a warm-up for what appeared to be the mountain's supreme challenge: the North Ridge, so forbidding no one had even bothered to attempt it.

The sun reflected off the snow into the couloir to reveal a mass of contorted ice. Debris, both ice and rock, cascaded out of it. It seemed the picture of unpredictability. The mountain seemed to be saying, "Here, I keep no pacts."

—*Grand Teton National Park Ranger Pete Sinclair, approaching a rescue on the Grand in 1965*

Teaming up with Fritiof Fryxell, a Grand Teton Park Ranger, Underhill took on the North Ridge in July 1931. The two moved up a snowfield on the north face called the Grandstand onto the ledges of the ridge proper. The climbing went brilliantly—until they came to the Chockstone Chimney, a broad vertical opening with a huge rock wedged into it. Underhill's solution called for Fryxell to stand on his shoulders and hope for a purchase high up into the chimney. For extra measure Fryxell stood on his partner's head but still finding no handholds, dismounted. His turn next, Underhill took the precaution of driving in a piton as high as he could and running his rope through the carabiner he had clipped into it. He scratched and thrashed—to no avail—and then heard Fryxell, speaking just above a whisper,

A climber works out a move high up on a Grand Teton classic, the Petzoldt Ridge, named for National Outdoors Leadership School founder Paul Petzoldt.

From the summit of the Grand Teton, the view south reaches down to the Wind River Range in west central Wyoming.

say, "Step on the piton." In the East, where many climbers considered artificial aid anathema, such advice would have constituted a form of ethical blasphemy. Underhill stepped, reached and hauled himself past the chockstone. Beyond the chimney the climbing eased off. Ten hours after they had started out, Underhill and Fryxell completed what to then was the hardest technical climb in the U.S. and is still considered one of the nation's finest alpine routes. In

one bold ascent, they had opened a whole new world of technical climbing.

There are currently more than twenty routes on the Grand, many of them more difficult but none with a greater impact on climbing in America than the North Ridge. While the roads to the trialheads may be congested, there is still plenty of solitude to be found on high up on the wonderful granite of the Grand.

This 1938 poster was part of a campaign mounted by Franklin Roosevelt's Works Projects Administration to support America's National Parks.

PITON: *A hardened steel spike with a ringed opening on the blunt end to which a carabiner can be attached, which is*  *hammered into a crack to provide protection or aid. Also called a pin. Because repeated placement and removal of pitons scars the rock at the point of placement, their use is now discouraged in favor of artificial chockstones and other clean climbing devices.*

MOUNT OWEN

ELEVATION	LOCATION	FIRST ASCENT
12,928 feet	*Grand Teton National Park, Wyoming*	*Fritiof Fryxell, Kenneth Henderson, Phil Smith, Robert Underhill, U.S., 1930*

Mount Owen, over-shadowed by the Grand just to the southwest, is the gem of the Tetons. It is the hardest of the all the peaks in the range to climb and the last of them to be summited. But for the climber with technical skills, the second highest Teton serves up the full range of mountaineering challenges: snow and ice, good rock and superb lines in every direction. From the east, Owen plummets 6,000 vertical feet down to the lush meadows of the Jackson Hole valley and the cool oval of Jenny Lake. Together with the peaks to the north and south, Owen forms a great spiky wall of granite that

The steep and endlessly varied rock of the Tetons offers some of the best climbing in North America.

is the most dramatic mountain-scape in the U.S.

Mount Owen was not climbed until 1930—and might have gone unclimbed even longer—were it not for the efforts of William Owen, a surveyor from Laramie, Wyoming, who laid out homesteads for the original settlement of Jackson Hole. After climbing the Grand with Franklin Spalding in 1898, Owen became inextricably linked with the range both as a surveyor and as a defender of his claim to the first ascent. He managed to get himself appointed to the committee that installed a bronze plaque on the summit of the Grand honoring his climb. It is not hard to imagine him exulting in becoming the namesake of the Grand's neighbor.

In 1925, Owen triangulated the height of Mount Owen and

began determinedly to push for a first ascent. He would have to be patient. In August 1927, a strong team—including Teton guides Paul Petzoldt and Fritiof Fryxell—made surprisingly good progress, only to discover they

Top, opposite: A bull moose sniffs out an intruder in the Grand Teton National Park.

Bottom, opposite: The longest segment of any ascent— the slog up scree and snow to the beginning of the interesting climbing.

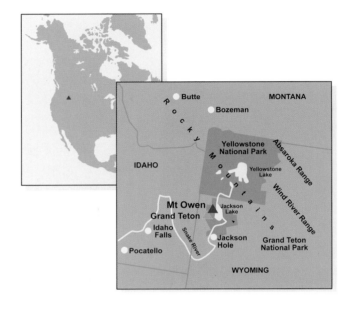

A mighty trinity: Grand Teton, Owen (separated from the Grand by a cleft in the ridge called the Gunsight) and Teewinot greet a new winter day dusted with snow.

had chosen the wrong couloir and climbed not Owen but neighboring East Prong. A week later two more attempts stopped well short. The following year, at William Owen's urging, Fryxell returned to the mountain. This time, his party got to within 100 vertical feet of the top, but there they were thwarted by the steep, smooth walls of the summit knob. A 1929 attempt also failed. The last of the Tetons' unclimbed summits finally succumbed in July 1930, when the talented alpinist Robert Underhill joined Fryxell and two others to solve the summit knob.

The summit, however, is not Owen's only difficulty. Every one of its dozens of routes and variations—some established as recently as the 1990s—requires mountaineering ability. Although a strong team can climb Owen in one long day, many parties establish a camp on the flank of

the mountain and go the summit on day two. For climbs from the east, this camp is best placed at Surprise Lake below Teton Glacier. From there the popular Koven Route, established in 1930 by Petzoldt, Glenn Exum and Theodore and Gustav Koven, reaches westward up the glacier to an 800-foot couloir that cleaves the lowest step of the South Face. The route ascends the couloir to a grassy ledge, then to the Great Chimney, a sixty-foot fissure that ascends to the first of two high snowfields. The route slants upward below this snowfield to bare rock and then the second snowfield, which is crossed to a weakness in the south face. From here 400 feet of face climbing reaches to just below the summit knob. A ledge leads to the deep West Chimney that proved to be the key to the steep wall which guards the summit.

Climbs on the less frequented

west side of the mountain start in Valhalla Canyon, a spectacular cirque below Owen and the Grand. To reach Valhalla, however, climbers must cross the swift Cascade Creek, a dicey undertaking in the early climbing season when the creek is swollen. Owen's west side presents a complex system of ridges and faces that put route-finding skills at a premium. But it also offers at least one passage, the West Ledges Route, that is accessible to climbers of moderate ability.

For those who accept Owen's challenges, there are splendid rewards: a respite from the crowds that throng to the Tetons and its more accessible peaks, a strenuous outing with terrain to suit a full range of technical ability and the rewarding—not to mention exclusive—view of the North Face of the Grand from the summit.

A Test of Will

FROM THE NEW YORK TIMES, 1983, BY AL ALVAREZ

Al Alvarez is a writer by profession and a climber by inclination. No one has articulated more eloquently what it is that would draw a person to steep places.

I started climbing in the summer of 1950, just before my twentieth birthday, hit my peak at the sport about fifteen years later, and have been on a gradually accelerating decline ever since. Yet I still try to get onto the rocks any Sunday when the weather is halfway decent, although my stamina and flexibility are sharply diminishing, and the rocks I usually go to—a little sandstone outcrop south of London—would fit comfortably into the foyer of the new A.T.&T. Building. These days, I climb mostly with my son. At fifteen, he is too young to know any better. Yet the fact is, whenever work or rain deprives us of our weekly fix of climbing, we exhibit identical withdrawal symptoms, restlessness, irritability, fretfulness, a glum conviction that our week has been spoiled. Climbing is an addictive sport that changes the psyche's chemistry as irredeemably as heroin changes the body's, and both of us are hooked.

When Mallory was asked why he wanted to climb Everest, he answered with a famous evasion: "Because it's there." I suspect that what he really meant was "Because you're here"—"you" being not only his aggrieved and aggressive questioner but also the town, the noise, the involvements, the problems, the routine. You climb to get away from all that, to clear the head, to breathe free air. Yet more weekend sportsmen—the fishermen and yachtsmen, golfers, even Sunday painters—do what they do in order to get away, without risking their necks in the process. Why, then does climbing exert such a curiously addictive power?

First, because it is one of the purest, least cluttered sports, requiring a minimum of equipment: a pair of special boots, a rope, a safety helmet, a few carabiners (snap links), nylon slings, and artificial steel chockstones or pitons for protection. The whole lot costs very little, lasts for years, and hangs easily around your neck and from your waist. Unlike other sports, if something goes wrong, the fault is nearly always in you, not in your gear. Conversely, the reward, when a climb has gone well, is an intense sense of physical well-being. On those rare occasions when mood, fitness, and rock all come together and every-thing goes perfectly, you experience an extraordinary combination of elation and calm—tension dissolves, movement becomes effortless, every risk is under control—a kind of inner silence like that of the mountains themselves. No doubt every athlete feels that on his best days, but in climbing that style of contentment is attainable long after you pass, as I have, your physical prime.

It is also not a competitive sport, however much the top climbers vie among themselves for first ascents or ascents in the best style. The competition is not even with the mountain or the rock face. You are competing, instead, with yourself—with your protesting body, your nerves, and, when the going gets really tough, with your reserves of character.

In 1964, for example, a companion and I spent a night belayed to a small ledge—a couple of feet long and 18 inches wide—1,300 feet up an overhanging face in the Italian Dolomites. We had been benighted on it by a sudden snowstorm and were soaked to the skin; but because this was August in Italy, we were climbing light, which meant we had neither protective clothing nor food. The route finished up a thousand-foot vertical corner, down which a waterfall of melted snow was pouring. It froze solid during the night, and privately both of us assumed that we would do the same. But neither of us mentioned the possibility, because to have done so would not only have undermined our confidence to complete the last 500 icy feet the next morning—if there was a next morning for us—it would also have been a violation of privacy. Our survival depended, as much as anything else, on tact. It was not just a question of being young enough and fit enough to withstand the cold, we also had to behave well and respect each other's feelings. Melodrama and self-pity would have done us in more surely than the freezing temperature.

I suspect that most men are secretly worried about how they will behave under pressure. Certainly I emerged from that night on the bare mountain with frostbitten fingers and a good deal more self-confidence than I had had before—a confidence that was quite apart from the pleasure of having got up a difficult climb in bad conditions. I had learned that the ability to sit quiet in a crisis and not fuss was more valuable than physical strength. I also discovered in myself an unsuspected, obstinate ability to survive and that, in some devi-ous way, seemed to absolve me from the youthful need continually to apologize and explain. As the poet Thom Gunn wrote, "I was myself: subject to no man's breath." Perhaps I should also add that I have not felt the need to repeat the experiment; the Via Comici on the north face of the Cima Grande di Lavaredo was the last serious climb I did without checking the weather forecast beforehand.

"Life loses in interest," wrote Freud, "when the highest stake in the game, life itself, may not be risked." Those who cultivate risk for its own sake, however, are probably emphasizing only their own inner torpor, just as the people who talk most fervently about the beautiful emotions induced by drugs are those who have most difficulty in feeling anything at all. The pleasure of risk is in the control needed to ride it with assurance so that what appears dangerous to the outsider is, to the participant, simply a matter of intelligence, skill, intuition, coordination—in a word, experience. Climbing, in particular, is a paradoxically intellectual pastime, but with this difference: you have to think with your body. Each pitch becomes a series of specific local problems: which holds to use, and in which combinations, in order to get up safely and with the least expense of energy. Every move has to be worked out by a kind of physical strategy, in terms of effort, balance, and consequences. It is like playing chess with your body.

And, that, for me, is the final satisfaction. To be a professional writer is, in the end, a sedentary, middle-class occupation, like accountancy or psychoanalysis, though more lonely. For five or six days each week, I sit at my desk and try to get sentences right. If I make a mistake, I can rewrite it the following day or the next, or catch it in proof. And if I fail to do so, who cares? Who even notices?

On a climb, my concentration is no less, but I am thinking with my body rather than my weary, addled head, and if I make a mistake, the consequences are immediate, obvious, embarrassing, and possibly painful. For a brief period and on a small scale, I have to be directly responsible for my actions, without evasions, without excuses. In that beautiful, silent, useless world of the mountains, you can achieve at least a certain clarity, even seriousness of a wayward kind. It seems to me worth a little risk.

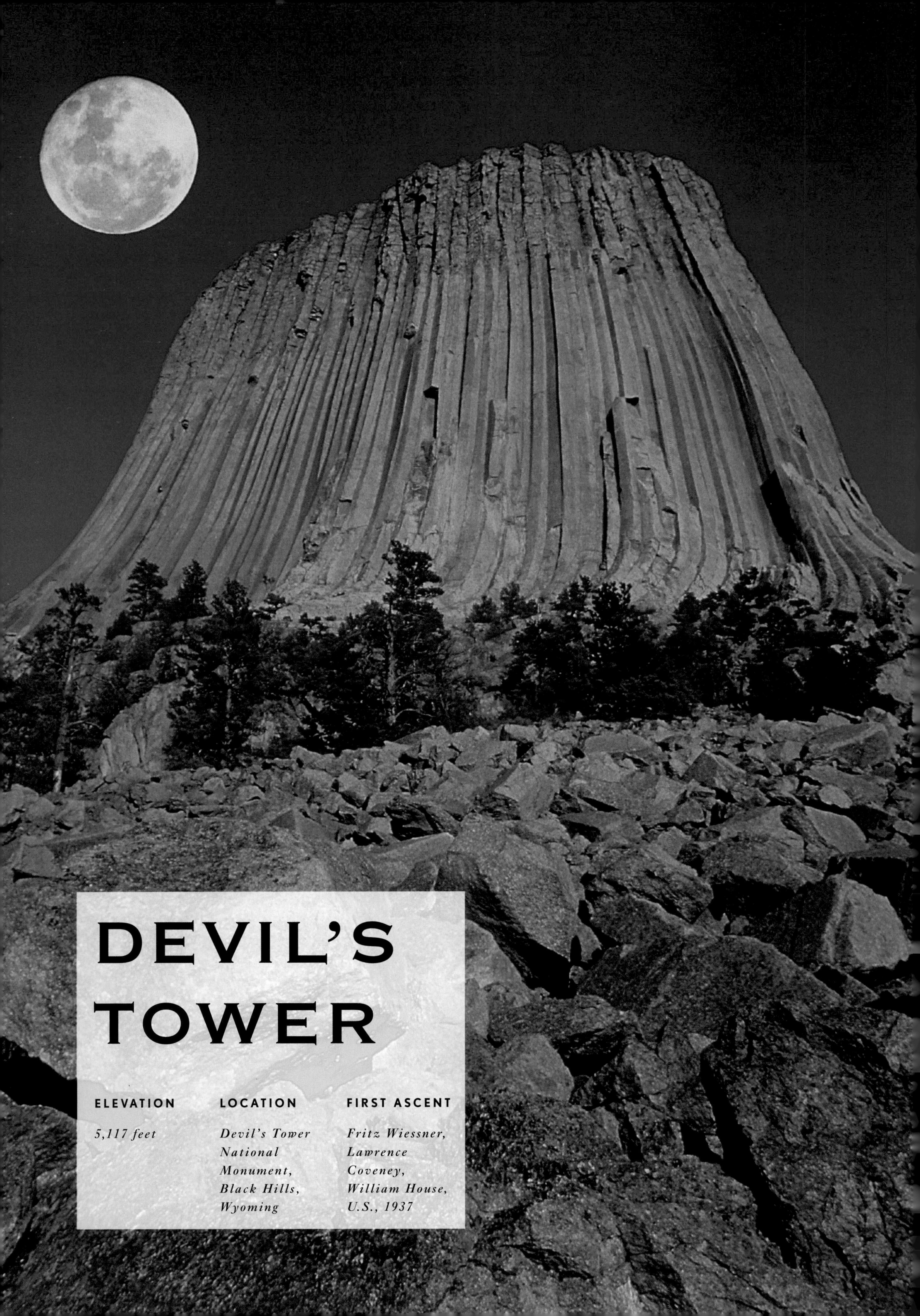

DEVIL'S TOWER

ELEVATION

5,117 feet

LOCATION

Devil's Tower National Monument, Black Hills, Wyoming

FIRST ASCENT

Fritz Wiessner, Lawrence Coveney, William House, U.S., 1937

L ong before Devil's Tower cast its eerie spell on the 1977 movie *Close Encounters of the Third Kind*, it was a theater for myth-making. Geologically, the monolith was created when an accumulation of molten phonolite porphyry just beneath the surface of the earth cooled, forming its mantel of columns. Eons of erosion exposed the monolith to the surrounding plateau.

Both the Lakota and the Sioux, however, had a different explanation for the tower and its long furrows: they were created by a giant bear that had clawed at its sides as it magically lifted a group of young girls out of harm's way. Today, says the legend, the girls can be spied in the heavens, as the group of stars we call The Pleiades.

In this century, it has served as a theater for a more modern sort of spectacle. In October 1941 parachutist George Hopkins, in one of his celebrated exhibitions of parachuting accuracy, landed a jump on the summit of the basalt column. The stunt came off perfectly—except for one thing. Hopkins had dropped a 1,000-foot coil of rope from an airplane for use on descent from the summit, but the rope missed its mark and snagged on a ledge far out of reach once he landed. Hopkins

---

ALSO KNOWN AS • Mato-tepee "Home of the Bear"

A stemming move solves a problem on McCarthy West Face.

Inset: Todd Skinner ascends an open book on "Hollow Men," one of more than sixty routes on Devil's Tower.

---

was stranded for six days while Jack Durrance of Dartmouth College, who had done the second ascent of the tower three years earlier, crossed the country by train to help get him down.

Today, park officials would not have to go far to bring in a rescue operation. Devil's Tower, its flut-

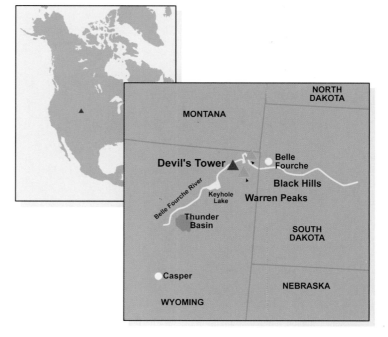

ed ridges rising like columns on a ruined Roman temple, has been climbed thousands of times. The first ascent, however, has never been repeated—at least in the style in which it was put up. In 1893 ranchers William Rogers and Willard Ripley nailed a row of two-foot stakes into a crack on the south side of the tower, thereby creating a ladder that ran clear to the summit plateau. On Independence Day Rogers and Ripley, with throngs of people, who had been alerted to the exhibition by a handbill, cheering them on, climbed the ladder to the top.

The first unaided ascent went to Fritz Wiessner, an alpinist celebrated both in the Dresden of his youth and in the U.S. to which he emigrated in 1929. In 1937 Wiessner, accompanied by noted American mountaineer William House and a friend Lawrence Coveney, traveled to eastern Wyoming to reconnoiter the tower. After a brief tour around the base of the monolith, they settled on a section of the southwest corner that seemed promising. The threesome scrambled up

Top: A three-cent stamp issued to commemorate the 50th anniversary of Devil's Tower's designation as a National Monument.

Left: Charley Mace takes the lead on the second pitch of McCarthy West Face.

CHALK: *A carbonate of magnesium gymnast powder used by climbers to absorb perspiration on fingers and hands, thereby enhancing their grip on rock. Although it is now generally accepted, chalk has been criticized for leaving unaesthetic blotches of white on the rock face and spoiling the adventure of route-finding for subsequent climbers.*

Top: The Tower floats on a pool of morning mist.

Right: Devil's Tower is a massive agglomeration of molten phonolite porphyry that cooled as it pushed up through the crust of the earth. When millions of years of erosion removed the less consolidated rock and soil around it, the strange obelisk was left standing on its own.

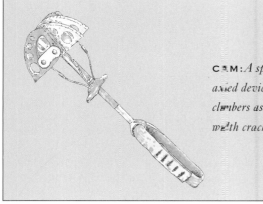

CAM: *A spring-loaded, double-axled device used by rock climbers as protection in off-width cracks.*

A climber enjoys the view from the top: the Belle Fourche River, and the seemingly endless plains beyond.

broken rock to a fissure between two columns and then to the base of a nearly vertical eighty-foot crack. Most climbers of the day would have been repulsed by the commitment demanded by this pitch, but to the astonishment of his partners, Wiessner attacked it head on and ascended it flawlessly. It was a supreme demonstration of European technique on American rock.

A year later Jack Durrance traveled to Devil's Tower intending to repeat Wiessner's route. But he spotted another line a little to the left and decided to give it a

go. It has since become one of the most popular climbs on the tower and is included in *Fifty Classic Climbs of North America*, the highly regarded technical climbing guidebook by Steve Roper and Allen Steck. The Durrance route ascends a leaning column, one of the few on the tower that is broken, to a seventy-foot jam crack just to the left of a slender column that must be traversed near its top. From there the climbing eases off for 100 feet straight up, then traverses right for a scramble to the summit. Three rappels put climbers back at the base.

Since then, more than sixty routes have been established on the tower. For an exhilarating outing with only occasional weather problems and no arduous walk-in, Devil's Tower has become a favorite.

JAM: *A rock climbing maneuver in which a finger, hand or foot is wedged into a crack in such a way as to carry the weight of the climber during a move; v. to perform such a maneuver.*

A 1938 Works Projects Administration poster issued to promote National Parks & Monuments.

RANGER NATURALIST SERVICE

CAMPFIRE PROGRAMS
WILDLIFE VIEWING
NATURE WALKS

AMERICA'S FIRST
NATIONAL MONUMENT
DEVILS TOWER
U.S. DEPARTMENT OF THE INTERIOR
NATIONAL PARK SERVICE

EST
1906

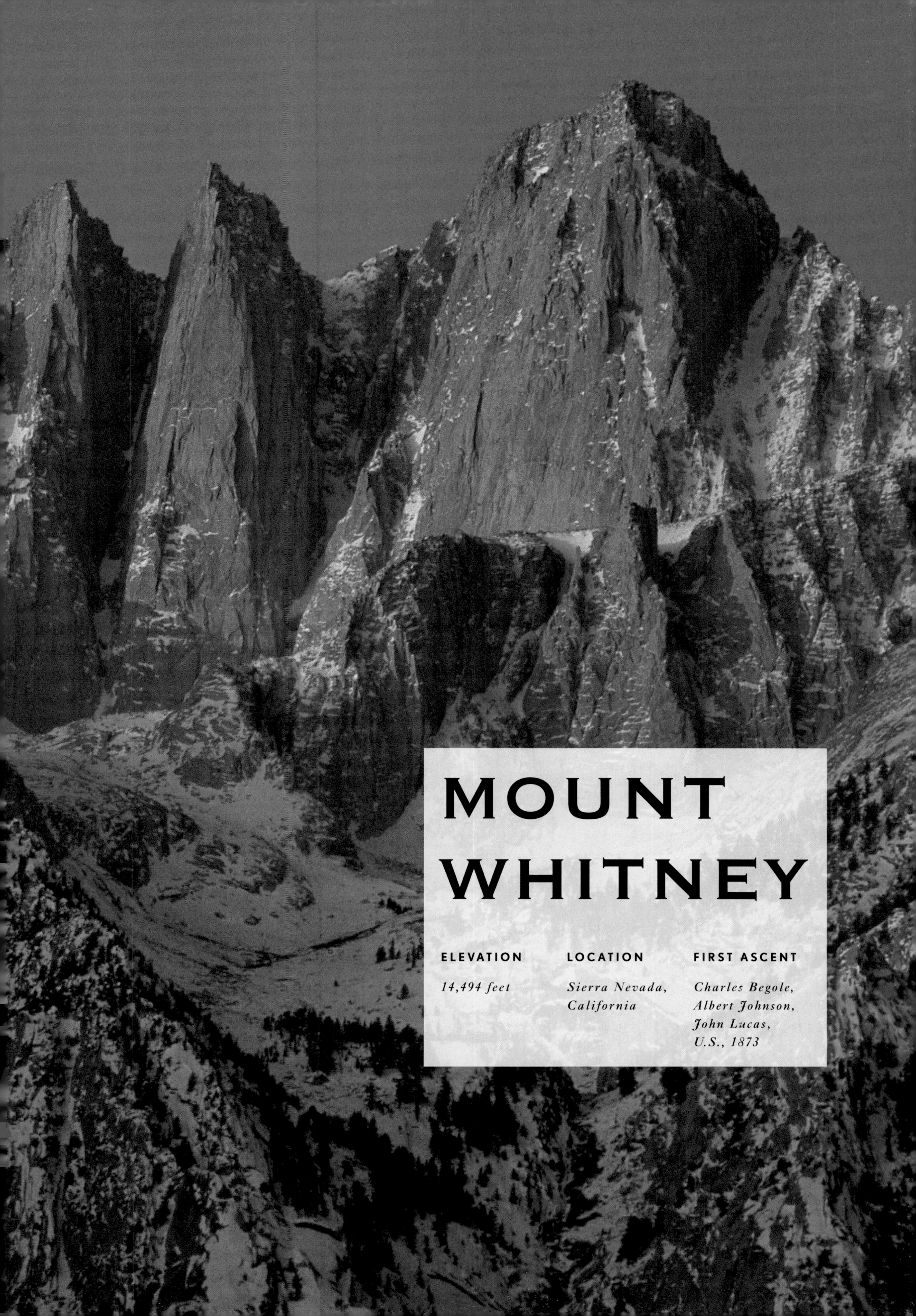

MOUNT WHITNEY

ELEVATION

14,494 feet

LOCATION

Sierra Nevada, California

FIRST ASCENT

Charles Begole, Albert Johnson, John Lucas, U.S., 1873

The three-room summit building, once used for high-altitude research by the Smithsonian Institution, is still maintained as an emergency shelter—and a windbreak for the summit register.

Y ou can be forgiven if traveling east of Mount Whitney you fail to pick out the highest point of the forty-eight contiguous states. Surveyor Clarence King failed—twice. In July 1864 King, then twenty-two, persuaded the California Geologic Survey to sponsor a first ascent of the recently discovered tallest mountain in the state, already named in honor of the Survey's leader, Josiah Whitney. Venturing into the rugged interior with a packer named Richard Cotter, King took aim at the highest peak in the area, and surmounting ice

encrusted rock near the top of the mountain, reached the summit. The view was breathtaking—and dismaying. Six miles to the south was a higher peak: the true Mount Whitney. King had, in fact, climbed nearby Mount Tyndall.

In 1871 King returned to settle the unfinished business. Starting this time from Owens

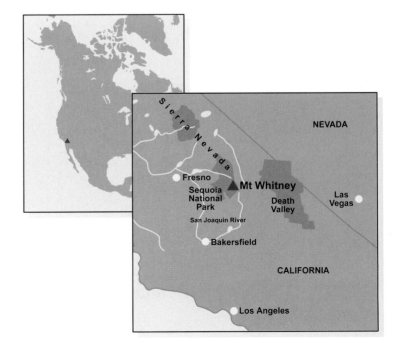

Valley, he climbed the most prominent peak to the west and finally felt justified in claiming the first ascent of Whitney. Wrong again. Two years later he learned from a party that had repeated his climb that he had summited not Whitney but a peak later named Mount Langley. That September King was back in the High Sierra, and this time he got it right. But he was too late to claim a first ascent. A month earlier a group of locals from Lone Pine had gone on a camping and fishing trip in the Sierras to escape the heat of Owens Valley, and three of them, Charles Begole, Albert Johnson and John Lucas, decided to climb Mount Whitney. Curiously, this group, too, wound up on an adjacent peak. But from this vantage point, a proper route was obvious, and early the following day they rode their horses to the southwest flank of the taller mountain and by noon were standing on the summit of the true Mount Whitney.

Since theirs was the first ascent, Begole, Johnson and Lucas took the liberty of naming the mountain Fisherman's Peak, a name favored by Owens Valley locals, who were only too glad to stick the unpopular Whitney with an inferior mountain. In the ensuing battle between pro- and anti-Whitney forces, a county assemblyman proposed legislation that would give official sanction to Fisherman's Peak as the mountain's name. When the state senate voted to call it Fowler's Peak, in honor of one of their own, the governor vetoed, calling the measure frivolous. "Whitney" won by default.

Foxtail pine, growing in the Sequoia National Park where Whitney is located, can, like the Bristlecone, live up to 2,000 years.

Opposite top: Sunrise Arch
frames Lone Pine Peak, right, and
the crenellated ridge of Whitney.

Surrounded by the stunning
California desert, Mount
Whitney rises out of a series of
granite towers without rival.
The Sierras are unique
mountains, whose geology is a
combination of phenomena
found nowhere else on Earth.
They have volcanoes, trap-door
ridges (ranges that rise steeply
on one side and gradually on the
other) and folded layers of rock
that result in a great variety of
terrain for climbers. Clarence
King described Whitney as "like
the prow of an ocean steamer";
others have described it as one
of the most dramatic and regal
peaks on the continent. No matter how you describe it, Whitney
and the Sierras are exceptional
in their creation, their appearance and their history.

Happily, Whitney is also
extremely accessible. Naturalist
John Muir, who first climbed
Whitney solo in October 1873,
wrote that "almost anyone able
to cross a cobblestone street in a
crowd may climb Mt. Whitney."
Indeed, one of the earliest trails
up the mountain was built to
let mules pack observatory
equipment to the summit.
Other trails on the southern and
western slopes of the mountain
call for perseverance, but
nothing more complicated
than scrambling up talus
couloirs and outcrops of rock.

The massive, 1,500-foot high
eastern face, however, presents a
wide range of challenging
routes. While some require
high-caliber technique, one is a
thrillingly exposed face climb

Left: Those looking for a more
challenging route up the mountain than Whitney's long but non-
technical west slope can follow
climber-photographer Galen
Rowell up buttresses on the
East Face.

National park service plaque reads:

NATIONAL PARK SERVICE
U.S. DEPARTMENT OF THE INTERIOR
MOUNT WHITNEY   ELEVATION 14,496.811 FT.
JOHN MUIR TRAIL — HIGH SIERRA TRAIL
SEPTEMBER 5, 1930
THIS TABLET MARKS THE CONSTRUCTION OF THE HIGHEST TRAIL
IN THE UNITED STATES, BEGUN IN 1928. IT WAS COMPLETED IN 1930
UNDER THE DIRECTION OF THE NATIONAL PARK SERVICE WORKING WITH
THE UNITED STATES FOREST SERVICE.

Far left: A climber checks his moleskin before suiting up for the twelve-mile hike back to the parking lot.

Left: The granite and quartzite rock of Mount Whitney form a wildly jagged ridgeline south of the main summit.

Climbers bivouacking on the summit get a front-row seat on the sunrise the following morning.

that can be done by capable climbers of moderate proficiency. In 1931 New Englander Robert Underhill, fresh from the North Ridge of the Grand Teton where he demonstrated the rockcraft he had learned in Europe, thought he saw a crack system on the right side of Whitney's East Face that would carry him to the summit. From Iceberg Lake at the north end of the face, Underhill's route scrambled to a pinnacle, the so-called First Tower, protruding from the lower section of the face. There he and three

California climbers who had joined him roped up and began a long, blocky ascent to the Second Tower. Their route, through a series of traverses, chimneys and dihedrals, led to a short ledge with a gap revealing a wildly exposed drop of 1,000 vertical feet—called, understatedly, the Fresh Air Traverse. From there a chimney and another traverse led them to The Grand Staircase, a series of ledges ending in an easy scramble to the summit. The Underhill party did the climb— Iceberg Lake to summit—in an

astonishing three hours and fifteen minutes. Even today, a fit team can take up to twice that time. The East Face is not a test of technique—beginning climbers have done harder moves. But for a test of composure, this is the route.

One of Whitney's beauties is the variety of its terrain. The summit on a summer afternoon frequently gathers together an amazing spectrum of talent. The mountain has something for everyone.

YVON CHOUINARD

1938 -

"Climbing is easy; writing is difficult."

HOME BASE ▪ *Ventura, California*

CLIMBING FEATS ▪ *first ascent of the North American Wall, Yosemite; South Face of Mount Watkins, Southwest Face of Fitzroy*

Yvon Chouinard was reared in a French Canadian family in Lewiston, Maine. Both at home and at the parochial school where he spent the first few years of his education, he was surrounded exclusively by French-speakers. As a result, when his family moved to Burbank, California, when he was seven, he felt isolated at the English-speaking school he attended. Yvon became a loner. He spent his time outdoors, fishing and exploring the Hollywood Hills on his bike. In high school he and his friends—"all the geeks. Couldn't dance, scared to death of girls " he once told a reporter—joined the California Falconry Club, which assisted in government bird counts by trapping and banding hawks. It was here that Chouinard discovered rock climbing and a new chapter in his life opened up.

When he was sixteen, he and some friends drove to the Wind River Range to climb Gannett Peak, Wyoming's highest mountain. Differing over which route to take they split up, and Chouinard soloed one of the mountain's faces. He was hooked. He drove north to the Tetons and persuaded two Ivy League college students that he was experienced enough to join them on a climb of Symmetry Spire. They put him in the middle of the rope, but when they both backed down from the crux, a wet and slimy chimney, they handed over a rack of pitons and invited Chouinard to lead it. "I didn't know what pitons were," Chouinard later admitted. "So I just faked it all and went up there and did the thing."

When Chouinard got better acquainted with climbing equipment, he didn't like what he saw. By age twenty-one he was fabricating his own carabiners and forging pitons of chrome molybdenum steel on a design invented by the legendary Palo Alto blacksmith-climber John Selathé. Chouinard sold the equipment directly to climbers from the back of his car and in 1964, after a two-year hitch in the Army, set up a fabricating facility, which, to be closer to his second passion, surfing, he moved to Ventura, California. The Great Pacific Iron Works (now Black Diamond) sprang from this operation and Patagonia, the apparel company that soon was setting the standard for outdoor gear, was close on its heels.

His first catalog, a one-page mimeographed price list, warned buyers not to expect speedy deliver during climbing season. Chouinard was not going to let a new company keep him away from the rocks—or the ice. He has done significant climbs from the Canadian Rockies to the towers of Tierra del Fuego. And wherever he goes he fiddles with equipment. It was discontent with European ice axes during a trip to France that led to one of Chouinard's most enduring designs, an axe in which the curve of the pick follows the arc of the axe as it is being thrust into the ice.

After almost being killed in an avalanche on a mountain in China, Chouinard swore off Himalayan size mountains. "You could be the world's greatest avalanche expert," he once said, "and if you're in the mountains much, you're going to get avalanched." Today, he has throttled back some, spending more of his time with his wife and family in Ventura or Moose, Wyoming, where they have a mountainside cabin Risk, however, seems to be imbedded in his genetic code. "There's no way I'm gong to stop taking risks," he has said. "Whatever confidence I have comes from striving, and I'm not going to sit back in my rocking chair and take it easy."

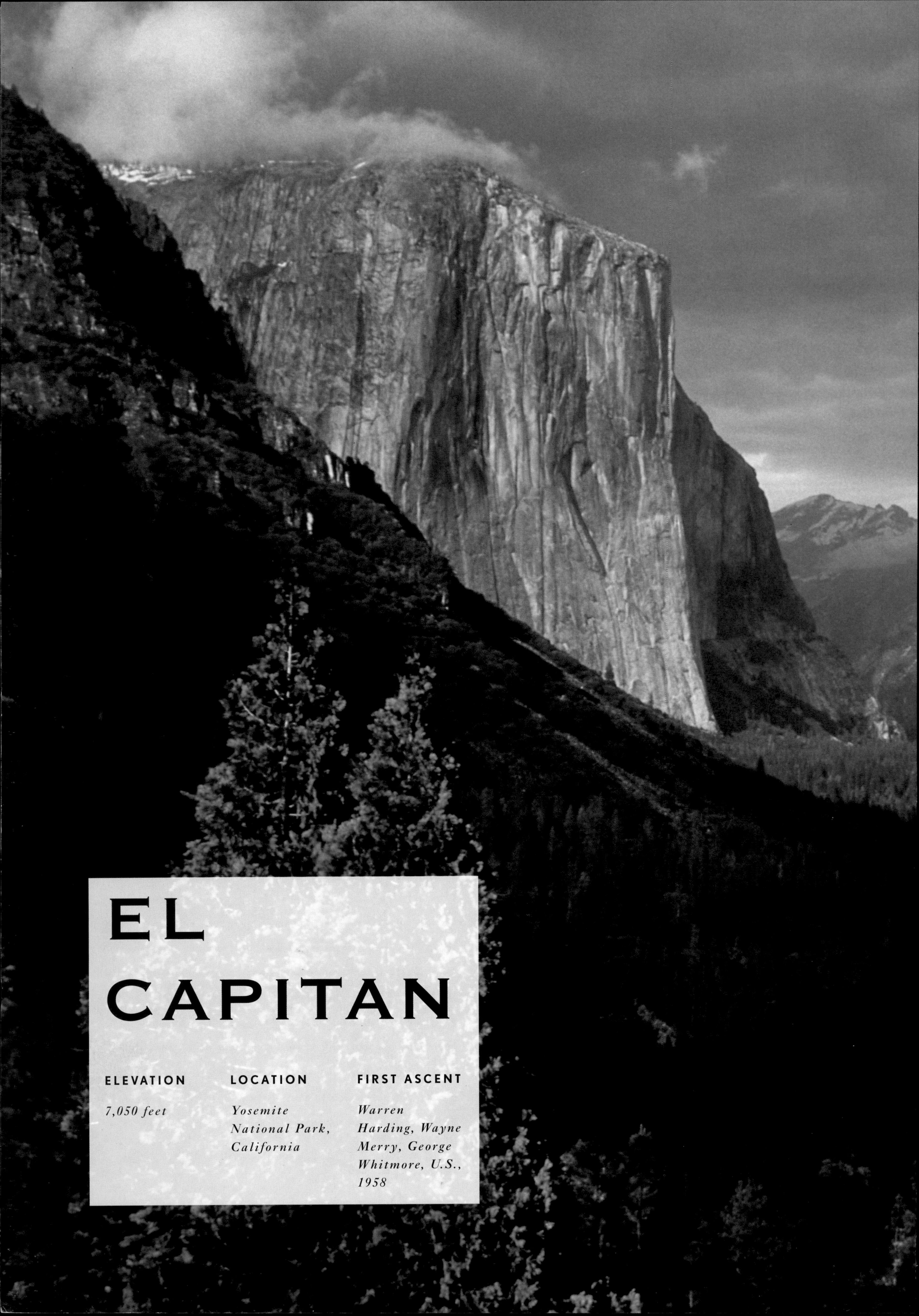

EL CAPITAN

ELEVATION	LOCATION	FIRST ASCENT
7,050 feet	*Yosemite National Park, California*	*Warren Harding, Wayne Merry, George Whitmore, U.S., 1958*

Yosemite pioneer Royal Robbins negotiates a chimney behind Texas Flake on the Nose route of El Capitan.

PROTECTION: *Also pro; devices such as nuts, pitons, bongs, Friends, Camalots and ice screws placed during a lead and connected via carabiners to the climber's rope so as to shorten the length of a potential fall.*

As storm clouds move in on El Cap, afternoon light illuminates Half Dome.

There is nothing else like it. El Capitan, with 2,900 nearly vertical feet of perfect granite glowing gray and orange in the California sunshine, haunts the dreams—and nightmares—of big wall aficionados the world over. Today, Yosemite Valley is a hurly-burly of commerce, gridlocked from May to September with visitors from every corner of the globe. But no amount of humanity can change the essential character of the valley: a bright green corridor of meadow, the Merced River a ribbon down its center and unworldly domes, spires and walls of rock—some of them adorned with bright spangles of waterfalls—on either side.

Climbers began to investigate the potential of Yosemite's incomparable granite in the 1930s, but two monolithic faces, Half Dome's famous northwest face and the awesome southern expanse of El Capitan, remained largely untouched. Huge overhangs and terrifying sections of blank wall put thoughts of ascent in the realm of giddy fantasy. The only way to negotiate these walls, it was believed at the time, would be to drill them full of bolt placements and hang them with ladders.

By the mid-1950s, however, Yosemite climbers had begun to imagine the unimaginable. In June 1957, after two years of unsuccessful attempts, Southern California climbers Royal

Robbins, Jerry Gallwas and Mike Sherrick caught other climbers off-guard—the first month of the season traditionally had been used to get into shape—by ascending the spectacular northwest face of Half Dome. The success of the Robbins team was greeted in the small, intensely competitive Yosemite climbing community with a mixture of admiration and chagrin. For twenty-eight-year-old Warren Harding, who himself had coveted a first ascent on Half Dome, the achievement was a signal to move on—to the dead-vertical, 3,000-foot buttress at the center of El Capitan: the Nose. At the time, it was the most awesome rock climbing challenge in America.

Harding was a less talented climber than Robbins, but they differed more sharply in one other respect. Robbins championed climbing as adventure: A route should be climbed in style, without rappels to the base for rest and resupply and without drilling into the rock for bolt placements unless it was absolutely necessary to connect natural weaknesses in the route. Harding had a less complex philosophy of climbing: Start at the bottom and get to the top. How one did it was hardly relevant. Necessary components of this

> I think most of us who are climbers recognize that we have a need for some sort of battle as part of our lives. I used to like getting up in the mountains and hiking around, but I knew I wanted something more exciting. I've said much more than that in the past, but I've come to see that it's that simple.
>
> —*Royal Robbins*

approach to the sport were patience, stamina and tenacity. As his ascent of the Nose was to demonstrate, Harding was supremely endowed with all three.

In early July, within a week of the Half Dome success, Harding had assembled his gear: 1,000 feet of rope, expansion bolts, a large assortment of pitons—including four jumbo-sized spikes fashioned from stove legs—and a winch for hauling it up the wall. Harding recruited Yosemite regulars Mark Powell and Bill ("Dolt") Feuerer, both of whom were also smarting from having been beaten to the Half Dome first ascent, and they headed for the base of the Nose.

A week of climbing showed them that they had seriously underestimated the enormity of the project. Fixing ropes to the high point of each day's progress allowed them to rappel to a campsite ledge for the night. But to begin anew the next day, they would have to re-ascend the rope, a laborious process in which two slings, one for each foot, were attached to the rope with mechanical ascenders designed to slip up the rope but not down it. The climb itself was strenuous almost without relief. The three men established a base of operations on Sickle Ledge 500 feet up. A thin crack system connected by

two pendulums—a maneuver in which the climber, hanging from a rope he has anchored to the rock above him, propels himself back and forth across the face until he has reached the new climbing position—led up to the awkwardly wide crack for which the stoveleg pitons had been designed. The stovelegs worked in their fashion but were damaged under constant placement and removal. And the three climbers, low on food and water and pounded by the southern California sun, were showing similar signs of abuse. They descended to the valley floor for rest and resupply. Once down, they were told they would have to wait until the end of the tourist season to go back up because drivers gawking at the specks on El Cap were creating monster traffic jams.

By the time they were allowed to resume the climb, Powell had injured an ankle, and without his leads progress slowed. Still, by Thanksgiving they had completed about a third of the climb, an accomplishment duly noted with the turkey and Chablis they had hauled to their bivouac ledge. The following spring they had to contend with foul weather and reached just beyond the half way point. After the enforced break for the tourist season, the group went back to their route, but they were soon riven with dissension. Powell and Feuerer dropped out, and George Whitmore, Wayne Merry and, temporarily, Rich Calderwood took their places. On November 11 Harding was approaching the last problem on the epic climb as daylight began to fail. In a night that has taken its

As this climber, in a hanging belay high on the Shield, demonstrates, a climb on El Capitan is among other things a severe test of equipment management.

Lynn Hill, one of the world's preeminent sport climbers, was the first person to climb the Nose without the use of aid.

place in Yosemite legend, he climbed through the darkness, placing 28 bolts to ascend a smooth overhanging wall and by the first light of the new day stepped off the climb and into a throng of journalists waiting at the summit.

Eventually the applause died down. As did the jeering. Many Yosemite climbers were displeased both with Harding's style—his team placed 125 bolts in all—and the publicity circus he had helped orchestrate. In the end, however, it was clear that Harding had ushered in a new era in rock climbing. Never again could it be said that face was unclimbable.

Two years later Harding's chief critic had formulated a response.

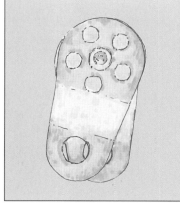

PULLEY: *a device used on multi-day rock climbs to assist in the raising of duffel bags containing equipment and provisions*

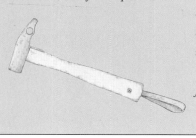

HAMMER: *a tool, slightly heavier than a carpenter's hammer, used for the placement and removal of pitons. On one end climber's hammers have a hole through which a carabiner and a length of webbing can be clipped, to add leverage and momentum to the act of "cleaning" protection devices from a rock face*

BOLTS: *Masonry anchors up to a half inch in diameter and three inches long used for aid and protection on rock faces in which there are no natural weaknesses for the placement of a piton or chockstone. Bolt holes are drilled into the rock with hand-hammered chisels or battery or gas powered drills. Bolts with a carabiner hanger attached are hammered, twisted or glued into the hole.*

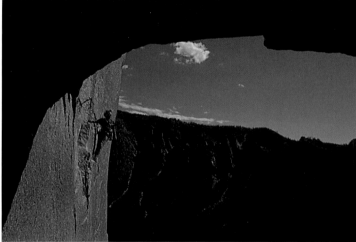

Warren Harding, who led the first ascent of the Nose, approaches his belayer on a pitch on the northwest face of Half Dome.

Conrad Anker pauses to take in the view during his one-day ascent of the Nose.

Royal Robbins, with Yosemite heavyweights Chuck Pratt, Tom Frost and Joe Fitschen, proposed to repeat the Nose climb, but in a single push without intermediate descents to the Valley. Seven days later they were at the summit.

Climbers negotiate the exceedingly thin Pancake Flake just beyond the Great Roof on the Nose, two pitches below a series of fine bivouac ledges.

Climbing the great face the sensible way—vicariously—from the El Capitan Meadow.

FREE SOLOING: *Rock climbing in which the climber dispenses with equipment of all kinds to complete a climb without protection.*

climber—male and female—to that time.

Usually, a first ascent follows the line of least resistance. Once a summit has been reached, mountaineers look for harder ways to the top. So too with Yosemite. Once the obvious routes had been done, climbers looked for variations, or like Hill, to climb free what had previously been done only with aid. Then, too, if someone links climbs in a new way—ascents of Half Dome and El Cap on the same day, for instance—it will be the talk of Camp 4, the Valley campground that the subculture of climbers has claimed as their own. Climbers from all over the world make the campground their home for months at a time, sometimes supporting their obsession for big walls by redeeming bottles and scrounging for discsarded food.

You needn't go for a new record to experience the thrill of the Nose. Almost from the ground up, the thirty pitches of the route offer breathtaking—if not mind-numbing—exposure. There are six ledges with space to accommodate two to four climbers and, between them, sections of rock that resonate with legend: the off-width Stoveleg Crack; the wild double pendulum around the crest of the buttress from Boot Flake; the huge overhang visible from the valley floor called the Great Roof. The Nose is no longer the most difficult route in Yosemite. But it has never been supplanted as the ultimate testpiece of big wall climbing.

Xavier Bongard, hanging under a severe overhang from one rope while he unsnags another, on an ascent of the Shield.

Camp 4 (Sunnyside to tourists) is the physical and spiritual center of climbing activities in the Yosemite Valley.

Yosemite's legendary Ron Kauk, one of America's most naturally gifted climbers, tunes up in the valley.

Robbins called it "the most magnificent and complete adventure of our lives." But knowing that history would overtake their feat, he predicted that the Nose would some day be climbed in five days or less. That day arrived in 1963 when the Nose was ascended in a little over three days. Inexorably, climbing times kept shrinking. In 1992, Canadian Peter Croft, born in the year the Nose was first ascended, climbed the famous route with Hans Florine in four hours and twenty-four minutes. Then in 1993 America's Lynn Hill succeeded with the most coveted remaining challenge in the valley: she made the first free ascent of the Nose, going from base to summit without ever once resorting to the aid that had assisted every

ZIPPER: *Climber jargon for the phenomenon of having a row of pieces of protection pull out under the weight of a falling climber.*

The Yosemite Valley is one of California's prize areas, and El Capitan is an instantly recognizable symbol for it, as evidenced in this antique postage stamp.

Camp 4

FROM MOUNTAIN, JULY 1969, BY DOUG ROBINSON

Climbers go to Yosemite Valley for the long routes, the clean granite and a social milieu like none other: Camp 4. Doug Robinson described it in 1969, and very little has changed since then.

Camp 4 is the physical and spiritual home of the Yosemite climbers. It lies near the geographical center of the Valley, where the old and stable talus, long since grown over with oaks and lichen, comes down from under the north wall to merge into the river-bottom meadows. It sits under a canopy of oak and pine. In spite of the spectacular setting, it has become the most trampled and dusty, probably the noisiest, and certainly the least habitable of all Yosemite's campgrounds. It is the only camp kept open all year, and was for many years the catch-all for pets, trailers, and other hard-to-classify and vaguely undesirable Yosemite visitors. Yet the Yosemite climbers will stay nowhere else.

By day, and in midsummer, it is "home" for tourist families, with their barking dogs and self-contained camping trailers complete with television sets. Toward evening, however, as the dust is being shaken from the last unwilling child before supper, the clanking horde begins to return. In twos and threes, talking and laughing—or with exaggerated weariness, set off by little sweat-etched lines on dusty foreheads—with their hands polished to a shiny slate color by carabiners, and with yet another pair of Granny Grundie pants hanging in tattered ribbons from their belts, they come to reclaim their campground. For, whether the tourists realize it or not, it is the climbers' campground. The campers have penetrated unaware into a magic circle; they stand undazed at the focus of a force field of tradition and emotion.

The National Park Service provides tables, and the climbers furnish them—their only vestige of home—in their own manner: oilskin tablecloth, stove, box of pots and pans, kerosene lantern, the inevitable red cover of Roper's *A Climber's Guide to Yosemite Valley*, various talismans—an onyx rain god, a broken one-and-a-half inch angle—and perhaps a battery record player with a collection of Beethoven and the Rolling Stones. An assortment of Klettershoes and boots, in various stages of decay, stand in a line under the table. The camp is completed by a collection of ropes, hardware, and hauling bags, piled against a tree; a bear-proof cache hanging overhead, and an open-air bed of pine needles—a comfortable several-months home. At peak season, in the spring and fall, almost half the campground is furnished in this fashion.

The boulders strewn around the campground probably first attracted climbers to Camp 4. Mostly small-hold face climbing and mantles, the boulder problems are basically unsuitable as training for the abundance of crack climbing on the walls. Yet they are quite popular; an hour of bouldering, while dinner is cooking, is common. The boulders serve other functions. They are a natural meeting place, where the lone climber can find a partner for a climb the next day. Also, for some reason, bouldering brings out the curiosity in tourist girls who come around to watch, chat, and perhaps get invited to a party—thus satisfying yet another perennial need of the Valley climbers.

Camp 4 evenings follow an irregular cycle of quiet nights and parties. The balmy evenings, a welcome by-product of the blistering hot days, banish any thought of seeking shelter. The climbers live outdoors for months at a time, and their parties are always held in the open air. There have, of course, been the legendary ones—as on the twentieth anniversary ascent of the Lost Arrow, when fourteen climbed the spire. They tyroleaned off, and were joined by thirty others, for beer and Teton tea around a fire on the rim. Parties are frequent, often spontaneous, and always unpredictable. By the time a party really gets rolling, it is late enough for the tourists to complain of noise—so the revelers must move out of camp or face the inevitable ranger. I remember one such evening when I had gone to bed early. I awoke to see Chuck Pratt, carrying a lantern and loudly calling directions, leading from the campground a ragged procession of figures clutching wine bottles. Bringing up the rear of the long line, quieter and rather more sure-footed than the rest, were two figures in Smokey-the-Bear hats.

Half a mile away, across the waving-grass meadows, the Merced River swings a wide arc, leaving Sentinel Beach in the quiet water of its lee. High above, Sentinel Rock watches all that transpires here, seeing without comment the climb-watching, girl-watching, dozing, swimming, and reading with toes wiggling in the sand. And sometimes, at night, the moon edges over Sentinel to see—brown tanned and wet-slick in its light, unselfconscious at last—dancers naked in the river, while part-full bottles of red wine list at crazy angles in the sand.

And the quiet evenings: a shirtsleeved group around a table; mugs of tea; endless discussions—of climbs, climbers, philosophy, religion, any and all subjects. And the silences. With the end of a thought trailing off into the lanternlight, the last of the transients shut up and gone to bed, the very darkness seems to take on a new dimension—a depth and silence that thickens before you until the night becomes palpable. The spiritual attachments, the feelings of home in this dusty campground and of companionship with one another, become almost visible for a few minutes at day's end, before we walk silently away to drop tired bodies on to pine needles in the dark ... to wake a few hours later, shivering slightly under oak-branch moonshadows, and crawl into the sleeping bag.

Morning: The sun climbs late into this deep valley, but in the morning light is already a promise of the heat of the day. The climbers are up early—not by Alpine standards, but compared to the tourists—and for a little while an expectant calm, broken only by the low familiar roar of a Primus making morning tea, hangs over the campground. Ropes, hammer, and swami are laid out on the end of the table. The hardware is racked, and hangs from its sling on a nearby oak branch. In this expectant hour, the climber's thoughts have already left Camp 4 and moved up the walls to the chosen problem of the day.

MOUNT LOGAN

ELEVATION

19,850 feet

LOCATION

St. Elias Mountains, Yukon Territory

FIRST ASCENT

Albert MacCarthy, Alien Carpé, William Foster, Fred Lambart, Norman Read, Andrew Taylor, U.S. and Canada, 1925

The Saint Elias Range rises up from the Yukon in dramatic, icy spires. Part of the Icefield Ranges, the Saint Elias Mountains are vast, continually snow covered and unique in their proximity to the ocean. Located just inside the Canadian border in the southwest corner of the Yukon Territory, Mount Logan not only is Canada's highest mountain but also has the largest summit plateau on earth—with eight peaks covering thirty square miles. Its glacial system, dominated by the Logan and Seward Glaciers, is more massive than any outside of Greenland or Antarctica. In the early part of the century, simply getting to the base of the mountain was a major undertaking, and the first ascent is still widely regarded as one of the most ambitious mountaineering achievements ever.

A party led by Albert

Mountaineering skis, which can be adjusted for either touring or downhill, speed progress over a high saddle on Mount Logan. Flagged wands are placed on the ascent to mark the route in case of whiteout on descent.

MacCarthy, a naval officer from Annapolis, Maryland who had moved to British Columbia in 1910, spent the summer of 1924 reconnoitering approaches to Logan across miles and miles of glacier that had never before had the imprint of a man's boot. MacCarthy determined that the ten tons of equipment and provisions—including three and a half tons of food for horses and dogs—would have to be cached during the winter while a river approach to the mountain was frozen over. It was cold work. During a February run, the sled harness on a team of horses

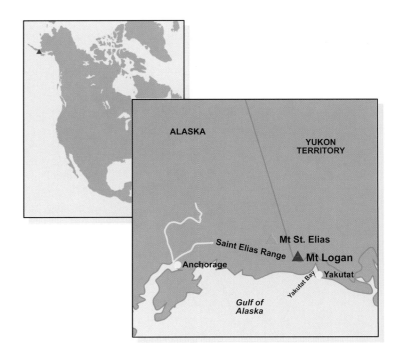

froze so solidly it could not be removed for two weeks.

During the ascent itself, weather conditions were hardly more hospitable. Starting out from McCarthy, Alaska on May 12, 1925, the eight-man climbing party took six days to reach the first of their supply caches eighty-eight miles away, and another eight days, carrying eighty-pound packs up the Logan Glacier, to advance to their furthest cache. From there, the siege of the mountain itself was finally under way. On June 6

the climbers reached a col between King Peak and Logan. But instead of being greeted by a smoothly sloping ridge to the summit, they encountered a thousand foot icefall, filled with viciously unstable blocks. Two days of carries stocked the col camp, and the party began an agonizingly slow ascent of the ridge. On June 20 they pushed through a storm to place their tents at 18,500 feet, at the time a record elevation for an alpine camp. Two days later, at 4:20 in the afternoon, six of the eight

climbers reached the nearer of Logan's two summits but were stunned to discover that the other summit, two miles distant, was clearly the higher one. Those final two miles took the haggard and exhausted climbers four hours to traverse.

The trip back to civilization was even more epic. The climbers remained for half an hour and had barely begun their descent when they were enveloped in clouds and wind-blown snow. They wandered in the whiteout for five hours and

Logan, with thirty square miles of summit plateau, contains more area covered by snow and ice than any other non-polar region in the world.

then waited out the darkness huddled pathetically in shallow holes they had hacked into the snow. It took another twenty-four hours to regain their high camp. By the time they had reached their base camp, some of them had been so badly frostbitten that their blackened skin had peeled back to reveal raw flesh. The eighty mile trip to McCarthy, part of it by crudely constructed rafts, took four days. In many respects it was astonishing that the party did not sustain more injury or even deaths. At any rate the mountain was not climbed again for twenty-five years when Norman Read, who was on the first ascent, and Swiss climber André Roch repeated the 1925 route.

Today, climbing parties generally fly from Haines Junction, west of Whitehorse, onto the Logan Glacier, putting them on a western shoulder of the mountain eighteen miles from the summit. Following the MacCarthy route, climbers ascend the western slopes to King Col, a saddle between Logan's main summit and the 17,125-foot King Peak. From there, an arduous ten mile traverse leads to Logan's summit. Ascents of the mountain can take four to five weeks even in settled weather. The weather on Logan, however, is rarely settled. Moist air driven in from the Pacific Ocean only sixty miles to the west is deposited on Logan in massive four-foot snowfalls. Canada's Kluane National Park, which administers the region, requires a climbing team of no less than four. They have only your interest at heart; safety in numbers has proven to be vital on Logan.

Logan's Central Peak, one of the mountain's eight summits, is the highest point in Canada and second only to Denali in North America.

Wrapping themselves in the flag,
Canadians celebrate a successful
ascent.

Logan's various ridges present a
challenging mix of snow, ice and
rock.

MOUNT ROBSON

ELEVATION

12,972 feet

LOCATION

Canadian Rocky Mountains, British Columbia

FIRST ASCENT

William Foster, Conrad Kain, Albert MacCarthy, Canada, 1913

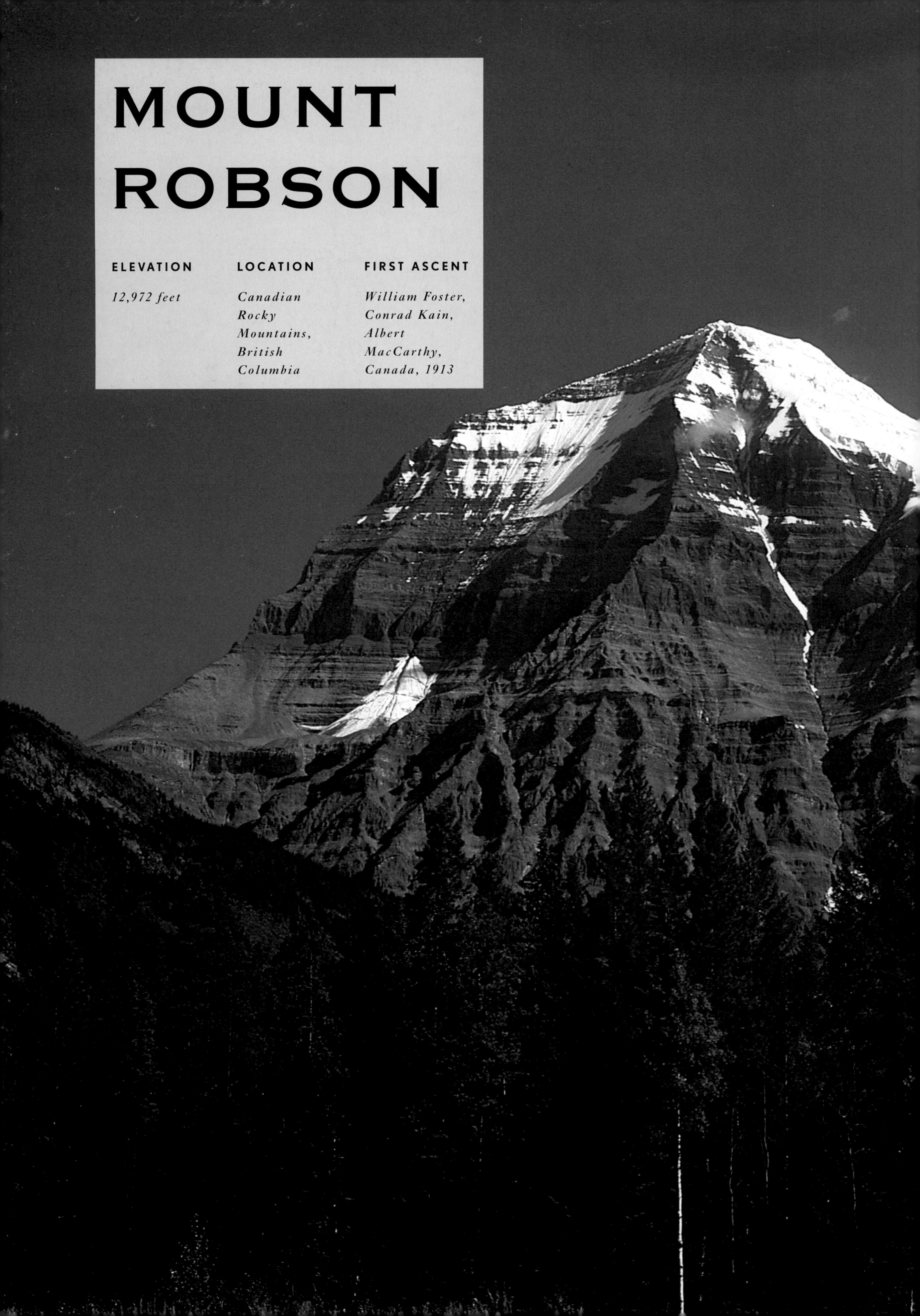

The very sight of Mount Robson intimidates. It looms nearly 10,000 feet above Kinney Lake to the south and 8,200 feet almost straight up over Lake Berg on the north. An ice-plastered monolith that is steep and stormy, Robson presents climbers with a classic Hobson's Choice: ascend one of its faces and risk being swept to the valley by an avalanche, or climb a ridge and contend with the "gargoyles"—strangely shaped ice pinnacles resembling "a host of white-cowled monks," in the words of one early climber, that block ascent. Robson's Emperor Face provides some of the most difficult climbing on the continent. Nowhere on the "Monarch of the Canadian Rockies," as it is called, is there an easy route, which may

If you're not hungry, you

brought too much food.

If you're not thirsty, you

brought too much water.

If you're not scared, you

brought too much gear.

If you made it to the top,

the route was too easy

anyway.

—*Climber's adage*

account for its dual status as one of Canada's most prized and least attempted challenges.

None drawn to the steep slopes of the pyramid-shaped mountain have been more obsessed by it than the Reverend George B. Kinney, a Canadian climber who joined Robson ascent parties in 1907 and 1908 and was turned back both times. The following year Kinney, in the grip of the mountain and unable to rest until he had made another attempt, set off on his own to trek the 200 miles from Edmonton to the foot of Robson. More than once, he almost lost everything in numerous crossings of the swollen Athabasca and

Top: A Canadian postage stamp showing Mount Robson from the shore of Berg Lake, whose brilliant turquoise color can be attributed to glacial silt that is suspended in the water.

ALSO KNOWN AS · Yuh-hai-has-kuh: "Mountain of the Spiral Road"

Rocky Rivers. Eventually he was joined by a young prospector named Donald Phillips, and the two continued together. On the mountain itself they were repeatedly thwarted by storms, avalanche and rockfall. Rocks, Kinney wrote, "fell from cliffs so high above us, that seemingly they came right out of the sky; without any warning they would scream past us in awful flight, to be engulfed in the silence below, for we could hear them strike nothing either coming or going." Kinney's claim that he and Phillips had reached the summit in the midst of a storm was later disavowed by Phillips, who admitted that a dome fifty or sixty feet high, too dangerous to climb, lay ahead of them when they decided to turn back.

That left the first ascent open to William Foster, Albert MacCarthy (who would later succeed in an epic assault on Mount Logan) and Canada's most accomplished guide, Conrad Kain. With the completion of the Trans-Canadian Railroad in 1913, the expedition was able to reach within five miles of the mountain by train. Kain chose the East Face, on the opposite side of the mountain from Kinney's attempt, and chopped steps on a zigzag route that reached high up the South Ridge. There, the party encountered the mountain's infamous gargoyles, requiring more of Kain's furious step cutting. As

Above: Climbers heading for the north and west faces of Robson pass Emperor Falls, an impressive sight on the Robson River that has been visited by Canadians for decades.

A mountaineer pauses during the walk-in to survey Mount Robson, which with its combination of steepness and storms may turn back a greater percentage of climbers than any other mountain

they reached the summit, finishing the most outstanding Canadian climb to that time, Kain, in a much quoted bon mot, turned to his clients and said, "Gentlemen, that's as far as I can take you."

A few days later, another of Robson's dramatic profiles came under assault. Swiss guide

ARÊTE: *French for ridge. Often connotes a sharp ridge with steep sides; on rock cliffs, an outside corner.*

Summiters on Robson greet a passing airplane.

Walter Schauffelberger with two clients took aim at the intimidating Southwest Ridge that leads elegantly right up to the summit pinnacle. About 1,500 feet from the top it is joined by a more westerly spur, forming an inverted V that has come to be known as the Wishbone Arête. In mid-August Schauffelberger led his party across a flank of the West Face to its southernmost edge and then proceeded up the ridge. They climbed the shattered limestone of the lower ridge and made their way over steeper rock to the apex of the V where gargoyles prevented them from going any higher. By that time,

A climber battens down the flaps on Robson's summit ridge as weather moves in.

Rising from the south end of Berg Lake is Robson's awe-inspiring Emperor Face, 8,000 feet of mixed climbing that is one of the most daunting challenges in the Rockies.

however, they had been on the ridge for fourteen hours and darkness had overtaken them. They bivouacked on a narrow shelf only 500 vertical feet below the summit, buffeted by a howling wind and coated with ice until the early sub-Arctic sun lit the route back down. Though they had failed to finish the climb because of weather, they got close enough to demonstrate the feasibility of one of the most stunning alpine routes in North America.

Over the next four decades thirty attempts were made on the Wishbone. None succeeded until 1955 when Don Claunch, an ice-climbing ace from Washington State, who had been driven off the route by storms two years previous, decided to try it again. "A feeling of admiration,

irresistible attraction and cold hostility is produced in the ambitious climber gazing at this spectacle," Claunch later observed. At a camp at the base of the mountain he recruited two Southern Californians: rock jock Mike Sherrick and medical student Harvey Firestone. By the end of the first day they had gained a broad step a little below the top of the V. They pitched the tent they had carried, and having left sleeping bags at the base of the mountain, relied on the heat of a candle for warmth during the night. A second day took them onto the gargoyle encrusted final ridge, but night caught them 300 feet short of the summit, and they spent another night, sleepless this time, fighting off the brutal cold. The final day, with Claunch

leading an ice-packed 60 degree chute and then a vertical headwall, brought them to the summit. It was, wrote Sherrick, "the greatest adventure, and the longest ordeal, of our lives."

Robson's final holdout was the fearsome North Face in 1978, a dangerous wall that can only be considered during stretches of fair weather when snow on the face has become well consolidated. Climbers intending to repeat this climb have been known to walk into a base camp at Berg Lake, take one look at the face and walk right back out again. There is no honor lost in being defeated by Robson; it is an extraordinary and powerful mountain that has been repulsing attempts on its summit for decades.

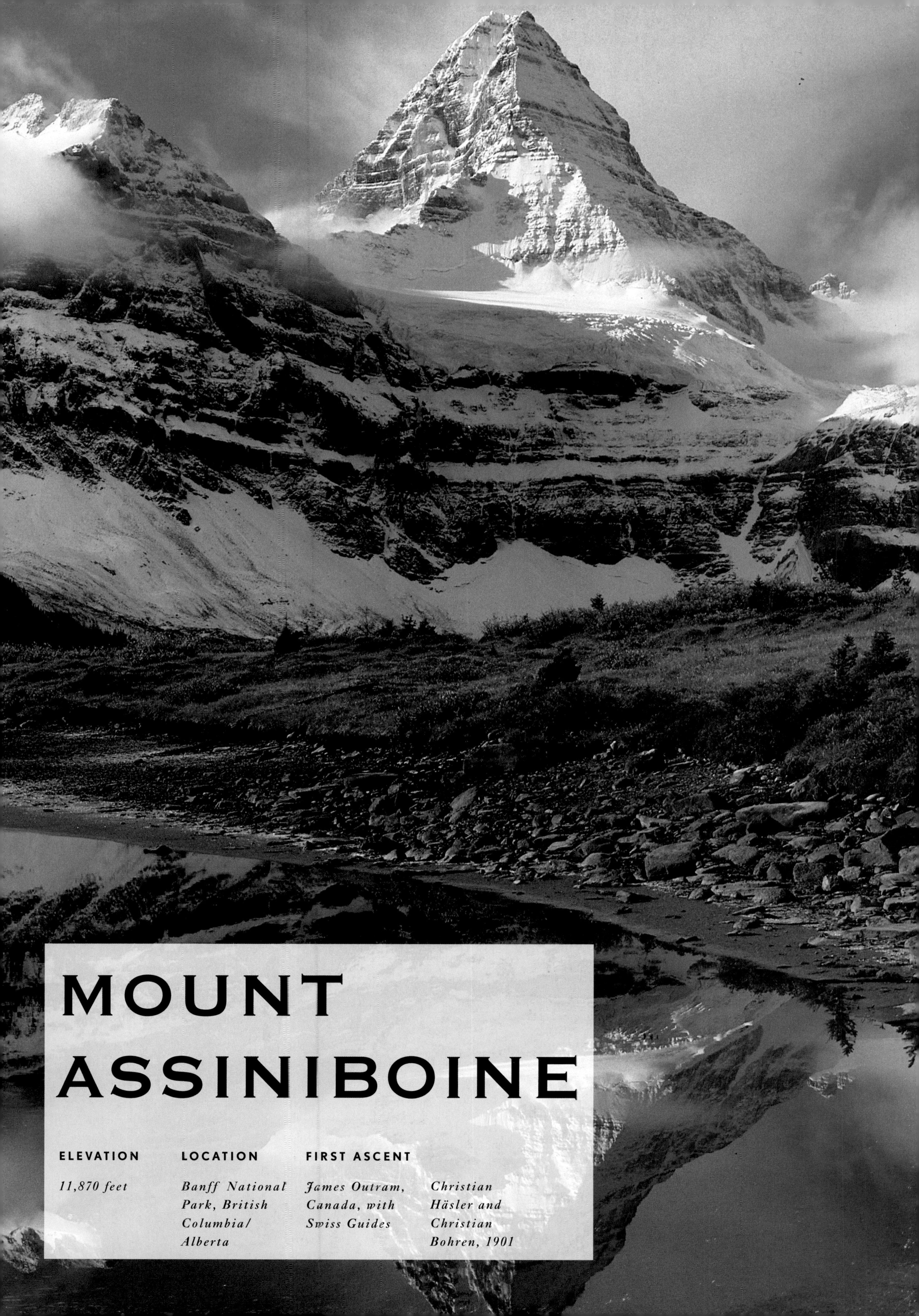

MOUNT
ASSINIBOINE

ELEVATION	LOCATION	FIRST ASCENT	
11,870 feet	*Banff National Park, British Columbia/ Alberta*	*James Outram, Canada, with Swiss Guides*	*Christian Häsler and Christian Bohren, 1901*

The tallest mountain in the southern Canadian Rockies, Assiniboine has a sculptured look, smooth limestone faces that are joined along classically elegant ridges. Surrounded by high alpine lakes and the spectacular beauty for which the Rockies are known, Assiniboine bears more than a passing resemblance to the Matterhorn—with one important exception. Unlike the hordes that line up at the base of the Hörnli Ridge of the famous Swiss Alp, midsummer traffic on Assiniboine's fine ridges and faces seldom exceeds four parties. Assiniboine, however, was among the first North American peaks to capture the attention of the English, who began to look to the Canadian Rockies for adventure once the Canadian Pacific completed its transcontinental railway in 1885. By 1900, Assiniboine still had not been climbed.

The mountain, named after the Assiniboine, a Sioux tribe whose name means "one who cooks by the use of stone," was first approached by Canadian explorers Tom Wilson and R. L Barrett in 1893. Years later, during

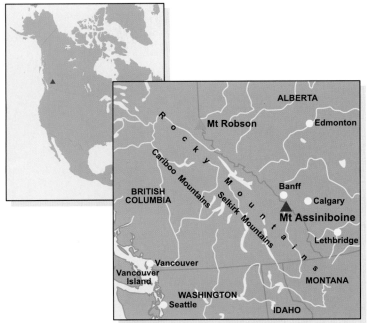

a trip to the Himalaya, Barrett wrote, "K2 at 28,000 feet didn't look as high and imposing and terrible as Assiniboine." In 1901 Walter Wilcox, also of Canada, came within 1,000 feet of Assiniboine's summit before he was turned back by a fusillade of avalanches. That was the summer Edward Whymper had elected to visit the Canadian Rockies, and the locals assumed that the world's

most famous mountaineer would surely claim their most celebrated summit. But Whymper, sixty-two at the time, chose not to risk his reputation on a highly visible defeat and moved on to more obscure objectives. He was joined by a young James Outram, a vicar in the Church of England who had suffered a nervous breakdown and had earlier immigrated to the Canadian Rockies in hopes it would improve his health.

In late August word of Wilcox's failure on Assiniboine reached the Whymper camp, which had hired an outfitter named Bill Peyto. Peyto had been to the base of Assiniboine six years before and confidently declared that he could lead a party there again. Outram took him up on the offer and was taken, with two of

Whymper's Swiss guides, to the foot of the North Face of the famous pyramid with only a day or two left before snows would end the climbing season. The three men, climbing westward, crossed one col and ascended another. From there they could view the southwest face, a long succession of steps intersected by gullies. They began to ascend the face, at one point scrambling through a cleft in a cliff, when a thick fog descended on them, forcing a retreat to their base camp. The mists cleared during the night and the team made a break for the summit the following morning. In six hours they were on the top of the mountain. Assiniboine, the invincible, had been conquered. Outram capped his triumph by traversing the summit and

Top: The normal route to the summit skirts Magog Lake, gains the saddle by way of a ramps right of the snow-filled gully, then ascends the North Ridge (parallel to the ridge on the right hand skyline).

Herds of elk forage throughout Banff National Park.

descending by way of the North
Ridge. The following day the
weather broke and a blanket of
snow closed off the mountain.

Today, Outram's descent route
is the most popular way to climb
Assiniboine. The approach begins
at the dead end of a rutted road
some thirty-two miles south of
Banff, Alberta. From there it is a
full day's walk along Bryant Creek
and over Wonder Pass to a
mountain lodge at Lake Magog.
Most routes on Assiniboine pro-
ceed from Hind Hut, which lies
two to three hours above a headwall to the north of the lake. To
get there, climbers must take care
to circumvent the gully that provides the shortest line to the hut
but also serves as a funnel for ice
chunks from the snow field above.

Most of the North Ridge,
which starts west of the hut, is a
pleasant scramble up the mountain's limestone bedrock. The
route (first ascent, 1903) is twice
interrupted by short pitches of
vertical rock. The Red Band, and
higher up, the Grey Band, require
moderate technical ability and for
most, roped protection. For
parties preferring a mixed climb,
the North Face route (put in by a
foursome led by Yvon Chouinard
in 1967 but requiring little of his
legendary expertise on ice) follows
a prominent snowfield and couloir
up the middle of the face and
gains the North Ridge above the
Grey Band. Both climbs, from
hut to summit and return, require
six to eight hours in good weather.
A snow covering increases the
time considerably.

The world is full of mountains
that are higher, harder, more
complex. Assiniboine comes by its
preeminence through a classical
simplicity. It has a straightforward
purity that will always be in style.

**Because of its resemblance to the
Matterhorn, Assiniboine was
coveted intensely by mountaineers
before its first ascent in 1901. Here,
the mountain rises majestically,
north of Magog Lake.**

FRED BECKEY

1923-

"The first ascent thing only matters . . . if I think it's a pretty good route, a classic line and is attractive from a climber's point of view."

HOME BASE ▪ *Seattle, Washington*

CLIMBING FEATS ▪ *First ascents of Mount Hunter, Mount Deborah, North Face of Edith Cavell in Canada; dozens of new routes in the Cascade Range; noted mountaineering author*

John Williams, Fred Beckey and Dave Statzman

Outer Space, Cat Burglar, Tomahawk, Phantom . . . they all have one thing in common: They are peaks, pinnacles and walls in the Cascade Range named by Fred Beckey. If you are on a mountain in the American West, Alaska or Canada, chances are good that Fred Beckey was there before you—or anyone else, for that matter. In a career that began while he was still in his teens, Beckey has bagged hundreds of first ascents in North America, though he has reportedly never kept count himself. Among them: Alaska's Mount Hunter, Mount Deborah and the northwest buttress of Denali; in Canada, Devil's Thumb, the winter ascent of Mount Robson, the east face of Snowpatch Spire in the Bugaboos, the north face of Edith Cavell; in the Cascades he was first up Liberty Bell and Rainier's Mowich face. His footprints are all over Wyoming's Teton and Wind River Ranges.

Born in West Seattle, Washington, Beckey was still a boy when he began scrambling up peaks on his own in the surrounding Cascades. Alarmed, his parents signed him up with the local Boy Scout troop to teach him outdoors fundamentals. At fifteen he joined the Seattle Mountaineers, where he learned technical climbing and four years later decided he was ready to take on a

serious challenge. In July 1942 he and his brother Helmy, not quite seventeen, traveled to British Columbia to climb Mount Waddington, which at 13,260 feet has no easy route to the summit. At the time, in fact, the first ascent of the mountain by Fritz Wiessner and William House in 1936 had never been followed. To the astonishment—and initial disbelief—of the Canadian climbing establishment the teenagers succeeded. Fred Beckey had discovered his calling

During World War II, he served with the U.S. Army Mountain Troops in Colorado, then attended the University of Washington. In the years since he has worked as a salesman in the printing and advertising industries and written a masterful and comprehensive book which covers peaks all over North America. But mostly he has climbed, perfecting the art of living out of his car as he traveled from one new challenge to another. His critics call Beckey obsessed and driven, and even his friends, inured to middle of the night phone calls recruiting them for a climb, consider him single-minded. "I'm not as competitive for getting first ascents as I used to be," Beckey recently told an interviewer. But in his heyday a tee-shirt he once wore for an ad campaign said it all: "Beware of Beckey."

BUGABOO SPIRE

ELEVATION

10,420 feet

LOCATION

Purcell Range, British Columbia

FIRST ASCENT

Conrad Kain with clients Albert and Bess MacCarthy, John Vincent, Canada, 1916

y the turn of the 20th century the European Alps had all been climbed. The great granite walls of Yosemite had long been enshrined in a National Park. But the Bugaboos, a wall of vertiginous spires that provide some of the cleanest, airiest climbing to be found anywhere on earth, remained untouched. In 1910 surveyor Arthur Wheeler, Canadian explorer Thomas Longstaff and a young mountain guide named Conrad Kain, who had immigrated from Austria to Canada the year before, ventured into British Columbia's Purcell range to find the so-called Spillimacheen Peaks. Hidden away in an area that had been traveled by prospectors but never documented, they saw a vast glac-

ier crowded with steep towers that looked all but unclimbable.

A half century later the spires would become a rock-climbing mecca, a paradise of clean, hard granite with towers as sharp and astonishing as the aguilles of Chamonix, France. For skiers the Bugaboos would come to be prized as the powder snow central of helicopter skiing. But six years passed before the wilderness was visited again. Then in August 1916 Kain returned with longtime client Albert MacCarthy—they had done a first ascent of Mount Logan together three years earlier —MacCarthy's wife Bess and John Vincent. Kain, who had spotted what looked like climbable ridges during the earlier trip, wanted to put his speculations to the test. Indeed, two of the towers

Looking south from the summit of Bugaboo Spire: Howser Spire and then a wilderness of snow and granite.

One of the most beautiful and charming spots I have seen.

—Canadian guide Conrad Kain on his first visit to the Bugaboos

offered little resistance. Then Kain turned his attention to Peak No. 3, as he called it, a thumb of granite in the center of the giant rock garden; the ascent of which looked dubious at best. But to the surprise and delight of the four–

> **GENDARME:** *A pinnacle that sits astride a ridge, frequently impeding passage on that ridge.*

From a lake near Boulder Camp, Pigeon Spire pokes insolently through the permanent snows of Bugaboo Glacier.

some, the ridge, an entertaining mixture of cracks, corners and chimneys, went smoothly for the first 1,200 feet. Then, they encountered the gendarme: a fifteen-foot pinnacle of rock that utterly closed off the upper 400 feet of the ridge. As Kain studied it, MacCarthy, according to some accounts, referred to the obstacle as a "veritable bugaboo," employing the term prospectors used for mining leads that turned out to be dead ends—and thus Peak 3 became Bugaboo Spire.

After due deliberation, Kain decided to attack the gendarme by a thin ledge on its west side. For thirty minutes, he edged out toward a crack system that would carry him over the gendarme, but he couldn't work out the final move into the crack. At last he gave up and returned to his party. Next, he tried the thin cracks on the almost vertical face, but again to no avail. At that point the group could have honorably turned around, but Kain would not surrender. The crack system of the west face was the key, he decided, and he ventured again and again to reach it. At long last there was a call from above. It had taken an hour and a half to climb seventy feet, but Kain had turned the gendarme, and the group was soon on the summit. Kain later called the ridge climb the hardest he had ever done.

With today's improvements in boots and equipment, Kain's route on the South Ridge of Bugaboo Spire is a rare classic that can be treasured by competent climbers who have mastered the fundamentals. Boulder Camp, base of operations for climbs in the Bugaboos, lies a short hike beyond

Right: Just south of Bugaboo, the clean granite of Snowpatch Spire forms a handsome pyramid.

A mountain goat wanders onto the glacier, below Howser and Bugaboo Spires.

a back road dead end thirty-four miles south of Parson, B.C., which is itself an easy drive from the resort town of Banff. From the camp, climbers ascend to the col between Bugaboo and the neighboring Snowpatch Spire—a one to two-hour hike for which crampons and ice axe are useful equipment. The first half of the climb is mostly a scramble up the right side of the ridge to its crest about mid way up. Then two chimneys and a ramp lead to the infamous gendarme. Today's climbers avoid Kain's thin ledge and follow a diagonal crack on the south face of the gendarme to friction slabs well above the ledge. More scrambling above the gendarme leads to a steep gully and then the summit and a view of an austere glaciated wilderness with peaks in every direction.

With morning shadows sharp as snow crystals, a climber crosses talus to the base of Bugaboo Spire.

CHOCKS: *(also nuts) Specially shaped chunks of aluminum or other metals of graduated sizes, threaded with a wire or rope loop so as to accept a carabiner, that are slotted into cracks during a rock climb to serve as protection.*

Chocks have generally replaced pitons (the placement and removal of which eventually scar and widen the cracks in which they are used), and their employment is regarded as clean climbing.

The gendarme on the South Ridge, "a veritable bugaboo," as the first ascent party called it, is climbed via a crack system to high on its west-sloping roof.

MOUNT ASGARD

ELEVATION	LOCATION	FIRST ASCENT
3,500 feet	*Auyuittuq National Park, Baffin Island, Canada*	*Paul Braithwaite, Dennis Hennek, Paul Nunn and Douglas Scott, England 1971*

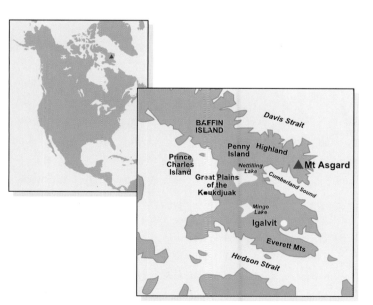

You may never have been to Mount Asgard, but there is a good chance you have seen it. In the opening sequences of *The Spy Who Loved Me* (James Bond thriller No. 10) Roger Moore's stunt double, accomplished climber Rick Sylvester, pursued by high-speed snowmobiles, skis off a high plateau and into a freefall as he pulls the ripcord on his parachute—that was Asgard.

Thirty miles inland from Overlord, an Inuit village on the east coast of Baffin Island,

An Inuit cairn on Frobisher Bay, on the southern end of Baffin Island.

Asgard's nearly identical north and south peaks jut into the Arctic sky like the towers of a medieval fortress. The mountain is among the loneliest on earth—given its remoteness and the challenge of its sheer walls, it's not surprising that it is also one of the most rarely climbed. As of the beginning of 1998, Asgard's granite towers had only nine ascents—each of them by a different route.

Near the Arctic Circle, inlets, frozen over until late spring, provide highways for snowmobiles and unlimited space for tent sites.

The Asgard chronicles begin in 1953 when a Swiss team ascended the steep couloir between the two towers. Unfortunately, their ascent ended there. Eighteen years later, a quartet of British climbers, Paul Braithwaite, Dennis Hennek, Paul Nunn and Doug Scott, claimed the first ascent of the higher North Tower by way of its Southwest Buttress, a climb of

severe difficulty but hardly Asgard's ultimate test. That honor falls to the breathtakingly vertical Northwest Face. Scott and Hennek looked at the dauntingly sheer face, but then, unwilling to drill the numerous holes the smooth rock would have required to bolt in protection, backed off.

That left the gate open for what is considered a truly historic

achievement in big wall climbing. In 1975 Charlie Porter, already the possessor of a passel of first ascents on Yosemite's El Capitan, flew to Baffin and spent the month of August hauling food and equipment the thirty miles from the coast to the foot of Asgard. There, he was joined by Sylvester, the Bond double, and another accomplished climber named Shari McVoy. The three set to

Given the seemingly unlimited quantity of fine granite and the isolation of Auyuittuq National Park, where Mount Asgard is located, first ascents are there for the picking.

Spiky and turreted rock characterizes the pristine wilderness on Baffin Island.

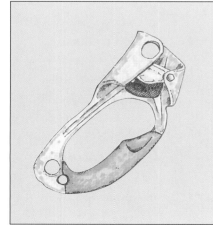

ASCENDER: *a device which, like the Prusik knot, slides freely when pushed up the rope to which it is attached but grips the rope tightly when weighted downward. Ascenders (see also Jumar) provide protection and aid on big wall and alpine climbs and are also used for hauling gear.*

Asgard looms above Arctic meadows of snow like a medieval fortress.

work solving the immense difficulties of the Northwest Face. They had worked their way two-thirds up the face, when storms hit the mountain and they had to back off, descending by way of fixed ropes. When Sylvester and McVoy, their food supplies running out, had to leave the mountain, Porter was left one-on-one with the face. Even before the weather settled he was back on it, regaining the previous high point. Battered by freezing rain and cold, he had to lick ice off of his ascenders just so they could grip the rope. After nine days of treacherous solo climbing, Porter stood on the slanting roof of Asgard's summit. But the cold had taken its toll on his feet, which swelled with frostbite. He, too, had run out of food. By the time he stumbled back to Overlord, he hadn't eaten for ten days.

For anyone wanting to repeat Porter's heroics, the first chal-

lenge will be to get to the mountain. Only one airline flies to Baffin, so ticket prices are steep—up to $1,200 round trip from Montreal or Ottawa. The twenty-mile trip from Pangnirtung, an Inuit village on the island's east coast, to Overlord by boat adds upwards of $100 per person. The thirty miles up the Weasel River to the foot of Asgard are free—Innuit outfitters will ferry parties to Overlord but do not hire out as porters, thus the carry to base camp entails either multiple trips or heavily-laden packs or both. Given the arduous walk-in— along a trail that crosses the Arctic Circle—it helps that the Weasel Valley serves up an utterly unique landscape. On either side are bleak granite towers separated by hanging glaciers, and on the floor of the valley, a riot of poppies, saxifrage and other wildflowers. The glacial

runoffs, some of which have to be forded thigh-deep, also provide distraction. The icy waters induce a painful numbing and thawing cycle for each crossing.

The time to visit Asgard is from late June to August, during which temperatures range into the upper 50s, and the sun virtually never sets. During the summer the ice pack on the Pangnirtung Fjord is sufficiently dispersed to allow boat travel to Overlord. In April and May the trip can be done on snowmobile. Asgard is still one of the most isolated mountains in the world. But if the Auyuittuq National Park ever gets congested, you can always travel further up the east coast of Baffin to Sam Ford Fjord, which is lined with dozens of 4,000-foot walls that have never been climbed, or beyond to 150 miles of peaks that have barely been charted.

MOUNT WASHINGTON

ELEVATION	LOCATION	FIRST ASCENT	
6,288 feet	White Mountains, New Hampshire	Darby Field, England, with two unknown	Native Americans, 1642

No longer in use, the Mount Washington meteorological observatory—the place where the highest wind velocity on earth was recorded in 1932—was housed in this clapboard summit building.

Being nineteen with strong legs—and stupid—was the right combination at the right time.

—Austrian skier Toni Matt describing his victory in the 1939 American Inferno ski race in which he schussed the headwall of Washington's Tuckerman's Ravine

Many geologists believe that the White Mountains of New Hampshire once soared to Himalayan heights but have been worn down by glacial action and erosion in the intervening millennia. Today, however, Mount Washington is a lot more than a once mighty has-been. Its proximity to the densely populated New York-Boston corridor makes it one of the most popular mountains in the world. And its diminished height notwithstanding, it has a history of turning against hikers and climbers with lethal ferocity.

Its main weapon is its wind. On April 12, 1934, a young radio operator named Alex MacKenzie was monitoring the gauges at Mount Washington Observatory when the wind began gusting to160 m.p.h. Then, as MacKenzie recalled it, the windows in the weather station hut seemed to bulge outward and the wooden structure, held to the summit with chains, shuddered. Next came the "Big Wind," as it came to be known, pushing the anemometer at the station to a reading of 231 m.p.h., to this day the highest wind velocity ever recorded. Winds reach hurricane force on the summit on average 100 days a year, and the wind-chill is as severe as that encountered in Antarctica. As the highest point for thousands of miles in every direction, and at the crossroads of three different weather systems, Washington gets extreme weather of every kind. During a three-day period in February 1969, eight feet of snow was dumped on the summit, and in June 1945 the temperature dipped to minus 8 degrees Fahrenheit. Some of the flora in the Alpine Meadows, east of the summit dome, can be found no other place south of the Arctic Circle.

Fortunately for Darby Field, weather on Washington was mild on the day in April or May 1642 when he made the first recorded ascent of any mountain in America. What is known of the climb comes from the journal of then Massachusetts Governor John Winthrop, who was told of the outing either by Field or a third party. An émigré from England to Boston in 1636 who later moved to New Hampshire, Field approached "the white hill," as it was called in the Winthrop journal, from the southeast and passed through a Native American settlement near the foot of the mountain. Some of the Native Americans "accompanied

Cairns, spaced closely enough to be followed from one to the next in a whiteout, guide hikers across a boulder slope to the head of Nelson Crag on Mount Washington.

The "Old Man of the Mountains," in a notch west of Mount Washington, has come to symbolize the state's crotchety conservatism.

him within eight miles of the top," wrote Winthrop, "but durst go no further, telling him that no Indian ever dared to go higher, and that he would die if he went."

In fact, the indigenous people of the region regarded the White Mountains as sacred. In an ancient, Noah's Ark-like myth, it was said that the land had been flooded, killing all but two of the tribe, who survived by escaping to the mountain heights. It was from these two that the earth was repopulated. "They had a superstitious veneration for the

VERGLAS: *A thin and treacherous coating of ice on rock.*

summit, as a habitation of invisible things; they never ventured to ascend it," Jeremy Belknap, wrote in a 1792 history of New Hampshire. In the end, two Native Americans continued with Field and not only survived but enjoyed an uncommonly calm visit to the summit.

Field guided a second party up the mountain a month later and brought down what he erroneously thought were diamonds. The mountain's true asset, it turns out, is its capacity to enliven generation upon generation of hikers and climbers. Every year from Memorial Day to Labor Day, thousands of people climb Washington and the adjacent Presidential peaks of Monroe, Jefferson, Adams and Madison on trails from both the east and the west. For those who want to range farther afield, the White Mountains have a European-style hut system that allows for multi-

Right: Ice-climbing routes in the White Mountains are among the most challenging in the Eastern U.S.

Bottom: The Mt. Washington Hotel on the west side of the mountain was the site of the famous Bretton Woods Conference in 1949 that set the course of post-World War II international economic policy.

day outings in the vast White Mountain National Forest. The area is best known for its superlative hiking, but in winter Washington's east-facing Huntington's Ravine becomes prime ice-climbing territory.

The shortest route to Washington's summit starts from Pinkham Notch and ascends to a shelter south of Tuckerman's Ravine, a steep bowl providing spring skiing well into May. From there hikers can either scramble up and over the lip of the bowl or take a ridge trail north of it to the

rocky Alpine Meadows that skirt the summit dome. The easiest way up Washington, however, is via a cog railway completed in 1869 from Crawford Notch on the west or a toll road finished in 1861, that climbs eight miles from Pinkham Notch to the east of the mountain to the summit through ninety-nine turns. Both took the carriage trade to the Summit House for dinner, an orchestral concert and a night's lodging. (This and three successive hotels on Washington have been destroyed by fire, and the present Summit House offers

food and souvenirs but no overnight facilities.) The road is also the venue of the Mount Washington ("Don't worry, there's only one hill") Run, a footrace held annually in mid-June since 1936. Best time so far: fifty-nine minutes, seventeen seconds by New Zealander Derek Froude in 1990.

The fastest time down the mountain was recorded by Austrian Toni Matt in the 1939 American Inferno ski race. In a run that instantly became the stuff of legend, Matt schussed the famously steep Tuckerman's Ravine and completed the four-mile race in six minutes, twenty-nine seconds.

A cog railway, running on coal-fired steam, has been carrying passengers to the summit of Washington since 1869. At "Jacob's Ladder," a thirty foot trestle near the treeline, the train chugs up the steepest grade of any cog railway in the world.

MIRIAM O'BRIEN UNDERHILL

1899-1976

"Very early I realized that the person who invariably climbs behind a good leader, guide·or amateur may never really learn mountaineering."

HOME BASE ▪ *Boston, Mass.*

CLIMBING FEATS ▪ *first all-female ascent of the Grépon; first all-woman ascent of the Matterhorn*

In August 1929 Miriam O'Brien, not yet married to Robert Underhill to become half of America's most highly honored mountaineering couple, hatched a revolutionary plan. She intended to climb the Grépon, a spiky needle on the ridge of aguilles above Chamonix, France, not only without a guide but without a man. In the male-dominated world of technical climbing, such a notion was practically seditious. So by the time she and a brilliant French climber, Alice Damesme, had reached crux of the climb, an exposed 60-foot pitch, called the Mummery Crack after the famed 19th century English alpinist who had first climbed it, a clutch of men had paused on a neighboring climb to watch. So novel was the sight of a woman on the lead of a hard pitch that when Damesme reached the top of the Mummery Crack, she was greeted with applause and cheers. That evening in Chamonix they encountered a member of the old guard, who lamented, "The Grépon has disappeared. Of course, there are still some rocks standing there, but as a climb it no longer exists. Now that it has been done by two women alone, no self-respecting man can undertake it."

"Manless climbing," as Miriam called it, had arrived. In 1932 she and Damesme went to Zermatt to attempt the Matterhorn. A number of women had summited Europe's most famous mountain but always accompanied by males. The two women succeeded—passing a rope of three men on the way—with surprising ease, but it was to be Miriam's last all-female climb. Her next outing was

with a group of friends in the Eastern Alps. One of them was Robert Underhill. They had climbed together in the past—notably on a first traverse of the pinnacles of the Aiguille du Diables near Chamonix, but this time something clicked. "Manless climbing is fun for a while," she wrote in her autobiography *Freedom of the Hills,* "but this other arrangement is better!"

The daughter of a Boston newspaperman, Miriam was taken to Europe by her mother when she was sixteen and was enthralled by her first view of the Matterhorn. She returned six years later and made her first Alpine ascents. In 1923 she met the renowned English alpinist George Finch, who told, her, "Don't waste time on trivial climbs." The advice seemed to galvanize her, and she went to become one of the finest American female climbers of her time. She and Robert Underhill raised a family, but that did not prevent them from continuing their lifelong love of climbing. Today, the most prestigious honor that can be bestowed on a U.S. climber is the American Alpine Club's Robert and Miriam Underhill Award.

SOUTH AMERICA

"A ndes" comes from anta, the Incan word for copper, which, happily, characterizes not the mining potential of the range but the burnished look of their rock. There is substantial evidence that the Incans got a close look at them: a burial site at nearly 20,000 feet in southern Peru; a wall at 17,000 feet; a stone pen for a beast of burden at 21,000 feet. In fact, Incans are believed to have climbed more than 100 Andean peaks, all the more remarkable given the stunningly etched ridges and vertiginous faces that characterize many of them. Five thousand miles long, more than three times the length of the Himalaya, the Andes have the highest mountains outside Asia and the highest volcanoes anywhere. Climbing in South America is abundant and varied—these mountains shine with a special beauty no matter what the season.

CHIMBORAZO

ELEVATION	LOCATION	FIRST ASCENT	
20,703 feet	Cordillera Occidental, Ecuador	Edward Whymper, England, with Italian guides	Jean-Antoine Carrel, Louis Carrel, 1880

Chimborazo is so imposing that from the mid-1700s to 1818 it was thought to be the highest mountain in the world. In one sense it is: Because of the slightly oval shape of the earth, the summit of Chimborazo, near the equator, is closer to the sun and further from the center of the earth than any other mountain. It sits on an immense massif; were it sheared off at half its height, the resulting plateau would be 40 miles long.

But even when loftier peaks were discovered, Chimborazo, a dormant volcano and the highest peak in Ecuador, continued to fascinate historians with its role in the formation of the nation. Unlike the Alps, which awaited venturesome Victorian gentlemen to be explored, the Andes show evidence of the presence of Incas, rulers of a vast Central and South American domain from the 13th to the 16th century. It was on the flanks of Chimborazo that Tupac-Yupanqui incorporated Peru into the Inca empire. And it was here that Incan Ruminahui lost a decisive battle to conquistador Sebastian Bellacazar to place Ecuador under the Spanish rule of Pizarro.

Recorded attempts on Chimborazo began with German naturalist Alexander von Humboldt, who climbed to 18,300 feet on the mountain in 1802. Until 1880 all subsequent attempts were thwarted at the

There have been joys too great to be described in words, and there have been griefs upon which I have dared not dwell; and with these in mind I say, 'Climb if you will, but remember that courage and strength are nought without prudence, and that a momentary negligence may destroy the happiness of a lifetime. Do nothing in haste; look well to each step; and from the beginning think what may be the end'.
—*Edward Whymper*

lowest section of Chimborazo's crater rim. That was the year Edward Whymper, long established as Europe's most famous alpinist, arrived in Ecuador. Accompanied by two crack guides, Jean Carrel (his onetime rival for the first ascent of the Matterhorn) and Jean's brother Louis, Whymper began a blitz of the country's highest peaks,

Chimborazo, the colossus of the Cordillera Occidental, has sixteen glaciers and a snowline at 15,000 feet.

A combination of elevation and proximity to the Equator puts the summit of Chimborazo nearer the sun than any other place on earth.

SNOWFIELD: *An area of permanent snow on summit domes, cols and other relatively level mountain locations. Snow that overfills a snowfield is carried downward by gravity and becomes the frozen head waters of a glacier.*

Llamas, grazing the high meadows west of the mountain, provide the wool knitted into famously intricate sweaters and caps.

starting with Chimborazo on January 4, continuing on to first ascents on six other mountains and ending with a second ascent of Chimborazo.

Until recently most climbs up Chimborazo followed Whymper's second route up the northwest flank of the mountain. But that requires a traverse under unstable seracs, which have broken off and caused several deaths. Today the preferred route, retracing Whymper's first ascent, begins southwest of the main summit (there are five) at the Refugio Edward Whymper, built in 1980 to celebrate the centennial of the climb. It can be reached by bus

or hired car from nearby Ambato, a town situated about 100 miles south of the Ecuadorian capital of Quito. Climbers should plan to spend a day or two at the Whymper hut, which is situated at 16,000 feet, to acclimatize. From the hut the route follows a scree slope to a broad corridor of snow and then a steep snowfield that reaches to Veintimilla, the most westerly of the mountain's peaks. From there, if the snow is still firm, the climb to the main summit takes less than half an hour—but three times that if it has softened in the morning sun. Climbers typically leave the comfort of the hut at around midnight to avoid getting mired in mushy snow. The return to the refugio takes three to four hours.

Well known for being an inexpensive, well-traveled route,

Chimborazo offers high-altitude experience and training without some of the dangers of other peaks. Because of its proximity to the equator, weather is remarkably stable and some of the surrounding mountains can be climbed year-round. The guides on Chimborazo and nearby Cotopaxi (19,384 feet) all have at least a rudimentary grasp of English, the huts are well-stocked with basic supplies and the mountains in this area offer astounding views.

The best climbing months

Chimborazo is a straightforward nontechnical climb, but as evidenced by these monuments at the base of the mountain, its crevasses and altitude can be fatally underestimated.

are June and July, and some recommend timing the push to the summit to a full moon. Cool lunar light on glacial snow can add a touch of magic to a climb that reaches closest to the sun.

HUASCARÁN

ELEVATION	LOCATION	FIRST ASCENT		
22 205 feet	*Cordillera Blanca, Andes Peru*	*North Peak: Annie Smith Peck, U.S., with Swiss guides Rudolf Taugwalder,*	*Gabriel zum Taugwald, 1908; South Peak: H. Bernard, P. Borchers, E. Hein,*	*H. Hoerlin, E. Schneider, Germany, 1932*

New England professor Annie Peck, forty-eight at the time of her arrival in Peru with her Swiss guides in 1908 . She went with the intention of climbing Huascarán and establishing the altitude record for a woman.

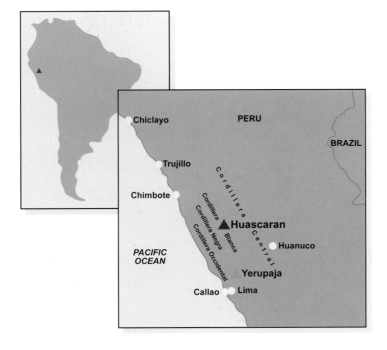

What Annie Smith Peck lacked in talent she made up for in tenacity. Studying in Europe in the 1890s, Peck, an archaeology professor from Providence, Rhode Island, was drawn to the Alps and in 1895 climbed the Matterhorn. But for an early feminist who wanted to demonstrate that women could be the equal of men in the mountains, that was an insufficient challenge. Seeking "some height where no man has stood before," Peck looked to the virgin peaks of South America and eventually set her sights on Huascarán, whose south summit is Peru's highest. Starting in 1903, Peck battled the mountain for six years and in the company of two Swiss guides reached the lower north summit in September 1908. She was fifty-eight. Three years later, Peck climbed to just below the 21,000-foot summit of Coropuna in southern Peru and planted a flag with the message, "Votes for Women."

Peck, in cold weather mask (and tied into her rope, ill advisedly, with a square knot), summited on the North Peak of Huascarán for a first ascent. But Peck's exaggerated estimate of its height was soon disproved by Fannie Bullock Workman, who thereby retained the woman's altitude record she had established in the Himalaya.

Competition among mountaineers was at full throttle at the turn of the century. And Peck's having made a feminist issue of her exploits on Huascarán only added fire. First there was the dispute with one of her Swiss guides, Rudolf Taugwalder, who according to Peck, unroped just below the summit and went to the top ahead of the expedition, an egregious breach of the mountaineering etiquette that called for the expedition leader to have that

A memorial near Huascarán honors climbers who have died on the mountain.

privilege. Later the guides said that Peck had ascended only to the saddle between the North and South peaks, though Peck's photos support her claim. The loudest row, however, took place between Peck and Fannie Bullock Workman, her rival among women climbers. Peck, who had failed in her attempt to measure the elevation instrumentally, estimated that the north peak probably rose above 24,000 feet, which would have given her the altitude record up to that time. Workman, the women's record holder up to then, contested Peck's claim by financing a survey of Huascarán that placed the height of the north summit, quite accurately it

turns out, at 21,812 feet.

Peck first tried to climb Huascarán from the east side but was turned away by its steepness (the mountain was not climbed from the east until 1961). The standard route, used by Peck and in 1932 by a German team that made the first ascent of Huascarán Sur, rises from the village of Musho on the west. The Garganta Route, named for the

prominent saddle between the two peaks, requires no technical climbing, but it is not a simple walk-up. The shifting blocks of the Garganta icefall, a chaotic jumble of seracs and ice blocks just below the saddle, can turn this section into a dangerous-

Alpaca, raised in the Peruvian highlands, are famous for the warmth of their wool.

ly complex maze of route finding.

The route leads east from Musho through a eucalyptus plantation and thence up the north flank of the valley to a base camp on a glacial moraine. Since this elevation can be reached in three hours, some climbers continue straight up the moraine or southward up rock slabs and across streams to establish a base camp below the icefall. Then comes the crux. To negotiate the icefall climbers should be roped up and equipped with crampons and ice axes. The normal route usually threads between seracs and rocks to the south. In some years it is possible to turn the icefall on the north. If the icefall proves impassable, the knife-edged, ice-covered

West Arête provides a potential detour. Climbers spend a second night in the saddle at 19,300 feet. The South Peak is still eight to twelve hours away up 30- to 40-degree snow slopes. The descent over the same route takes two days.

Legend has it that Huascarán was a woman who had castrated her husband and then fled with her children—the tears she shed made the streams that feed the Río Santa Valley. Whatever wrong she was avenging has not been recorded. But Huascarán seems to have been linked to strong women long before Annie Peck took her stand on one of its summits.

SERAC: *An unstable tower of ice that forms in an ice fall. Also, ice pinnacles that result from the sculpting of sun and wind.*

ALPAMAYO

ELEVATION

19,510 feet

LOCATION

*Cordillera
Blanca, Peru*

FIRST ASCENT

*Jacques Jongen,
George Kogan,
Raymond
Leininger,*

*M. Lenoir,
France/Belgium,
1951*

Until the 1930s the peaks and valleys of the Cordillera Blanca were uncharted territory. Then in 1932 and again in 1936 the Austrian surveyor-photographer Edwin Schneider and German Hans Kinzl completed an extensive exploration of the range that resulted in a stunning book of photographs, *Cordillera Blanca*, published in 1951. In one of their pictures, the strikingly symmetrical summit of Alpamayo was reminiscent of a wilderness cathedral shimmering in a mantel of ice. It so inspired a Peruvian travel agent that he had a poster produced of the mountain above an inscription that read: La Montaña mas Bella del Mundo. Despite the fact that the poster featured a different, much more mundane photograph of the mountain—and that its name, derived from the alluvial overflow from the glacial lakes at its base, means "muddy river,"—the sobriquet stuck. Alpamayo, with its fluted North Face rising to a crenellated summit ridge, is still widely described as the most beautiful mountain in the world.

The Andean landscape surrounding the mountain is arid, with just enough grass to support small herds of cattle. The pathway from the roadhead ascends stepwise through a spectacular canyon, passing small mountain lakes filled by windspun ribbons of falling water. With horses and burros to help carry supplies, the trip to base camp, a vertical mile above Hacienda Colcas, west of the range, can be covered in three days.

No attempt on the mountain was made until 1948 when a Swiss team climbed the North Ridge. Their progress was abruptly halted when a cornice they had surmounted broke, sending them 600 feet down the steeply curving North Face. As testament to the porcelain smoothness of the face, none of the climbers was seriously injured.

Günther Hauser negotiates a steep pitch on the first ascent of the Alpamayo's South Peak, the higher of the mountain's twin summits, in 1957.

The first ascent is generally credited to a loosely organized French-Belgian group that included acclaimed Belgian climber Georges Kogan and his wife Claude but no designated leader. The 1951 expedition hadn't even bothered to secure the sponsorship of an alpine club, as was generally the case in the highly nationalistic efforts of the day. Still they succeeded where the Swiss had not. The amateur status of the party was lauded by Maurice Herzog, then the most celebrated mountaineer in the

A climber makes his way past a foreboding ice cave below the South Ridge.

world by dint of his first ascent of Annapurna the previous year. "The most perfect satisfaction," Herzog wrote, "is reserved for those who risk all merely so that they shall not come short of their own ambitions."

There was a small flaw in their accomplishment. The summit party reached the North Peak at 7 PM just as darkness overtook them. They saw a steep descent to the south but not the South Peak, which rises fifty-seven feet higher on the other side of a knife-edged col. Upon study of the Kinzl-Schneider photographs, a German party led by Günther Hauser suspected the oversight and reached the true summit via the dangerously corniced South Ridge. In the interim, the North Peak has flattened somewhat and is now considered merely a continuation of the North Ridge, but most histories continue to regard the French-Belgian effort as Alpamayo's first ascent.

Some of the most dramatic ascents came two and three decades later as climbers tackled the southeast and southwest faces. In 1980 Americans Peter Millar and James O'Neill had planned an ascent of the brutally steep southwest face. When they were slow to rouse themselves from sleeping bags after a cold night at the foot of the face, two French climbers, Serge Beriol and Bernard Lay started up ahead of them. The Frenchmen, nearing the summit ridge, were 300 feet above the Americans and out of sight on the other side of a flute when Millar and

O'Neill heard a loud roar. Suddenly the channel they were ascending was filled with chunks of ice shooting by like asteroids, but the face was so steep that most of them passed over the Americans, who had hugged up against the face. A cornice on the summit rim had broken—or

teen pulled—free, sweeping both Frenchmen with it. When the ice stopped falling, writes O'Neill, "I looked up to find one of the French climbers hanging upside down ten meters from me. He must have been killed instantly." The second body was discovered the following day

nearly 1,000 feet down the face.

What is now considered the standard route on Alpamayo was established by an Italian team led by climber Casimiro Ferrari in 1975. From a base camp looking onto the southwest face, a cairn-lined path leads to a saddle, containing good campsites, between Alpamayo and Eitaraju, a less distinguished but slightly higher peak to the south. From there the route slants northward along glacial moraine and then turns east to ascend the South Ridge leading to the summit. The final section of the climb, traversing 700 feet of 45 to 50 degree ice that must be protected, requires steady nerves. Col to ridge will take fit parties three to six hours,

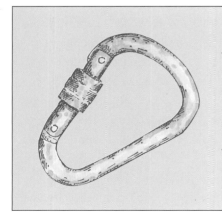

CARABINER: *(also biner)*
An aluminum alloy loop commonly oval or D-shaped and about 3 inches long that is used as a link between climber and rope and rope and protection. A spring-loaded gate allows the rope to be passed inside the carabiner or removed from it.

The Cordillera Blanca, viewed from the wind-scalloped North Ridge of Alpamayo, is set afire by the morning sun.

Next page: Climbers approach the spectacularly fluted North Face

the entire outing a week.

The top of Alpamayo, of course, is one of the few places in the area from which the world's most beautiful mountain cannot be seen. A trek to the mountain's base may provide the best view of all.

YERUPAJÁ

ELEVATION	LOCATION	FIRST ASCENT
21,711 feet	*Cordillera Huayhuash, Peru*	*James Maxwell, David Harrah, U. S., 1950*

Its towering ridge flanked by steep, fluted faces presents a stunning profile along the Huayhuash skyline 100 miles north of Lima. But there is something sinister about Yerupajá. For one thing there are no easy routes on the mountain; it so frequently rejects attempts on its summit that it has acquired another name: Carnicero, the butcher. But more ominously, among the several deaths that have taken place on the mountain, no body has ever been found.

ALSO KNOWN AS • Carnicero "The Butcher"

Paths that wander in the alpine valleys of the Cordillera Huayhuash encounter exotic forests, mountain lakes, and dazzling floral displays, like these yellow orchids near the ruins of Sayamarca on the Inca Trail.

Interest in Yerupajá was sparked by the publication of superb photographs of the Huayhuash taken in the mid-1930s by the German exploration team of Dr. Hans Kinzl and Erwin Schneider and published in 1951. The entire range, running northeast to southwest, is only twenty miles long, but the peaks along its knife-edge ridge present some of the hard-

est climbing anywhere. Right in the center of the Huayhuash sits the Carnicero, Yerupajá, Peru's second highest mountain. By June 1950, when the Harvard Andean Expedition landed in Lima, its summit still had never been reached. On July 4 the students established a base camp between two lakes west of the mountain. From there they pushed up a crevassed glacier to the col between Yerupajá and Rassac, an 18,200-foot peak directly to the west. The high camp was placed on the Southwest Ridge above the col. From this camp on July 31 James Maxwell and David Harrah made their push for the top. To minimize the danger of frostbite, they waited until 10:30 AM for the sun to warm their route before starting out. Seven

A trekker in the Peruvian Andes receives a welcoming committee of Quechua girls.

hours later they stood—one at a time—on the fragile summit cornice. Then the real adventures began.

The pair had begun to descend the ridge and had paused on a snow ledge to take pictures. Suddenly, a section of the ledge broke off, and Harrah pitched over into a sickening freefall. As the coil of rope connecting the climbers whipped off

the ledge, Maxwell rammed his ice axe into the snow and threw himself into a prone position. Fifty feet down Harrah hit the steep west face and kept going. The rope went taut and jerked Maxwell toward the lip of the ledge. He drove his axe in a second time, then a third— it held. Miraculously, Harrah hadn't let go of the two ice tools he had been holding, and despite badly

Finely wrought ridges and delicate cornices, like those on Yerupajá, center, are signature characteristics of the Huayhuash mountains.

A good one is a live one.

—Don Whillans, when asked to define a good mountaineer

bruised ribs was able to claw his way back—on the face and then on flutings—to his partner. They picked their way down the ridge in darkness and were still an hour above their highest camp when they found refuge in a crevasse. The following day they were helped to safety by fellow members of the expedition, but their ordeal took its toll: Harrah lost all his toes to frostbite; Maxwell, parts of three.

The magnitude of the

Harvard team's achievement became apparent over the next fifteen years as one attempt after another was turned back by Yerupajá's well defended summit. Through 1965 nine expeditions from seven different nations failed, one of them within 500 feet of the summit. Then in 1966 another pair of climbers, Lief-Norman Patterson of the U.S. and Jorge Peterek of Poland, established a new route on the West Face of Yerupajá while Americans John Crowley and David Isles repeated the Southwest ridge climb of 1950. Today, there are still only a half dozen routes on the mountain, and it remains one of the superlative challenges of world mountaineering.

SELF ARREST: *A technique for decelerating and then stopping a falling slide on a snow slope, in which the climber rolls onto his or her ice axe and twists the pick so that it gouges a furrow into the snow and thereby acts to brake the descent.*

The Final Choice

FROM *Touching the Void* BY JOE SIMPSON

Americans Joe Simpson and Simon Yates had just completed an ascent of Siula (20,808 feet), a mountain that neighbors Yerupaja in the Peruvian Andes, and were starting down when Simpson broke a leg in a fall from an ice ledge. The descent continued with Yates lowering Simpson on a rope, from ledge to ledge, down the steep face. Then something went wrong: The rope had nearly played out, but Simpson, suspended below an overhang, had nowhere to stand. Yates hung on, but he was gradually being pulled off the narrow belay seat that had been hacked into the steep slope. In one of the most gripping survival epics ever recorded, Yates describes the terrible decision he faced.

Simon is writing . . .

Joe had smiled as I let him slide away from me. It wasn't much of a smile. His pain twisted it into a grimace. I let him go fast and ignored his cries. He was quickly gone from my torch beam, and as another avalanche swept over my head the rope disappeared as well. Apart from his weight on my waist there was no sign of his existence.

I kept the speed going. The belay plate was easy to control despite my deadened fingers. They were bad now. I worried about them, as I had done since we left the col. I knew Joe's climbing days were over, but now I was scared for my hands. There was no telling how bad they

would be. I had a quick look when it was light but I couldn't see how deep the damage was. Four fingertips were blackened, and one thumb, but there was no saying whether the others wouldn't also go the same way.

I heard a faint cry from below, and the rope jerked slightly. Poor bastard, I thought. I had hurt him all the way down. It was strange being so cold about it. It had been hard not to feel for him. It was easier now. We had made such fast progress. Efficient. I felt proud about it. We had held it all together, and that was good. The lowering had been easier than I had expected, especially with Joe digging the seats for me. He had really held it together. That was some control! I'd never asked him to dig the seats, but he just went ahead and did it. Wonder whether I would have done that? Who knows.

My hands were stiffening again. They always got bad before the knot; stiff, like claws. The rope ran out smoothly. I had been careful to avoid any tangles. The idea of holding Joe with one hand and trying to unsnarl a tangled and frozen rope didn't bear thinking about. The pull at my harness increased. The slope must be steepening again, I thought. There were another seventy feet to go before the half-way knot had to be changed over. I increased the rate of descent. I knew it was hurting him. When it had been light I could see his pain for a

long way down, but we had got down. It was necessary. Another faint cry came from the darkness. A rushing flow of snow poured over me again. I hunched deeper into the seat, feeling the snow settle and crumble slightly. The seats lasted for the lower but by then they were well on their way to collapse.

Suddenly I jolted heavily forward from the waist and nearly came out of the seat. I threw my weight back and down into the snow, bracing my legs hard against the sudden pressure. Christ! Joe's fallen. I let the rope slide slowly to a stop trying to avoid the impact I would have got if I had stopped it dead. The pressure remained constant. My harness bit into my hips, and the rope pulling tautly between my legs threatened to rip me down through the floor of the seat.

As the rope ran out I realised that the pressure wasn't easing. Joe was still hanging free. What in hell's name was I lowering him over?

I looked down at the slack rope being fed through the belay plate. Twenty feet below I spotted the knot coming steadily towards me. I began swearing, trying to urge Joe to touch down on to something solid. At ten feet I stopped lowering. The pressure on the rope hadn't changed.

I kept stamping my feet. I was trying to halt the collapse of the seat but it wasn't working. I felt the first shivers of fear. Snow hit me again from behind, surging over and around me. My thighs moved down fractionally. The avalanche pushed me forward and filled the seat behind my back. Oh God! I'm coming off.

Then it stopped as abruptly as it had started. I let the rope slide five feet, thinking furiously. Could I hold the rope with one hand below the knot and change the plate over? I lifted one hand from the rope and stared at it. I couldn't squeeze it into a fist. I thought of holding the rope locked against the plate by winding it round my thigh and then releasing the plate from my harness. Stupid idea! I couldn't hold Joe's weight with my hands alone. If I released the plate, 150 feet of the free rope would run unstoppable through my hands, and then it would rip me clear off the mountain.

It had been nearly an hour since Joe had gone over the drop. I was shaking with cold. My grip on the rope kept easing despite my efforts. The rope slowly edged down and the knot pressed against my right fist. I can't hold it, can't stop it. The thought overwhelmed me. The snow slides and wind and cold were forgotten. I was

being pulled off. The seat moved beneath me, and snow slipped away past my feet. I slipped a few inches. Stamping my feet deep into the slope halted the movement. God! I had to do something!

The knife! The thought came out of nowhere. Of course, the knife. Be quick, come on, get it.

The knife was in my sack. It took an age to let go a hand and slip the strap off my shoulder, and then repeat it with the other hand. I braced the rope across my thigh and held on to the plate with my right hand as hard as I could. Fumbling at the catches on the rucksack, I could feel the snow slowly giving way beneath me. Panic threatened to swamp me. I felt in the sack, searching desperately for the knife. My hand closed round something smooth and I pulled it out. The red plastic handle slipped in my mitt and I nearly dropped it. I put it in my lap before tugging my mitt off with my teeth. I had already made the decision. There was no other option left to me. The metal blade stuck to my lips when I opened it with my teeth.

I reached down to the rope and then

stopped. The slack rope! Clear the loose rope twisted round my foot! If it tangled it would rip me down with it. I carefully cleared it to one side, and checked that it all lay in the seat away from the belay plate. I reached down again, and this time I touched the blade to the rope.

It needed no pressure. The taut rope exploded at the touch of the blade, and I flew backwards into the seat as the pulling strain vanished. I was shaking.

Leaning backward against the snow, I listened to a furious hammering in my temple as I tried to calm my breathing. Snow hissed over me in a torrent. I ignored it as it poured over my face and chest, spurting into the open zip at my neck, and on down below. It kept coming. Washing across me and down after the cut rope, and after Joe.

I was alive, and for the moment that was all I could think about. Where Joe was, or whether he was alive, didn't concern me in the long silence after the cutting. His weight had gone from me. There was only the wind and the avalanches left to me.

ACONCAGUA

ELEVATION	LOCATION	FIRST ASCENT	
22,835 feet	*Cordillera Andes, Argentina*	*Matthew Zurbriggen, Swiss guide on*	*an English expedition, 1897*

In a ratio of elevation to effort, Aconcagua may be the world's best mountaineering bargain. The highest mountain outside of Asia has been climbed on skis and mountain bikes. Motorcyclists have rumbled to within 180 vertical feet of the summit. In the winter of 1985 and 1986 Fernando Garido of Spain spent sixty-six days camped just below the summit, setting a new longevity record for high-altitude habitation.

The first ascent of the mountain remains an intriguing mystery. Since archeologists have found signs of Incan presence above 22,000 feet in the Andes,

High up on the mountain, Seven Summiter Christine Janin of France traverses wind- and sun-sculpted neve.

there is credible speculation that some Andean peaks were climbed before the Spanish Conquest. In 1947 the skeleton of a guanaco, a relative of the llama, was discovered far above its natural habitat on the crescent ridge connecting the North and South peaks of Aconcagua (the name is derived from an Incan phrase meaning White Sentinel), and in 1985 a mummy, preserved in the moun-

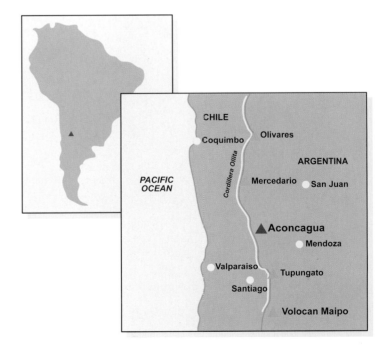

tain's cold, dry air, was found on Aconcagua's Southwest Ridge at an elevation of 17,060 feet. The first recorded ascent came in 1897, when wealthy English adventurer Edward Fitzgerald spent two months on the mountain and finally succeeded in

At Nido de Condores, climbers bare their soles as they acclimatize to an elevation of 18,000 feet.

putting Austrian guide Matthias Zurbriggen on the summit on the fifth attempt. Fitzgerald, wracked by mountain sickness, never quite made it.

As it turned out, Fitzgerald, who ran into one dead end after another, finally discovered a route requiring no technical expertise whatsoever. Its very accessibility, however, has proved lethal: since the first known

death in 1926, more than fifty people—including almost every member of a 1944 expedition—have died on Aconcagua. Some of them were felled by the most insidious danger on the mountain: lack of acclimatization. Adapting one's physiology to the increasingly thinner air at altitude takes some people longer than others—some don't adapt at all, even at 8,000 to 10,000 feet. Because the normal route on Aconcagua presents no objective difficulties, it is easy to climb beyond one's acclimatization, risking headaches and nausea or the potentially fatal conditions of pulmonary or cerebral edema.

With proper acclimatization and an eye out for deteriorating weather, reasonably fit climbers taking the normal route can expect to reach the summit in four to six days: two days'

Climber Mark Harvey, shielded against the intensity of the sun, documents his ascent to the highest point in the Western Hemisphere.

walk-in from the roadhead and two to four days of ascent. Climbers start from the village of Puenta del Inca, 120 miles west of Mendoza, Argentina, where mules are available to carry food and equipment to the trail head at the Plaza de Mulas. Because the Plaza lies at an elevation of 13,874 feet, nearly 5,000 feet above Puenta del Inca, most parties acclimatize by stretching the trek over two days. From the Plaza de Mulas a well trod trail wends northward, then ascends a steep scree slope to the east. Most parties bypass the first group of huts (Camp Canada at 16,000 feet) and the second (Camp Alaska, 17,100 feet) and ascend directly to Nido de

Condores, a level area with rock outcrops that make good windbreaks for tents.

At this point Fitzgerald's party headed straight for the summit across a vast and featureless scree field. But because of the loose footing and lack of shelter, climbers now turn southward onto the crest of the ridge. Some stop for the day at Camp Berlin, three ruined huts at 19,520 feet; some continue a little higher to White Rocks, a group of boulders providing tent site protection and less congestion than Berlin. From these camps it's seven to ten hours to the summit. The final impediment is the Canaleto, a 1,300 foot chute at a steady incline of 33 degrees that is filled with infuriatingly loose rock, which exits onto a saddle between the North and South Peaks. An aluminum cross on the North Peak marks it as the true summit of Aconcagua. The descent to Punta del Inca can be done in two or three days.

The classic technical route on Aconcagua lies on its famed South face, 10,000 feet of ice and rotting rock that was first climbed alpine-style by a six-man French team in 1954. The climbers were on the face eight days and suffered severe frostbite, but they established an astonishing new level of accomplishment in the Andes, heralding some of the world's hardest routes.

Aconcagua's accessibility and its prominence as the highest peak outside of Asia draws hundreds of climbers to the mountain in Argentina's summer months of December and January, so the available hut space is generally taken. Bring your own tent—and a leisurely pace. On Aconcagua the crux of the climb is proper acclimatization.

Midway along the walk-in to the
base of the normal route on
Aconcagua, mules do double duty:
ferrying both supplies and
climbers across the Rio Vacas.

Mountain Sickness

BY CHARLES S. HOUSTON, M.D.

Why do climbers get headaches, nausea and hallucinations in the mountains? Why do their lungs sometimes fill with fluid? Physician and climber Charles S. Houston has spent more than four decades studying these questions. Here is what is known.

The explosion of interest in mountaineering and the availability of amazing new technologies have expanded our understanding of cause, prevention and treatment of a widening spectrum of altitude illnesses. The basic cause of altitude illness is lack of oxygen (hypoxia), but we are gradually recognizing that other factors are also involved. Millions of people visit mountainous country every year, and even those who go no higher than 8,000 to 10,000 feet may be vulnerable to several kinds of altitude sickness.

Acute Mountain Sickness (AMS), which does not discriminate for gender but is less common in older than younger individuals, is the most common of the illnesses induced by altitude. It affects twenty-five percent of all persons who ascend rapidly from low to even moderate altitudes, such as those of resorts in the Rockies. AMS is characterized by headache, fatigue, nausea and insomnia. It can also disturb water balance in the tissues, resulting in swelling of feet, hands and even the face. These symptoms usually disappear in two or three days, but in most people they can be prevented by going high gradually—taking an extra day or two to reach 10,000 feet. A 125 mg or 250 mg tablet of acetazolamide (Diamox) taken once a day when starting out also prevents AMS and only rarely has side effects. Dexamethasone (two to five mg several times a day) minimizes symptoms once they appear but is not as good as Diamox for prevention.

We now believe that some symptoms of AMS are due to small, reversible changes in brain chemistry and/or circulation. In the rare instances when these changes are dominant, the illness escalates to a condition called High Altitude Cerebral Edema (HACE). Symptoms of HACE are a staggering walk, confusion, perhaps hallucination and, if it is not treated, coma. These symptoms indicate a serious condition that calls for immediate descent. If this is impossible, intravenous dexamethasone and supplementary oxygen will buy time.

Also less common but more serious than AMS is High Altitude Pulmonary Edema (HAPE), a condition that results in the accumulation of fluid in the lungs. It is marked by weakness and shortness of breath out of proportion to the effort being expended and cyanosis, a blue color in fingernails and lips that results from insufficient oxygenation of the blood. Crackles, gurgles and wheezes can be heard in the lungs. A slight cough grows worse and soon produces frothy or sometimes bloody sputum. Pulse rate is rapid; there is often a slight fever; and the patient looks really sick. A rise in pulmonary arterial pressure that accompanies HAPE is now attributed to a deficiency of nitric oxide, a simple chemical found in most mammalian tissue. Certain chemicals (endothelins) released from the lining of blood vessels during hypoxia contribute to HAPE—and possibly to HACE also.

In contrast to AMS, men are four times more likely than women to develop HAPE; younger persons are only somewhat more susceptible to it. The incidence of HAPE has been difficult to pin down, but the best estimates place it between two and five percent of visitors to resorts in the Rockies. Strenuous exertion soon after arrival increases its likelihood. At very high altitudes, even acclimatized climbers can develop both HAPE and HACE if they exert themselves too aggressively.

Some individuals especially susceptible to HAPE are at risk whenever they go high. Recent studies suggest that this is a genetic trait, perhaps related to the auto-immune system. Those who live at high elevations can develop HAPE upon returning home after a few days at sea level.

Milder cases of HAPE recover with supplementary oxygen and rest. HAPE victims can also be helped by spending a few hours in a so-called Gamow bag, an air-tight cylindrical bag that is pressurized to simulate descent to a lower elevation. Nifidipine by mouth or vein relieves HAPE rapidly by lowering the high pressure in the pulmonary artery—though it does not help AMS or HACE. This drug is not advised for prevention except in the rare cases in which a person is HAPE-susceptible. Both HAPE and HACE may progress very rapidly to a serious or even fatal outcome, so rapid descent to a lower altitude is wise—and the victim improves more quickly than with any medication.

The best therapy for these conditions, however, is prevention—allowing time for the body to adjust to the lack of oxygen. This means going to moderate altitude more slowly, even stopping overnight at lower elevations on the way. Given time, our physiology is able to sustain normal oxygenation by increasing respiration and heart rate, making more red blood cells and adjusting the alkalinity of the blood. Most people who live at or near sea level will feel almost completely at home after a week or so of acclimatization to 10,000 feet.

Three other forms of mountain sickness have been recognized, but they are all quite rare. Chronic Mountain Sickness (CMS) affects a few individuals who though they have lived without difficulty at 12,000 to 14,000 feet suddenly begin to make a surplus of red blood cells. Within a few months they start suffering from aches and pain, and blood clots develop in limbs and lungs. The condition will result in heart failure unless the patient goes down to a lower elevation. Recovery is slow, and the condition will recur if the victim returns to high altitude.

Subacute Infantile Mountain Sickness, occurring only in Han Chinese infants born high up or brought to altitude when very young, causes heart enlargement and failure. Descent is the only treatment. A variant, Subacute Adult Mountain Sickness, which also can cause heart failure, has occurred in some soldiers who have been stationed for months at 20,000 feet or higher and have been engaged in prolonged strenuous activity. Again, descent is essential.

High Altitude Retinal Hemorrhages (HARH) can be seen in the retina of the eye in 15 to 35 percent of everyone who goes above 15,000 feet. These rarely cause any change in vision and disappear in days or weeks with no lasting effect, except for the rare instance when the hemorrhage is in the macula or area of central vision. But they raise troubling questions: Do they occur in the brain as well? If so, might they damage delicate brain tissue? Thus far most researchers doubt that such damage takes place, while conceding that repeated climbs to high altitudes might result in lasting changes. The issue continues to be debated.

There are other ways in which those who do not have an obvious form of mountain sickness will be affected above 18,000 to 20,000 feet. Many, perhaps even most of the tragedies that have been occurring with increased frequency on the highest mountains are due to clouding of judgement and perception from the subtle impacts of hypoxia. Above 22,000 feet, no one is as alert, wise or prudent as at sea level. Foolish mistakes, flawed decisions, disrupted teams have caused scores of fatalities—even among veteran and well acclimatized climbers. It is not simply for theatrical effect that this area is often referred to as the Death Zone. Supplementary oxygen can help at this elevation, but reliance on it risks serious consequences should supplies run out.

Only a few hundred thousand people may be at risk from mountain sicknesses, but many millions become hypoxic from chronic or acute illness or injury at sea level. The potential for application to more common forms of hypoxia is what gives altitude research its special fascination and value. What happens to hypoxia victims everywhere will be better understood as we learn more about the responses of healthy men and women in the mountain environment.

FITZROY

ELEVATION

11,289 feet

LOCATION

Andes, Patagonia, Argentina

FIRST ASCENT

Lionel Terray, Guido Magnone, France, 1952

Most of the world's great mountains are higher; few are harder. Fitzroy rises off the pampas of Patagonia like a beautiful nightmare, a vision out of Edgar Allen Poe, as French mountaineer M.A. Azema imagined it from his readings of Charles Darwin. Darwin had seen Fitzroy in the early 1830s when he ventured into Patagonia during his round-the-world trip aboard the Beagle as he gathered evidence for his theory of natural selection. (The region's highest peak, called Chaltel until the end of the 19th century, took its present name from the Beagle's captain, Robert Fitzroy.)

So forbidding were the sheer, ice-coated faces and ridges of Fitzroy that no one seriously considered climbing it until 1937. That year an Italian team got as far as the col between Fitzroy and a neighboring peak to the south, marking the first time anyone had actually set foot on Fitzroy.

Failed attempts over the next fourteen years seemed to confirm the mountain's reputation as insurmountable. When a renowned team of French alpinists, including Lionel Terray, who had been on the successful Annapurna expedition the year before, arrived in Buenos Aires on their way to Fitzroy in late 1951, the Argentineans were impressed. They wined and dined the climbers, and Argentine President Juan Perón offered two army trucks to transport them to within ten miles of the mountain. But disaster struck even before the climbers reached their base camp. While crossing the Rio Fitzroy, which had become swollen by glacial runoff, one of the team slipped. When the safety line to which he was clipped broke free of its mooring, he was pulled under and drowned. As a memoriam, Fitzroy's neighboring tower was named Poincenot for the perished climber.

The French team established a base camp under the Italian Col just before the New Year and for two weeks hauled supplies to a snow cave on the col itself. Then, bad weather arrived, as it inevitably does in Patagonia. The climbers retreated to a forest east of the mountain and waited. January 30 dawned clear and still, and the team resupplied the snow cave. Two days later Lionel Terray and Guido Magnone set out onto Fitzroy's awesome southeast face with pitons, ice axes, a bit of food and two sleeping bags. Fourteen hours of strenuous climbing took them up less than 800 vertical feet.

Top: A camper checks the weather—and his resolve—as he notes cloud formations over the wild array of peaks that make up the Fitzroy massif.

Opposite: South of Fitzroy, a stately procession of spires: Poincenot, Rafael and Saint-Exupery.

They settled down for the night on rocks at the base of a gully—and discovered that the flasks they had carried with them contained not water but fuel. Ruefully, they resorted to eating snow.

With the dawn, they started

PITON: *A hardened steel spike with a ringed opening on the blunt end to which a carabiner can be attached, which is* hammered into a crack to provide protection or aid. Also called a pin. Because repeated placement and removal of pitons scars the rock at the point of placement, their use is now discouraged in favor of artificial chockstones and other clean climbing devices.

up again. The final pitch onto
the summit ramp almost
stymied them. It required a
thin piton called an Ace of
Hearts, but they had used their
last one far below. Suddenly,
Terray recalled that he had
employed just such a piton as a
can opener and then thrown it
into his rucksack. Luckily, it
was still there. Half an hour
later they were on the summit.
Terray later proclaimed this
first ascent of Fitzroy, "the
hardest climb of my life." It
was hard enough that the
mountain was not climbed
again for thirteen years.

Today, Fitzroy's normal
route, established by an
American party in 1968, goes up
the southwest ridge. The five
climbers, led by equipment
innovator Yvon Chouinard of
California, called themselves the
Funhogs, a name they had
adopted before they were forced
to wait out a twenty-five-day
storm in a snow cave and were
reduced in the end to telling
each other their dreams to drive
off their boredom. When they
got their chance, however, all
five made it to the summit and
back in twenty-three hours. Of
the seventeen leads on this popular route, only three required
aid.

No matter how it's climbed,
Fitzroy remains one of the great
adventures in mountaineering. For
some, it is the achievement of a
lifetime. "I felt a state of grace,"
said twenty-year-old Argentinean
climber José Luis Fonrouge upon
making the second ascent of
Fitzroy in 1965, "ultimate calm,
the end of a dream."

Opposite: On a rare blue-sky day in Patagonia, a climber ascends a couloir to take on one of Fitzroy's eleven routes.

Right: As winds the winds pick up and visibility declines, a climber on the lower slopes of Fitzroy runs for cover.

Bottom: Mists over the massif create an ethereal and foreboding mountain landscape.

GLOSSARY

A cheval: French for on horseback, a technique in which a narrow ridge is climbed with legs straddled to either side.

Abseil: German for rappel.

Aid climbing: A rock climbing technique in which such equipment as pitons, chocks or bolts are used not simply for protection but to support the weight of the climber. Typically, aid is employed where free climbing techniques appear to be unavailing. Many aid routes have later been freed by subsequent climbers.

Aiguille: French for needle. On a mountain, a needle-like peak; a spire or a pinnacle.

Alpine style: An approach to multi-day climbs in which a team or an individual progresses toward the summit in one continuous push, using neither stocked camps or fixed ropes in the ascent.

Anchor: The fixed point or, preferably, points to which a belayer is secured so as to be able to hold the weight of a partner in case of a fall.

Arête: French for ridge. Often connotes a sharp ridge with steep sides; on rock cliffs, an outside corner.

Back rope: An auxiliary rope that prevents the second climber from an uncontrolled pendulum in case he or she falls on traverse. The back rope, tied into the second climber and run through protection at the start of the traverse, is paid out by the belayer while the main rope is gathered in. After completing the traverse, the climber unties from the back rope, which is then pulled through the protection at the beginning of the traverse.

Belay: n. A secure position on a rock or ice climb in which one of a pair of roped climbers prepares to arrest the fall of the other. v. To provide protection through belay.

Bergschrund: Also simply 'schrund. A broad crevasse or series of crevasses occurring at the head of a glacier where moving ice separates from static ice or rock.

Bouldering: Free climbing on boulders, up to about 25 feet high, without protection. Historically bouldering was done to hone technique. Since the 1980s bouldering has gained status as a subcategory of climbing with its own rating system.

Brake hand: In a belay, the hand that holds the dead end of the rope (rather than the end of the rope that runs toward the climber, i.e. the live end), and is used to lock the rope against the body or a belay device in case of a fall.

Buttress: A shallow ridge projecting from a face.

Chimney: A crack in a rock cliff wide enough for a climber to enter and ascend by means of applying pressure to the opposing walls. v. To ascend a chimney.

Chockstones: Naturally occurring rocks or stones jammed into chimneys and cracks, sometimes a barrier to ascent, sometimes useful for handholds or placement of protection.

Cirque: An area ringed by mountains; also called a cwm (Welsh) or corrie (Scottish).

Clean climbing: Rock climbing that abstains from the use of pitons in favor of protection that does not deface the rock.

Col: The low point or saddle on a ridge connecting two peaks.

Cornice: A cap of windblown snow overhanging the leeward side of a ridge. Cornices pose two kinds of hazards: They can break off, smashing into climbers moving below them, or they can give way under the weight of climbers crossing them.

Couloir: French for gully. A cleft in the side of a mountain that rises to a ledge, a ridge or the summit itself. Since couloirs can serve as funnels for loose rock and avalanches, they pose a special danger to climbers.

Crevasse: A crack in a glacier that can be tens, even hundreds of feet deep. Because crevasses can be hidden under a covering of snow that can give way under the weight of a climber, sound climbing practice calls for climbers on a crevassed glacier to be connected to each other by rope and spaced out perpendicular to possible fractures.

Crux: The hardest pitch of a route; also the hardest move within a pitch.

Dihedral: A vertical section of a cliff in which two slabs meet to form a more-or-less right angle. Also called a diedre (French), an inside corner or an open book.

Expedition style: An approach to mountaineering in which climbers establish progressively higher camps and fix rope over difficult sections of the route to assist in ascent and descent.

Firn: Snow, granular in texture, that has compacted because of repeated thawing and freezing. Also, the permanent snow that remains after the spring thaw.

Fixed line: Rope that is left in place on steep snow slopes or rock faces to facilitate subsequent ascent and descent in an expedition-style climb.

Free climbing: Rock climbing in which the ascent is made by way of the rock alone. Equipment is used only for protection.

Free soloing: Rock climbing in which the climber dispenses with equipment of all kinds to complete a climb without protection.

Front pointing: A climbing technique in which the front two points of the crampon, which project forward rather than down, are kicked into snow or ice to provide purchase for ascent or descent of steep or vertical slopes.

Gendarme: A pinnacle that sits astride a ridge, frequently impeding passage on that ridge.

Glacier: A river of ice, fed by snow and pulled inexorably by gravity down the mountainside where it resides

Hanging belay: A belay on a sheer rock face in which the belayer, lacking a surface to stand on, hangs from protection placed at the point of the belay.

Icefall: A steepened section of a glacier in which faster flow results in numerous ever-changing crevasses and seracs that can topple without warning. On some climbs they comprise the most dangerous section of the route.

Jam: A rock climbing maneuver in which a finger, hand or foot is wedged into a crack in such a way as to carry the weight of the climber during a move; v. to perform such a maneuver.

Lead: In technical climbing, the upward progress of the first climber, the lead climber, on a rope. Having completed a pitch, the lead climber establishes himself or herself in a belay and protects the second. In well balanced climbing teams, the second will typically lead through, continuing beyond the belay stance of his or her partner and lead the next pitch.

Moraine: The rocks and soil pushed along the path of a glacier and deposited along its sides, a lateral moraine, along its center, a medial moraine or at its snout, a terminal moraine.

Off-width crack: A crack that is too narrow to accept a climber's body and too wide to hold a fist or boot placed inside it.

Pendulum: An aid technique in which the climber traverses a blank section of rock—typically to get from one crack system to another—by swinging from the rope after having clipped into a fixed point and then descended far enough to provide a radius of rope on which to swing.

Pitch: The section of a climb between two belay positions. The length of a pitch is limited by the length of rope, typically 150 or 165 feet, between the climbers.

Protection: Also pro; devices such as nuts, pitons, bongs, Friends, Camalots and ice screws placed during a lead and connected via carabiners to the climber's rope so as to shorten the length of a potential fall.

Prusik: A knot, adapted to mountaineering from violin string repair by Dr. Karl Prusik of Austria, that can be moved upward on a rope to which it is attached but holds when weighted downward. In emergency situations, it performs like the mechanical ascenders that have superseded it.

Rappel: A means of descent in which the climber makes a controlled slide down a rope, governing the rate of descent by applying friction between the rope and the body or a device specially constructed for this purpose. v. To descend via rappel.

Scree: Layers of loose rocks and stones that collect in gullies and at the bases of cliff and ledges, the ascent of which is typically frustrating and laborious.

Self arrest: A technique for decelerating and then stopping a falling slide on a snow slope, in which the climber rolls onto his or her ice axe and twists the pick so that it gouges a furrow into the snow and thereby acts to brake the descent.

Serac: An unstable tower of ice that forms in an ice fall. Also, ice pinnacles that result from the sculpting of sun and wind.

Sherpa: A member of a Buddhist clan that inhabits the Khumbu district of Nepal, a region south of Mount Everest generally at an elevation of 9,000 feet and higher. Because of their lifelong acclimatization to altitude, their loyalty and their ingrained hospitality to visitors to their land, the Sherpa people are a prime source of Himalayan porters, guides and base-camp workers. With a few exceptions—Tenzing Norgay, who summited on Everest with Sir Edmund Hillary in 1953, and Nawang Gombu, with Jim Whittaker in 1963—the exploits of individual Sherpas have gone unsung, yet several have made multiple ascents of 8,000-meter peaks and are celebrities among their own people.

Siege: An expedition style of ascent in which a mountain or big wall climb is accomplished in stages with multiple trips from base camp to higher camps, both for supplying camps and promoting acclimatization.

Snowfield: An area of permanent snow on summit domes, cols and other relatively level mountain locations. Snow that overfills a snowfield is carried downward by gravity and becomes the frozen head waters of a glacier.

Step cutting: The practice, before the advent of modern front-pointing crampons and ice tools, of cutting a stairway into a snow slope to facilitate ascent.

Talus: A jumble of large rocks at the base of a cliff.

Top rope: A rope, one end of which is tied into a climber, the other held by his or her belayer at the base of a climb, with the midpoint inserted into a carabiner at the top of a pitch above them. Typically used for practice or training, the top rope is gathered in by the belayer as the climber ascends the pitch, eliminating the need for intermediate protection.

Traverse: a section of a route on a steep or vertical face that is horizontal or slanting, connecting lines of weakness where upward progress can be resumed; v. to execute a traverse.

Verglas: A thin and treacherous coating of ice on rock.

Zipper: Climber jargon for the phenomenon of having a row of pieces of protection pull out under the weight of a falling climber.

EQUIPMENT

Ascender: a device which, like the Prusik knot, slides freely when pushed up the rope to which it is attached but grips the rope tightly when weighted downward. Ascenders (see also Jumar) provide protection and aid on big wall and alpine climbs and are also used for hauling gear.

Bolts: Masonry anchors up to one-half inch in diameter and three inches long used for aid and protection on rock faces in which there are no natural weakness for the placement of a piton or chockstone. Bolt holes are drilled into the rock with hand-hammered chisels or battery or gas powered drills. Bolts with a carabiner hanger attached are hammered, twisted or glued into the hole.

Cam: a spring-loaded, double-axled device used by rock climbers as protection in off-width cracks.

Carabiner: (also biner) An aluminum alloy loop commonly oval or D-shaped and about three inches long that is used as a link between climber and rope and rope and protection. A spring-loaded gate allows the rope to be passed inside the carabiner or removed from it.

Chalk: A carbonate of magnesium gymnast powder used by climbers to absorb perspiration on fingers and hands, thereby enhancing their grip on rock. Although it is now generally accepted, chalk was initially criticized for leaving unaesthetic blotches of white on the rock face and spoiling the adventure of route-finding for subsequent climbers.

Chocks: (also nuts) Specially shaped chunks of aluminum or other metals of graduated sizes, threaded with a wire or rope loop so as to accept a carabiner, that are slotted into cracks during a rock climb to serve as protection.
Chocks have generally replaced pitons (the placement and removal of which eventually scar and widen the cracks in which they are used), and their employment is regarded as clean climbing.

Climbing rope: a kern-mantle rope, typically 150 to 165 feet long and .44 inches in diameter, composed of continuous strands of nylon (the kern) enclosed in a braided nylon sheath (the mantle) and sufficiently elastic to absorb the energy of a falling climber

Crampon: A metal platform of spikes that is strapped to the boot to provide purchase in hard snow and ice. The frontmost pair of spikes on most modern-day crampons protrude outward so that they can be kicked into steep ice or snow, in a technique called front pointing.

Etriér: A three- to five-step ladder typically constructed from nylon webbing that, when clipped into a piton, nut or bolt, supports a climber on an aid climb.

Gear sling: a loop of nylon webbing worn over the shoulder of a rock climber to which the pieces of protection needed for a pitch of technical climbing are clipped.

Hammer: a tool, slightly heavier than a carpenter's hammer, used for the placement and removal of pitons. Some hammers have a hole through which a carabiner and a length of webbing can be clipped, to facilitate jerking protection devices from a rock face.

Hanging bivouac tent: a tent shelter designed to maintain its shape when suspended from a vertical wall.

Helmet: a safety device specially designed to protect climbers' heads from falling rock and ice. Climbing helmets must be light, strong and comfortable.

Ice axe: a mountaineering tool with many uses, such as to aid stability on steep snow, for cutting bivouac ledges into a snow slope, belaying or as a walking stick.

Ice screw: a hollow cylinder with a prominent thread that is screwed into ice to provide an anchor for a belay or as protection on a lead.

Jumar: The most widely known brand-name mechanical ascender; v. To ascend a rope using such a device.

Overboot: footwear worn over climbing boots to provide added warmth.

Piton: A hardened steel spike with a ringed opening on the blunt end to which a carabiner can be attached, which is hammered into a crack to provide protection or aid. Also called a pin. Because repeated placement and removal of pitons scars the rock at the point of placement, their use is now discouraged in favor of artificial chockstones and other clean climbing devices.

Probe: A long wand used in avalanche rescue to feel for bodies that may be buried in snow.

Pulley: a device used on multi-day rock climbs to assist in the raising of duffel bags containing equipment and provisions.

Rock shoes: tight-fitting climbing boots designed to provide maximum adhesion between climber and rock.

Seat harness: a matrix of heavily stitched nylon webbing worn around the legs and the waist that provides the point of connection between climber and rope.

FACTS & FIGURES

RATING SYSTEMS

From Climbing: The Complete Reference *by Greg Child*

Various systems indicate the comparative difficulty of climbs. Separate rating systems are used for Free Climbing, Aid Climbing, Alpine Climbing, and Ice Climbing. Several systems are in current use, each devised in different countries and at different periods during the climbing history of those countries.

All rating systems begin from a baseline rating of the earliest climb and progress upward. Some systems take into consideration technical difficulty only. Others consider factors like, exposure, loose rock, and poor protection. Though criteria exist to determine ratings, ratings are largely subjective and frequently contentious. For example, a free climb that may require a very long reach may be easy for a tall person and may be rated moderately, but for a short person the move may be several grades harder. Also, a 5.11 climb established during the 1970's , may seem easy compared with a 5.11 established in the 1990's. Even within the same country, ratings often vary from one area to another.

FREE CLIMBING RATING SYSTEMS

The American System

The U.S. rating standard is the Yosemite Decimal System (YDS). This system evolved from the old Welzenbach System, used in Germany during the 1920's, which the Sierra Club in California began using in 1937. The American system divides mountain travel into six classes:

Class	Meaning
Class 1	Hiking.
Class 2	Easy scrambling. Hands used for balance on rocks.
Class 3	Steep scrambling. Handholds and footholds are used. Exposure is such that a beginner may require a rope for safety.
Class 4	Belayed climbing, with the need for equipment to anchor the belay. A leader fall on class 4 would be serious, but the climbing is easy and protection is usually not necessary.
Class 5	Technical climbing requiring ropework, protection and belays and basis for American 5-ratings (such as 5.9 or 5.11).
Class 6	Too steep or featureless to climb without aid climbing techniques. Now replaced by A1–A5 system.

During the 1950's at Tahquitz Rock in Southern California, free climbs reached such a high level of technical difficulty that class 5 was divided into a closed-ended decimal system with 10 ratings from 5.0 to 5.9. However, this system proved inadequate as harder and harder climbs fell into the 5.9 category. In 1959 5.10 was established. Then 5.10 was divided into 5.10a, b, c, and d. The same divisions later arose within the categories 5.11, 5.12, and 5.13 during the late 1970's and 1980's. During the 1990's, 5.14 is in the process of expansion. Some areas append Yosemite Decimal System ratings with a note regarding the seriousness of a Pitch. A rating of 5.10x would indicate a 5.11 route with long stretches between protection and the risk of a long fall.

In areas like Yosemite Valley, with climbs between 100 and 3,000 ft (30 and 915 m) long, climbers found that an overall ranking like 5.8 (free climbing ranking) A1 (aid climbing rating) could include anything from a short outing of a few hours, to a multi-pitch climb lasting several days. In the late 1950's Mark Powell conceived a system using Roman numerals from I to VI to augment the Yosemite Decimal System (free climbing ratings) with a grading system that took length and time commitment into account. As used today, its principal function is as an indication of the amount of time a climb requires. Therefore typical Yosemite routes are given three grades or ratings: Grade IV (length), 5.10 (free climbing rating), A4 (aid climbing rating).

Grade	Duration
I	Several hours.
II	Half a day.
III	Most of a day for ascent and descent.
IV	A full day for ascent and descent.
V	The route requires one Bivouac en route.
VI	More than two days are needed. Several bivouacs on the climb may be required.

A U.S. system still used to rate the difficulty of bouldering problems is the B1-B3 system, devised by the boulderer John Gill. Gill developed this system during the 1960's and 1970's to rate boulder problems that at the time incorporated harder moves than the roped climbs of the day. B1 represents a move of extreme difficulty that may require repeated attempts; B2 is markedly harder; harder again, B3 is only solved after many tries, and traditionally designated a problem that has seen one ascent only and has resisted all attempted repeats.

Other rating systems have emerged from the United States over the years, but most are no longer used. Among these are the Teton Grading System, Appalachian Mountain Club System, American Classification System, and Universal Standard System. Certain areas use other systems. The National Climbing Classification System (NCCS) is still used in some journals. This system rates difficulty only from F1 to F13.

The British System

Three systems have evolved in Britain. The original system is the Adjectival System. A numerical system developed in the Gritstone areas is used in conjunction with the adjectival system. The numerical system rates objective difficulty only, i.e., pure difficulty of a move. Because of the nature of British climbing, which traditionally incorporates loose rock, scant protection and an ethic of boldness a system to indicate seriousness was necessary. In the early 1980's the E Grade System (the most extreme levels of the adjectival system) was devised to describe the seriousness of a pitch in terms of the difficulty of placing protection and runouts. The numerical system usually coexists with E grades, i.e. E5 6c.

The Australian System

Also called the Ewbank System, after John Ewbank who devised it, this system is open ended and goes from 1 to 33.

The European Systems

In Europe, several systems exist. The UIAA system was developed in 1968 with the intention of its being adopted as the international standard for all areas. Though used in Europe alongside domestic rating systems, it did not gain acceptance in the United States or Britain.

MOUNTAINEERING RATING SYSTEMS

Alpine Rating System

Mountaineering ratings are hard to pinpoint due to the vagaries of mountain weather. For this reason alpine ratings apply largely to technical difficulty. An alpine route climbed during bad weather will always present a greater challenge than the same rout climbed in perfect weather.

Used primarily in the European Alps, this system gives an overall rating to a mountain climb. The system uses six grades, I-VI, with the distinctions Sup. (Superior) and Inf. (Inferior) to add detail within a grade. Individual pitch ratings are indicated by the UIAA system.

An older French system still used in the European Alps uses adjectives to rate climbs.

French

F	Facile (Easy)
PD	Peu Difficile (Slightly Difficult)
AD	Assez Difficile (More Difficult)
D	Difficile (Difficult)
TD	Tres Difficile (Very Difficult)
ED	Extrement Difficile (Extremely Difficult)

ICE CLIMBING RATING SYSTEMS

Because frozen waterfalls and ice formations are an ever-changing medium, dependent on the temperature, precipitation and weather of a given day, rating ice climbs has always proven difficult. Most systems are closely related to each other, and account for technical difficulty only. The Canadian System has added the grade VI for extremely long climbs found in the Rocky Mountains.

Scottish	New England Ice (NEI)	Canadian
I	I	I
II	II	II
III	III	III
IV	IV	IV
V	V	V/VI
		VI

AID CLIMBING RATING SYSTEMS

The American aid rating system has denominated other systems. In the Welzenbach System, from which the Yosemite Decimal System sprang, all aid climbs are included in the grade 6, from which the American "A" system evolved. As American aid climbing developed during the 1950's and 1960's, more specific ratings were found to be necessary. The Australian system is open ended. M stands for Mechanical.

American	Australian	Meaning
A0	M1	Extremely solid placements.
A1	M1	Very solid placements.
A2	M2	Less solid, more difficult to place.
A3	M3	Placements can hold short falls.
A3+	M4	Increased chance of longer falls.
A4	M5/M6	Placements hold only body weight.
A4+	M7	Numerous body weight placements
A5	M8	Continuous A4.

INTERNATIONAL RATING SYSTEMS COMPARISON CHART (ROCK CLIMBING)

Germany (UIAA)	France	British (adjectival)	British (technical)	British (E)	USA
I	I	Easy (E)			Class 1
					Class 2
					Class 3
					Class 4
		Moderate (MOD)			5.0
					5.1
					5.2
II	2	Difficult (DIFF)			5.3
		Very Difficult (VDIFF)			
III	3	Severe (S)			5.4
IV	4a	Hard Severe (HS)	4a		5.5
V-	4b				
	4c	Mild Very Severe (MVS)	4b		5.6
V	5a				
V+	5b	Very Severe (VS)	4c		5.7
	5c				
VI-	5c+				5.8
VI	6a	Hard Very Severe (HVS)	5a		5.9
VI+	6a+		5b	E1	5.10a
VII-	6b			E2	5.10b
VII	6b+				5.10c
VII+	6c		5c	E3	5.10d
	6c+			E4	5.11a
VIII-	7a				5.11b
VIII	7a+		6a	E5	5.11c
	7b				5.11d
VIII+	7b+			E6	5.12a
IX-	7c		6b	E7	5.12b
					5.12c
IX	7c+				5.12d
IX+	8a		6c	E8	5.13a
X-	8a+				5.13b
X	8b			E9	5.13c
X+	8b+				5.13d
	8c		7a		5.14a
XI-	8c+				5.14b
XI	9a				5.14c
					5.14d

REPRINT ACKNOWLEDGEMENTS

Excerpt from *K2: The Story of a Savage Mountain* by Jim Curran reprinted by permission of Hodder and Stoughton Limited

Excerpt from *All 14 Eight-Thousanders* by Reinhold Messner reprinted by permission of The Crowood Press

Excerpt from *Annapurna* reprinted by permission of Sterling Lord Literistic, Inc. Copyright 1952 by Maurice Herzog

Excerpt from "Nanda Devi from the North" by Willi Unsoeld reprinted with thanks to the American Alpine Club for permission to excerpt from its 1977 AAJ

Excerpt from "Life is a Mountain: *Into Thin Air* and Beyond" reprinted by permission of Thomas Hornbein

Excerpt from *Into Thin Air* reprinted by permission of Random House, © 1997 Jon Krakauer

"Sherpas on Everest" reprinted by permission of NOVA Online, Liesl Clark & Audrey Salkeld

Excerpt from *Storm and Sorrow in the High Pamirs* reprinted by permission of Robert Craig, past President of the American Alpine Club, a member of numerous Himalayan, Alaskan and South American expeditions and recently retired as Founder and President Emeritus of the Keystone Center in Keystone, Colorado.

Excerpt from *One Man's Mountains* reproduced with permission of Curtis Brown Ltd, London, on behalf of the Estate of Tom Patey. © Tom Patey 1978

Excerpt from *Solo Faces* reprinted by permission of Sterling Lord Literistic, Inc. Copyright 1989 by James Salter

Excerpt from *A Soldier of the Great War* copyright © 1991 by Mark Helprin, reprinted by permission of Harcourt Brace & Company

Excerpt from *On Mountains: Thinking about Terrain* copyright © 1978 by John Jerome, reprinted by permission of George Borchardt, Inc. on behalf of the author.

"Camp 4" by Doug Robinson copyright © 1969, 1996 from *A Night on the Ground, A Day in the Open*

Excerpt from "A Test of Will" copyright © by The New York Times Co. Reprinted by Permission.

Excerpt from *Touching the Void* copyright © 1989 by Joe Simpson, reprinted by permission of HarperCollins Publishers, Inc.

Facts & Figures reprinted from *Climbing. The Complete Reference* by Greg Child. Copyright © 1995 by Greg Child. Reprinted by permission of Facts On File, Inc.

BIBLIOGRAPHY

Adcock, David, "Yerupaja: N.Z. Andean Expedition, 1968," *New Zealand Alpine Journal,* 1969

Allison, Stacy with Carlin, Peter, *Beyond the Limits: A Woman's Triumph on Everest,* Dell Publishing, New York, 1993

Alvarez, A., *Feeding the Rat: Profile of a Climber,* Atlantic Monthly Press, New York, 1988

Anthoine, J. V., "Trango Conclusion," *Alpine Journal,* 1977

Anthoine, J. V., "Trango Tower," *Alpine Journal,* 1976

Ashton, Steve, *Ridges of Snowdonia,* Cicerone Press, Cumbria, England, 1985

Athearn, Lloyd F., "Nanda Devi by a Narrow Margin," *Rock & Ice,* No. 84

Barrington, Charles, "First Ascent of the Eiger," *Alpine Journal,* August 1882 to May 1884

Bass, Dick and Wells, Frank with Ridgeway, Rick, *Seven Summits,* Warner Books, New York, 1986

Bates, Malcolm S., *Cascade Voices: Conversations with Washington Mountaineers,* Cloudcap, Seattle

Baume, Louis C., *Sivalaya: Explorations of the 8000-metre Peaks of the Himalaya,* The Mountaineers, Seattle, 1978

Beckey, Fred W., *Mountains of North America,* Sierra Club Books, San Francisco, 1982

Bender, Friedrich, *Classic Climbs in the Caucasus,* Diadem Books, London, 1992

Bernbaum, Edwin, *Sacred Mountains of the World,* Sierra Club Books, San Francisco, 1990

Birkett, Bill and Peascod, Bill, *Women Climbing: 200 Years of Achievement,* A. C. Black, London, 1989

Boardman, Peter D., *Sacred Summits: A Climber's Year,* Hodder and Stoughton, London, 1982

Bonington, Chris, *Everest the Hard Way,* Random House, New York, 1976

Bonney, Orrin H. and Lorraine G., *Guide to the Wyoming Mountains and Wilderness Areas,* Sage Books, Chicago, 1960

Borchers, P., "In the Cordillera Blanca," *Alpine Journal,* 1933

Borneman, Walter R. and Lampert, Lyndon L., *A Climbing Guide to Colorado's Fourteeners,* Pruett Publishing, 1952

Bousfield, Bruce, "Ever So Humble, Ecuador's Sleeping Giants," *Climbing,* May 1998

Bowen, Mark, "Behind the Indonesian Veil," *Climbing,* September 15, 1997

Breemer, Chris, "The Other Alps, Mountaineering in New Zealand," *Climbing,* April/May 1993

Bueller, William, *Mountains of the World: A Handbook for Climbers and Hikers,* The Mountaineers, 1977

Buhl, Hermann, *Nanga Parbat Pilgrimage,* Hodder and Stoughton, London, 1956

Child, Greg, *Climbing: The Complete Reference,* Facts On File, New York, 1995

Clark, Gary L. "Pik Kommunizma," *American Alpine Journal,* 1978

Cleare, John, *Mountains,* Macmillan London, London, 1975

Cleare, John, *The World Guide to Mountains and Mountaineering,* Webb and Bower, London, 1979

Craig, Robert, *Storm & Sorrow in the High Pamirs,* The Mountaineers, Seattle, 1977

Curran, Jim, *K2: The Story of the Savage Mountain,* The Mountaineers, Seattle, 1995

Davidson, Art, *Minus 148 Degrees F: The Winter Ascent of Mt. McKinley,* W.W. Norton, New York, 1969

Dawson, Louis W. II, *Dawson's Guide to Colorado's Fourteeners,* Blue Clover Press, Monument, Coloado, 1994

Demler, Helmut and Burkhardt, Willi P., *High Mountains of the Alps, Vol. 1: 4000m Peaks,* The Mountaineers, Seattle, 1993

Diemberger, Kurt, *The Endless Knot: K2, Mountain of Dreams and Destiny,* The Mountaineers, Seattle, 1990

Dietz, Richard, "Peak Communism—American Style," *Summit,* April-May 1979

Dougherty, Sean M. *Selected Climbs in the Canadian Rockies,* Rocky Mountain Books, Calgary, 1961

Dubin, Marc S. and Lucas, Enver G., *Trekking in Turkey,* Lonely Planet Publications, Victoria, Australia, 1989

Else, David, *Mountain Walking in Kenya,* Robertson McCarta, London, 1991

Everett, Boyd N. Jr., "The West Ridge to Logan," *American Alpine Journal,* 1967

Fanshawe, Andy and Veneables, Stephen, *Himalaya Alpine-Style: The Most Challenging Routes on the Highest Peaks,* The Mountaineers, Seattle, 1995

Farquhar, Francis P., *History of the Sierra Nevada,* University of California Press, Berkeley, 1965

Filley, Bette, *The Big Fact Book about Mount Rainier,* Dunamis House, Issaquah, Washington,

1996

Fraser, Esther, *The Canadian Rockies: Early Travels and Explorations*, M. G. Hurtig, Edmonton, 1969

Frass, Hermann, *Dolomites: Mountains of Magic, Discovery and Conquest*, Athesia, Bolzano, 1977

Frison-Roche, Roger and Jouty, Sylvain, *A History of Mountain Climbing*, Flammarion, Paris, 1996

Garden, John F., *The Bugaboos: An Alpine History*, Footprint Publishing, Revelstroke, B. C.

Gardiner, Steve. *Why I Climb: Personal Insights of Top Climbers*, Stackpole Books, Harrisburg, Paennsylvania, 1990

Gilbert, Richard, *260 Challenging Walks in Britain and Ireland*, Diadem Books, London, 1990

Goedeke, Richard, *The Alpine 4000m Peaks: By the Classic Routes*, Diadem Books, London, 1991

Green, Randall, and Bensen, Joe, *Bugaboo Rock: A Climber's Guide*, The Mountaineers, Seattle, 1990

Harrer, Heinrich, *The White Spider: The Story of the North Face of the Eiger*, Palladin Grafton Books, London, 1959

Harrer, Heinrich, *I Come from the Stone Age*, E. P. Dutton & Co., New York, 1965

Harris, George and Hasler, Graeme, *A Land Apart: The Mount Cook Alpine Region*, A.H. and A.W. Reed, Wellington, N. Z., 1971

Herzog, Maurice, *Annapurna: Conquest of the first 8,000-metre Peak*, Dutton, New York, 1954

Hesse, Mark, "The Forgotten Classic," *Climbing*, June 1988

Hewitt, Rodney and Davidson,

Mavis, *The Mountains of New Zealand*, A.H. and A.W. Reed, Wellington, N. Z., 1954

Hodgson, Bryan, "Grand Teton," *National Geographic*, February 1995

Holzel, Thomas and Salkeld, Audrey, *First on Everest: The Mystery of Mallory and Irvine*, Henry Holt and Co., 1986

Hornbein, Thomas F., *Everest: The West Ridge*, Sierra Club Books, San Francisco and Ballantine Books, New York, 1966

Houston, Charles S., M.D., *Going High: The Story of Man and Altitude*, Charles S. Houston, M. D., Burlington, Vermont, and The American Alpine Club, Golden, Colorado.

Hunt, John, *The Ascent of Everest*, Dutton, New York, 1954

James, Ron, *Dolomites: Selected Climbs*, Alpine Club, London, 1988

Jerome, John, *On Mountains: Thinking About Terrain*, Harcourt Brace, New York, 1978

Jones, Chris, *Climbing in North America*, The Mountaineers, Seattle, 1997

Kandarian, Paul, "The Worst Weather in the World," *Sunday Journal Magazine*, Providence, Rhode Island, March 1992

Kearney, Alan, *Mountaineering in Patagonia*, Cloudcap, Seattle, 1993

Kelly, Rob, "The Pamir International Camps," *Summit*, December-January 1979

Kelsey, Joe, *Climbers and Hikers Guide to the Worlds Mountains*, 3rd Edition, Kelsey Publishing, Provo, Utah, 1990

Kielkowski, Jan, *Mount Everest Massif*, Explo Publishers, Gliwice, Poland, 1993

Kinney, George, "To the Top of Mount Robson, the Highest Peak in the Canadian Rockies," *Appalachia*, 1910

Krakauer, Jon, *Eiger Dreams*, Anchor Books, New York, 1997

Krakauer, Jon, *Into Thin Air*, Villard, New York, 1997

Lange, Harald, *Kilimanjaro: The White Roof of Africa*, The Mountaineers, Seattle, 1982

Le Bon, Leo, *Myths in Mountains: Roaming the Great Mountain Ranges of Six Continents with Leo Le Bon*, Harry N. Abrams, 1989

Lipton, Chet, *Walking Easy in the Italian Alps*, Gateway Books, Oakland, California, 1995

Logan, Hugh, *The Mount Cook Guidebook: A Climber's guide to the Mt. Cook Region*, New Zealand Alpine Club, Christchurch, 1987

MacInnes, Hamish. *Scottish Climbs: Volume 1*, Constable, London, 1971

MacInnes, Hamish, *Scottish Winter Climbs*, Constable, London, 1982

Marts, Brian S., "American Antarctic Mountaineering Expedition" *American Alpine Journal*, 1967

Matthews, W. V. Graham and Harrah, David, "Up Yerupaj," *American Alpine Journal*, 1951

Mazel, David, *Pioneering Ascents: The Origins of Climbing in America, 1642-1873*, Stackpole Books, Harrisburg, Pa., 1991

Mazel, David, *Pure and Perpetual Snow: Two Climbs in the Andes of Peru*, The FreeSolo Press, Alamosa, Colorado, 1937

McNaught-Davis, I. I., "British-Soviet Pamirs Expedition, 1962," *Alpine*

Journal, 1962

Messner, Reinhold, *All Fourteen 8,000ers*, Cloudcap Press, Seattle, 1988

Miler, John. "Mt. Washington, New Hampshire, U.S. A." *Summit*, Spring 1993

Miller, Maynard M., "The First American Ascent of Mount St. Elias," *National Geographic*, February 1948

Molenaar, Dee, *The Challenge of Rainier*, The Mountaineers, Seattle, 1971

Moore, Robert T., "Chimborazo, Bolivar's 'Watchtower of the Universe'" *American Alpine Journal*, 1930

Morrow, Pat, "Carstensz Pyramid," *Rock & Ice*, September-October 1990

Morrow, Pat, *Beyond Everest: Quest for the Seven Summits*, Camden House, Camden East, Ontario

Neate, Jill, *Mountaineering in the Andes: A Sourcebook for Climbers*, Expedition Advisory Centre, London, 1994

Newby, Eric, *Great Ascents in Mountaineering*, Viking, New York, 1977

Noyce, Wilfred and McMorrin, Ian, editors, *World Atlas of Mountaineering*, Thomas Nelson & Sons, London, 1969

O'Connell, Nicholas, *Beyond Risk: Conversations with Climbers*, The Mountaineers, Seattle, 1993

O'Neill, James, "Kitaraju, Allpamayo, Southwest Face and Tragedy," *American Alpine Journal*, 1981

Ortenburger, Leigh N. and Jackson, Reynold G., *A Climber's Guide to the Teton Range*, The Mountaineers, Seattle, 1996

Osmaston, H. A. and Pasteur, D., *Guide to the Ruwenzori: The Mountains of the Moon*, The Mountain Club of Uganda, Kampala, 1972

Ostertag, Rhonda and George, *100 Hikes in Oregon*, The Mountaineers, Seattle, 1992

Patey, Tom, *One Man's Mountains*, Victor Gollancz, London, 1971

Patterson, Lief-Norman and Isles, David, "Yerupaj·1966," *American Alpine Journal*, 1967

Pause, Walter and Winkler, Jurgen, *Extreme Alpine Rock: The 100 Greatest Alpine Rock Climbs*, Granada Publishing, London, 1979

Perrin, Jim, "Snowdon," *High*, May 1986

Rachowiecke, Rob and Wagonhauser, Betsy, *Climbing and Hiking in Ecuador*, Bradt Publications, 1994

Randall, Glenn, *Mount McKinley: Climber's Handbook*, Chockstone Press, Evergreen, Colorado, 1992

Rébuffat, Gaston, *On Ice and Snow and Rock*, Oxford University Press, New York, 1971

Rébuffat, Gaston, *Starlight and Storm: The Ascent of Six Great North Faces of the Alps*, J. M. Dent, London, 1956

Reichardt, Louis F. and Unsoeld, William F., "Nanda Devi from the North," *American Alpine Journal*, 1977

Reid, Don and Meyers, George, *Yosemite Climbs: Big Walls*, Chockstone Press, Evergreen, Colorado, 1993

Reuther, David and Thorn, John, editors, *The Armchair Mountaineer*, Menasha Ridge Press, Birmingham, Ala., 1989

Ricker, John F., *Yuraq Janka: Cordilleras Blanca and Rosko*, Alpine Club of Canada, Banff, Alberta, and American Alpine Club, Golden, Colo., 1977

Righter, Robert W., editor, *A Teton Country Anthology*, Roberts Rinehart, Niwot, Colorado, 1990

Roach, Gerry, *Colorado's Fourteeners: From Hikes to Climbs*, Fulcrum Publishing, Golden, Colorado, 1992

Roberts, David, "Five Who Made It to the Top," *Harvard Magazine*, January 1981

Roberts, David, "Rewriting Annapurna," *Climbing*, December 1997

Rockwell, Robert S. "The 'Peak of Communism' and the Soviet Pamirs," *Summit*, May-June 1987

Roper, Steve and Steck, Allen, *Fifty Classic Climbs of North America*, Sierra Club Books, San Francisco, 1979

Rossiter, Richard, *Teton Classic: Selected Climbs in Grand Teton National Park*, Chockstone Press, Evergreen, Colo., 1991

Rowell, Galen, *Vertical World of Yosemite*, Wilderness Press, Berkeley, 1974

Salkeld, Audrey, "High Witness," *High*, April, 1998

Salkeld, Audrey and Bermúdez, José Luis, *On the Edge of Europe: Mountaineering in the Caucasus*, The Mountaineers, Seattle, 1993

Sayre, Woodrow Wilson, *Four Against Everest*, Prentiss Hall, New Jersey, 1964

Secor, R. J., *Aconcagua: A Climbing Guide*, The Mountaineers, Seattle, 1994

Secor, R. J., *The High Sierras: Peaks, Passes and Trails*, The Mountaineers, Seattle, 1992

Sharman, David, *Climbs of the Cordillera Blanca of Peru*, Whizzo Climbs, Aberdeen, Scotland, 1995

Sherman, Paddy, *Cloud Walkers: Six Climbs on Major Canadian Peaks*, The Mountaineers, Seattle, 1965

Sherwonit, Bill, editor, *Alaska Ascents: World-class Mountaineers Tell Their Stories*, Alaska Northwest Books, Seattle, 1996

Siebert, Dieter, *Classic Routes on the Eastern Alps*, Diadem Books, London 1992

Simpson, Joe, *Touching the Void: The Harrowing First Person Account of One Man's Miraculous Survival*, Harper & Row, New York, 1988

Skinner, Todd, *Storming the Tower*, National Geographic, October 1996

Smith, Karl, *The Mountains of Turkey*, Cicerone Press, Milnthorpe, Cumbria, 1994

Smoot, Jeff, *Summit Guide to the Cascade Volcanoes*, Chockstone Press, Evergreen, Colorado 1992

Starr, Walter A. Jr., *Starr's Guide to the John Muir Trail and the High Sierra Region*, Sierra Club Books, San Francisco, 1974

Stone, Peter B., editor, *The State of the World's Mountains: A Global Report*, Zen Books, London, 1992

Styles, Showell, *The Climber's Bedside Book*, Faber and Faber, London, 1968

Synott, Mark, "A Tough Act to Follow, Charlie Porter's Wilderness of Pain: Baffin Island," *Climbing*, March 15, 1998

Tabin, Geoffrey, "Antarctic Solitude," *Climbing*, October-November 1991

Thomas, Lowell, *Book of the High Mountains*, Julian Messner, New York, 1964

Unsworth, Walter, *Encyclopaedia of Mountaineering*, Hodder & Stoughton, London, 1992

Unsworth, Walter, *Because It Is There*, Victor Gollancz, London, 1968

Unsworth, Walter, *Hold the Heights*, Hodder and Stoughton, London, 1994

Voge, Hervey H. and Smatko, Andrew J., editors, *Mountaineer's Guide to the High Sierra*, Sierra Club Books, San Francisco, 1972

Wala, Jerzy, "Routes Leading to Pik Kommunizma," *Alpine Journal*, 1973

Washburn, Bradford and Roberts, David, *Mount McKinley: The Conquest of Denali*, Harry N. Abrams, New York, 1991

Webster, Ed, "Roof of the World: Rock Climbs of Huntington Ravine," *Rock & Ice*, May-June 1991

Weston, the Rev. W., "Fujiama in May," *Alpine Journal*, November 1892

Wielowchowski, Andrew, *East Africa International Mountain Guide*, West Col Productions, Goring Reading Berks, England, 1986

Workman, Fanny Bullock, "Letter to the Committee of the American Alpine Club," *Appalachia*, 1910

Wrobleski, Brad, "Welcome to Vinson Beach," *Rock & Ice*, January-February 1994

PHOTOGRAPHY CREDITS

INDEX

W

Wahlstrom, Richard W., 116
Wales, 124
Walker, Horace, 138, 139
Walker Spur, 139
Wallaston, A.F.R., 106
Washburn, Bradford, 21, 184, 185, 187
Washington, Mount, 275-286
Watson, Vera, 52
Waugh, Andrew, 56
Wells, Frank, 117, 118
Wheeler, Arthur, 266

Whillans, Don, 52, 61, 120, 300
White Mountains, 276
Whitmore, George, 238, 240
Whitney, Josiah, 196, 232
Whitney, Mount, 231-236
Whittaker, Jim, 9, 60, 62, 63, 69, 195, 202, 206
Whittaker, Lou, 206
Whymper, Edward, 139, 155, 156, 157, 159, 160, 161, 162, 261
Wiessner, Fritz, 226, 228, 230
Wilcox, Walter, 261
Williams, John, 264
Williams, Martyn, 106
Wilson, Maurice, 59

Wilson, Tom, 260
Winthrop, John, 276, 278
Wood, Rev. T.A., 193, 196
Wood, Walter, 187
Woolf, Virginia, 151
Workman, Fannie Bullock, 289
Works Project Administration, 198, 220
Wyoming, 32, 215, 221, 226

Y

Yamabushi, 81
Yates, Simon, 301
Yerupajá, 297-300

Young, Geoffrey Winthrop, 67, 125, 139
Yuh-hai-has-kuh. See Robson, Mount
Yukon Territory, 188, 249

Z

Zaire, 97
Zenho, 81
Zermatt, 156, 157, 159, 160
Zipper, 317
Zumtaugwald, Johann, 167
Zumtaugwald, Matthias, 167
Zurbriggen, Mattias, 113, 302, 303-4